O'NEILL'S
OWN COUNTRY

O'NEILL'S
OWN COUNTRY

A History of the Ballinderry Valley

To Dessie with best wishes

KEVIN JOHNSTON

Kevin

N

For Jack

First published 2009

Nonsuch Publishing
119 Lower Baggot Street
Dublin 2
Ireland

www.nonsuchireland.com

British Library Cataloguing in Publication Data.
A catalogue record for this book is available from the British Library.

ISBN 978 1 84588 956 2

Typesetting and origination by The History Press
Printed in Great Britain

CONTENTS

ACKNOWLEDGEMENTS

I wish to thank:

Michael McGuckin and the officers of Cookstown District Council, who helped and encouraged me in this project;

Ian MacNeill, who spent many long hours trying to teach me the basics of botany;

Seamus Ryan, Ballyronan, for his information about fishing on Lough Neagh;

Alan Keys and Frank Mitchell of Ballinderry Fish hatchery, for telling me all I needed to know about the Ballinderry River;

Mark Horton of the RIPPLE Project, for introducing me to so many useful contacts;

And mainly my wife Maura, for tolerating my obsession for so many months.

INTRODUCTION

Viewed on a map, the outline of Camlough bears an unusual resemblance to Lough Neagh, some twenty miles to the east. It is roughly rectangular, but about halfway down its longer sides it narrows slightly, as if it had aspirations to a waist. Not very large, perhaps 500m north to south, and 300m east to west, it is a relic of the last Ice Age. Once a huge block of ice stood here, so large and so bulky that it remained while all the ice around it melted away. Like all good things, however, this block came to an end; it melted eventually, and left a deep trough in the ground. This held the water of the melting ice and since then has held to itself the water of numerous springs. It must have been a lonely place once, even when Camlough Lodge was first built on a green bank to the south of the lough. For some years, however, the demand for building material has meant that sand has been extracted from numerous quarries in the hills around, and the driver is likely to meet a tipper lorry full of sand as he or she negotiates the narrow, twisty roads. There is a small lay-by to the north of the lough and here some locals come to try for the sweet trout of the hills.

At the south-western end of the lough, near the green grass and the lodge, a small but steady stream of water overflows, and falls quickly before steadying itself and moving under the road bridge. The Ballinderry River has started its journey.

To begin with it moves quite slowly, meandering through a sandy heath that has changed hardly at all since the great ice sheets left it. Even sheep are scarce here. A long esker turns it northward where it finds a more definite slope gives it more speed and more power to erode a path for itself. It gains water from drains on either side and from another stream that comes from the tiny Loughnagay, further west. By the time it reaches the main Cookstown to Omagh Road at Creggan Bridge, it has become a power to be reckoned with. Below the bridge it has dug out for itself a deep channel and it continues to flow fast, cutting always at its banks, looking for a quicker way, until it steadies itself near Teebane and starts to flow through good agricultural land. For much of this stretch, it is possible to follow the river bank. If you move quietly, this is a good area in which to see otter. In summer, the river is sinuous with ranunculus weed, the long fronds waving like hair in the stream. There are walks and a picnic area near Dunnamore, so here at least the visitor need not worry about damaging a farmer's fence.

At Kildress the Ballinderry is joined by a short but powerful tributary. It is now a fully fledged river. A good spot to view this part of the river is at Wellbrook Beetling Mill, a reminder of the linen industry which was the backbone of the local economy for many years. Here the National Trust has preserved not only the mill, but a walkway that follows the mill race. From this vantage point it is possible to see a unique part of the river; this is a small, boulder-strewn gorge that cannot have changed much since the ice vanished. It gives a real sense of how the river must have appeared to our stone-age ancestors as they explored it in search of prey. Beech has replaced the original hazel scrub, but only a purist would carp at that when the vegetation takes on the beautiful reddish-browns of autumn.

Below Wellbrook the river meanders between low hills and rich farming country until it reaches Cookstown, the larger of the two towns that are situated on its banks. There was a time when the sheer size of Cookstown meant that its waste had a very negative effect on the river. Modern sewage works have meant that the river below the town is as pure as it was above. It passes to the south of the town, flowing under the King's Bridge. Just downriver from here there is another vantage point, where a walkway has been constructed through Cabin Wood. There is an interesting contrast between the old fishermen's path along the river and the neat rows of trees planted on the hill behind. The Environment Agency has made itself a hostage to fortune by siting its sewage treatment works just opposite, so that it is under the constant supervision of passersby.

Just below Cabin Wood, the first of the river's major tributaries joins it from the south. This is the Killymoon River, itself made up from the joining of the Rock and Claggan Rivers near the little village of Sandholes. In terms of history, this is one of the most important watercourses in the valley. About two miles upstream it passes through a narrow glen. Near its east bank are the remains of Tullahogue Fort, where the leaders of the O'Neill clan were inaugurated in times past. On the west bank is an establishment with a slightly more recent claim to fame. Although it is now a college specialising in food production and technology, Loughry College still contains the house that was home to the [?] family. A close friend of the family in the early eighteenth century was Jonathan Swift, and the irascible Dean often stayed there, using as a private study a summer house, which

The Ballinderry at Wellbrook.

The Ballinderry at Ardtrea.

still stands. The Claggan River rises very close to Hugh O'Neill's own home, near what is now called Stewartstown. He had a lake dwelling on an artificial island know as a crannog, and he knew the site as 'an Craobh', which means 'the Branch'. The site of the crannog is still visible in the lake to the east of Stewartstown.

Below the junction the river takes on a mature look, meandering through some excellent farming country. Between here and Lough Neagh it is intensely fished, for brown trout for most of the season and for salmon and the large lake trout known as dollaghan in late summer and autumn. There are fishermen's paths along most of the banks, although they do not make easy walking. The author on more than one occasion has stepped on 'grass' only to find himself up to his waist in water. A good sense of this more mature river can be had at Ardtrea Canoe Steps, near what is called Ardtrea Bridge in the Ordinance Survey map, but which all the locals call Big Bridge.

Not far below this the river, which has been exclusively a Tyrone river up to now, becomes a county border. From now on the north bank is in County Derry (or County Londonderry, if you prefer), while the southern bank remains in Tyrone. It is a border not simply between counties but between baronies. In Tyrone, the land is in the Barony of Dungannon, while on the Derry side is the Barony of Loughinsholin. Followers of Gaelic football observe this border with great zeal, since their annual championships are based on county boundaries. There is a certain irony in the fact that Loughinsholin was also a part of Tyrone,

The Footgo.

400 years ago. The two baronies, Dungannon and Loughinsholin, were Hugh O'Neill's personal holding, and the two together were known as O'Neill's Own Country. From the north, formed by several small streams rising high on the slopes of Slieve Gallion, yet another tributary joins the main river. This is the Ballymully River, which once flowed through the mighty forests of Glenconkeyne and Killetra. Now, after an exciting dash off the hillside, often through deep, wooded glens, the Ballymully flows through Moneymore and along a rich flood plain to the Ballinderry. Its stream is still powerful enough to cut steep banks as it meanders along, and this is a good place to see kingfishers and dippers.

The Ballinderry has reached its full power by the time it has reached the bridge at Coagh. Here, in October, fishermen watch as dollaghan as heavy as 12lb spawn on the ford just below the bridge. There is a series of fords and corries below here, each with a deep pool below it where salmon and dollaghan lie in late summer and autumn. There are many woods along this stretch, and mature trees hang out over the river. Here and there are remnants of deserted houses, and even some industrial remains. At Ballinderry Bridge the river passes under the last road bridge before Lough Neagh. There is a small village here, in the townland of Derrychrin. Even after the penal laws had been repealed, and people were allowed to practise the Catholic religion, Mass was said here around a large boulder. It was not until a chapel was built nearby, at Ballylifford, that locals could be sheltered while they prayed.

A good place to view the peaceful progress of the river is Cot Lane. This is a walkway that begins just in front of the chapel at Ballylifford – confusingly known as Ballinderry chapel – and goes down through thick hedgerows until it reaches the river. Here it crosses the Footgo, a footbridge built to link the two halves of Ballinderry Parish so that, in the days when people had to walk most places, neither scholars nor churchgoers were inconvenienced by having to detour via the road bridge. Below the Footgo, around the final sweeps of the river, the Ballinderry opens out into the lough. It is no dramatic entrance; there is a sandbar at the mouth which gets so shallow that fishing boats have trouble crossing it. In a dry summer, it can even prevent fish returning to the river. It is also a difficult place to reach, since there is private ground on both sides of the river.

Never mind! Turn around on the Footgo and look upstream, back the way you have come. As you look towards the distant hills you are contemplating the piece of Ireland that the Great O'Neill saw as his own. Through it like an artery flows the Ballinderry, O'Neill's own river.

AFTER THE ICE

THE RETURN OF LIFE

For about a million years the ice seemed to have a life of its own, coming and going across the land, planing the ground right down to the bedrock, as if it were trying to wipe the slate clean, to remove all trace of the past. It grew and shrank and grew again, in a rhythm so slow that a human lifetime would scarce have seen a change. Sometimes it disappeared for thousands of years at a time before returning. Then, about 13,000 years ago, it began to melt away. There had been three main ice sheets in north-west Ireland at the time. From Lough Neagh, ice flowed westward up the slopes to the Sperrin ridge, then down through Glenshane and elsewhere. Another advance went up the Ballinderry River valley until it met the ice from the Tyrone glacier. Finally, a glacier that formed around Lower Lough Erne and south-east Donegal flowed down the Mourne and Foyle valleys.

But the ice was gone a long time before men returned. The huge ice mountains that rose 5,000ft above Lough Neagh, and higher over Omagh and south Donegal had been overcome by the improving climate and had melted away and left the damage they had done exposed to the skies. The bare rock in places had been polished to a smoothness that reflected the lightening skies. Elsewhere, great dunes of sand dominated the landscape, hundreds of feet deep. At the old edges of the glaciers, and where they had melted, moraines of huge boulders blocked river courses. With the exception of bacteria within the rocks, and of small plants whose spores were so light that they could be carried round the world, there was no biological life.

The earth was not dead, however. Ever dynamic, its processes began to work on the exposed rock immediately. Extremes of heat and cold on the higher ground, by causing rock to expand and contract, broke little fragments off its surfaces. This happened, and still happens, because different minerals within the rock have different rates of expansion and contraction. In summertime, rainwater gathering in the new crevices or on the surface began to dissolve chemicals out of the rock. In wintertime, the same water could be turned to ice and its expansion broke up the rock even more. Each time that the rock broke, it released some of its nutrients into the environment, ready for a seed or a spore to take advantage. And life came. On cracks in the bare rock of the watershed, on land that is still called Creggan (or stony), wind-blown seeds took hold. The living was not easy. The plants grew slowly, because the nutrients had to be worked for, and because there were times of year when the land dried up and there was no water. Grasses and sedges would probably have been first, followed by low-lying, frost-tolerant species like juniper and dwarf willow, and trees like hairy and silver birches. As silt and humus gathered around the river valleys, and the thinnest of layers covered the hills, a fresh influx of plants came from the south and east. It seems likely that a land bridge joined Ireland and Spain, and another one, which moved north after the glaciers, crossed the Irish Sea. In the hundreds of years before trees grew closely enough together to form canopies blocking out the sun, there would have been an explosion of colour every spring. Such a place still exists in Ireland: the Burren. The land there has never been covered by forest, and each spring a veritable collage of flowers comes into bloom, with alpine Mountain Avens rubbing shoulders with Sea Pinks.

The start of the flow.

There was no human there to see the annual spring display, and it was only a temporary phenomenon. As soil accumulated and the climate improved, trees began to grow. Birch would have been first, then pines, followed by hazel and the first, twisted oaks. By about 8,000 years ago, most of the lowland, and the hills up to about 2,500ft – in other words all of the Sperrins – were covered in trees. In their search for sunlight, herbs that could tolerate frost went to the mountains, while salt-tolerant species settled along the coast. Not many had made it to Ireland by the time the waters had closed round its shores and made it an island.

THE COMING OF MAN

As yet there was no trace of humankind. In terms of evidence rather than conjecture, humans came to Ireland at a very late stage. Leaving Africa, they had settled in Tierra del Fuego long before they reached Ireland's shores. The first to arrive on this western island were different from the brutish caricatures often portrayed in lurid books and children's comics. Except for their unusual clothes and lifestyle, they would have been difficult to distinguish from the modern inhabitants of Ireland. Although the few remains that have been discovered in Ireland confirm the findings, most of what we know about these people has been obtained from studies done in England and, in particular, at Star Carr in Yorkshire. They survived off nature, gathering fruits and herbs in season, hunting animals for the protein that they needed. They were of that era that archaeologists call 'Mesolithic', or 'Middle Stone Age', when new lifestyles were beginning to develop in response to the improving climate. They were a nomadic people, moving in cycles driven by the seasons, setting up campsites near each source of food as it came into season, returning each year to the same places at the same time until their food sources became depleted or, if they were lucky enough to be a thriving group, increased numbers forced them to split up and seek new territory. They were intelligent people, with the same power to think that modern humans have. For all that, they were like shadows, leaving little trace in the land, and the archaeologist must assume the role of detective, striving to gain as much information as possible from the few clues that they left.

The most long-lasting of the clues are the tools that they used. Like a modern tradesman, each family group had a tool kit and, just as you can tell from a tradesman's tools whether he is a plumber or an electrician, so you can place a prehistoric group within a culture by examining the artefacts that they have left behind. The first humans in Ireland came in the early Mesolithic, about 7000 BC. A camp has been found near to where the Lower Bann meets the sea, at Mountsandel, on the outskirts of Coleraine. Archaeologists became interested

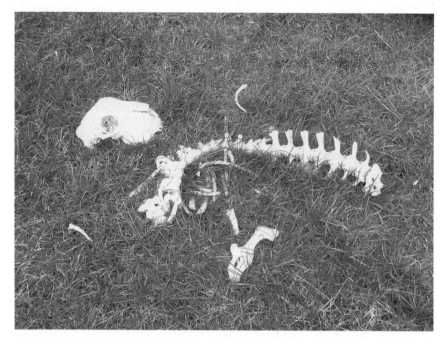

Moorland remains.

Moorland remains, detail.

when workmen at a nearby building site began turning up flint tools. After the site was studied, these archaeologists were able to paint quite a detailed picture of the lifestyle of these first Irish, and also to draw some clues as to their origins. It was the tools that provided the evidence for this.

Like most Mesolithic peoples, those living at Mountsandel made their tools from nodules of flint. These appear like large pebbles in the white chalk cliffs that occur all along the north and east coasts of Ireland and large numbers are still found at the base of cliffs as the sea erodes them. A couple of techniques could be used to shape them. The simplest was to hit the flint with another hard stone, such as quartzite. More detailed work could be done with a hammer and chisel fashioned out of the antlers of red deer. When flints are shattered, the fragments have extremely sharp edges, which can be used in a variety of ways. The largest pieces were used as axes. These were often made from the core of the flint and were sharpened by striking small pieces off the edges. If an edge became dull, it was easy to use the same technique to re-sharpen it. Core axes were used for chopping wood.

Another form of axe was made by striking large flakes from the core of the flint. These would then be shaped so that they had a sharp, straight edge. These were used like a chisel or a plane, to shape wooden tools. Other flakes could be used as scrapers, cleaning and working the skins of animals, particularly red deer, without damaging the hide. There were very few of these at Mountsandel, perhaps indicating that deer was not a major prey item. This theory is supported by the fact that no red deer remains were found at the site.

The most interesting flint products found at Mountsandel were tiny blades known to archaeologists as microliths. The word means 'small stones', and these were tiny splinters that were deliberately fashioned into a number of shapes. This is where the antler hammer and chisel came into their own, allowing very detailed work. These tiny blades were not weapons in themselves, but could be used as arrow-points or barbs on a wooden arrow or harpoon, or could even be inserted in a line on a piece of wood to form a rudimentary saw. Microliths used in this way were shaped like scalene triangles. Many of these were found in pits that also contained pig bones, suggesting that they had found their way into the pig when it was killed in the hunt. Other microliths were shaped like rods, but archaeologists have not been able to come up with a theory as to how these tools were used.

Microliths have a particular importance in the study of the origins of these first inhabitants. First of all, microliths like this did not appear in Scotland or in Northern England till some time later, whereas they did exist in Northern France. It is possible, therefore, that Ireland's first settlers had migrated along the south coast of Britain before crossing the sea to Ireland. This begs the question as to why they did not stop off along the way. Since hunter-gatherers require vast ranges to support them through the year, perhaps there simply wasn't room.

Another possible explanation is that microliths did exist in Britain at the time, but that archaeologists simply haven't found the evidence. Whatever their origins, the sea crossing would have been well within their capabilities, whether they used skin boats or dugout canoes. The fact that there is a great uniformity among the microliths found at different sites in Ireland indicates a uniformity of culture. It is unlikely that one or two small family groups would have survived to populate the entire island, so it may make sense to suppose that a number of groups from the same clan made the crossing over a period of years, bringing the population up to a viable total of several hundred.

The other major find at Mountsandel was a pattern of post-holes which allowed archaeologists to estimate the size and shape of the shelters that these early people used. These were grouped together in a hollow that showed signs of being enlarged. Post-holes are formed when a piece of wood that has been driven into the ground rots. The space it leaves is gradually filled with other material: top-soil or even charcoal. It becomes darker in colour than the surrounding soil, and is easily picked out by a trained eye. What the archaeologists found was the remains of a series of huts, each of them about 6m in diameter, and each with a hearth in the centre. There were no post-holes in the centre to support a roof, so it is believed that the hut was formed by ramming saplings into the ground in such a way that they could be pulled over and tied at the centre. In the draughty climate of the Coleraine district, something must have been used to cover the walls and keep out the weather. Brushwood or skins might have been used with, perhaps, a layer of turfs on top to keep out the cold. A group of between six and nine people could have lived comfortably in this accommodation. Several of these shelters may have been built together in times of plenty, such as when the salmon were running in the river below. In times of hunger, like late winter or early spring, the clan may have spread out over a greater range.

Around the site the excavators found the remains of pits. They guessed that these had been used to store food, for example hazelnuts. Other foods such as crab apples and the roots of water lilies would not leave any trace. As they had been emptied of their stores, they were refilled, accidentally or otherwise, with the rubbish from the campsite. Here was found definite evidence of what these people hunted and what they gathered. A favourite prey was wild pig, and there were many burnt bones of pig among the rubbish. These remains were well enough preserved for scientists to be able to tell that the pigs were not fully grown, and were probably killed in the late winter. This is the time that boars begin their rut, and they would have driven last year's young males away from the sounder. Used to being protected by the group, these inexperienced young animals would have been easy meat for the hunters of the tribe. Other mammals were surprisingly rare, with only Irish hare appearing more than once. There were quite a few remains of birds, although in this case hunting or trapping does not seem to have been so specialised, and a wide variety of species is represented. The most common remains were of fish, in particular salmon and trout, although there were also considerable numbers of eel and sea bass. The salmon, trout and sea bass show that the group was there in summer, while the eels would have been taken as they migrated towards the sea in autumn. Another autumn foodstuff found in large quantities was hazelnut, and it was probably these that were stored in the food pits, set aside to see the group through the lean times. It was possible, therefore for some, if not all, of the clan to remain in the area all year round.

The group or clan probably had little formal social structure. Evidence from contemporary groups of hunter-gatherers suggests that these societies are usually egalitarian. A man – or woman – might gain a position of leadership through his or her personal achievement, by demonstrating wisdom or skill at hunting or ability to choose suitable stretches of the river for fishing. To get the others to perform his will it was necessary to have moral authority, or be powerful enough to bully them into doing it.

The pressure to find food would have been relentless and, even in times of plenty, there would have been pressure to explore the hinterland in order to evaluate its potential for future use. These early explorers stuck close to the rivers. The presence of bears and wolves in the forest may well have made this a prudent policy. Where they found suitable locations, they set up camps. There is a series of these up the valley of the Lower Bann, particularly around Lough Beg and where Lough Neagh flows into the Bann at Toome. Further sites are located down the west shore of the lough. As well as food, they needed regular access to chalk, so that they could have a continuous supply of flint tools. Chalk underlies the basalt rock of much of north-east Ulster, coming to the surface in outcrops along the Antrim coast and in a few other places. One of the most important of these lies a few miles to the west of Lough Neagh, where a chalk escarpment runs between Coagh and Magherafelt. On the River Ballinderry, near here, and on the Lough Neagh shore near the river mouth, there are early Mesolithic sites, indicating that they knew of this resource.

It would probably be too much to say that they were masters of the land. That is not how they interacted with their environment. What was crucial for them was the maintenance of a balance in their relationship with nature. They were masterly in keeping this balance, and lived relatively unchanged lives for many generations, for over 3,000 years. That is not to say that there was no development. At some stage, around 5500 BC, someone realised that, instead of the complicated way in which the earlier microliths were used, it was much easier to strike off large flakes of flint and use them as tools. The resulting tools are much cruder that those of the early Mesolithic and some archaeologists have used this to suggest that there was a second wave of colonisation about this time. These tools are unique to Ireland and the Isle of Man, perhaps indicating that those living in Ireland had become isolated from the rest of their kind. Because so many of the earliest discoveries of these tools were found along the Antrim coast and especially around Larne, these later Mesolithic people were described as having a 'Larnian' culture.

Sites along the coast were industrial ones, only occupied for a few days or weeks while enough tools were prepared to last the coming year. To try to make sense of the day-to-day lives of these people, it is necessary to look at some of their inland sites. There are several along the Lower Bann and on the shores of Lough Neagh. One of the most important of these was found where the waters of Lough Beg emptied into the Bann, near the area known nowadays as Newferry. The soil here is made up largely of the tiny remains of creatures known as diatoms, and is known as 'diatomite'. The diatoms flourished in the freshwater lake that gathered here just after the last Ice Age. The quality of these soils saved many lost tools from damage and erosion, and the resulting collection gives a good history of the progression of late Mesolithic tools used over a period of nearly 2,000 years.

The basic tool was one that was so common along the river that it became known as the Bann flake. One end is a basic leaf shape, almost like a spearhead, with other end trimmed to form a thick butt. This butt is too thick to be attached to a spear shaft and it probably had a short, thick handle, and was used as a hand tool, in the same way that a modern boy scout might use his hunting knife, for cleaning out fish that he caught, or for descaling them. There is no waste material among the remains, indicating that the people would have worked the flint nodules on site, near the coast. Better that than carry the weight of waste stone perhaps twenty miles or more to their fishing and hunting camps.

A slight puzzle is caused by some mudstone axes that are found among the Bann flakes. The nearest source of this is a band stretching from County Down to County Longford, passing through southern Ulster. Since there is little evidence of Mesolithic settlement in these areas, it is possible that people from around Lough Neagh would occasionally travel to what is now south Tyrone and south Fermanagh. Their most obvious route would be up the Ballinderry Valley and over the Carrickmore hills. No base camps resembling Mountsandel have been found for these late Mesolithic people, and there is no sense of how they spent their winters. They were people almost constantly on the move. It has been calculated that, depending on the richness of the environment, a group of humans at the time would require between six and sixty square miles to support each member. In poor land, this could mean that a group containing ten adults would need a territory of up to 600 square miles to feed itself. The whole of County Derry might have been needed to support two such groups, if they did not have access to the richest of the rivers.

Burnavon weir.

Fish must have been one of their primary sources of food. To catch them, they made tools such as fish weirs and harpoons. This may be why there was a change to much cruder stone tools than had been the case before; the most important tools were now being made from wood or bone. There is some evidence that red deer were being hunted by this time, and their antlers can also be used as tools. Something was about to happen, though, that was about to change their way of life much more profoundly than anything they could ever have imagined.

IRELAND'S FIRST FARMERS

While the people we have been considering eked out their existence on the most westerly land in Europe, a revolution, the birth of the Neolithic, or New Stone Age, had taken place thousands of miles away and perhaps thousands of years previously. In south-west Asia and the area we now think of as the Middle East, other people had found a way to abandon the nomadic way of life and to come together in communities which were based on agriculture and the keeping of domestic animals. The increased manpower which resulted from living together allowed them to undertake projects (such as irrigation) that were beyond the capabilities of smaller groups. This increased their efficiency in food production. Because they were no longer moving from place to place they had time to build proper shelters. The most vulnerable in the community, the very young, were less exposed to the twin dangers of hunger and the diseases which accompanied it. At the other end of the scale, adults were no longer subject to the dangers and stresses of the hunter-gatherer and their life expectancy increased. The very old no longer had to struggle to keep up. This lowered the death rate while the birth rate increased. More children survived to have children themselves, and the population increased.

This would have been seen as a good thing at first, since it would mean more hands for work. There would have come a time, even so, when the population would have become too great for the resources in a particular area. This would have put pressure on some of the people to leave the home area and to seek out new land suitable for cultivation. Probably, after the harvest had been gathered in, they would have sent scouts out in different directions. They would look for the right combination of soil and water. When they reported back, a decision would be made by the tribal elders as to where they should go. Colonising would have been a job for young people, who would be expected to live long enough to see the project through. They would have taken a supply of seed, and enough food to see them through to the first harvest. They would also have taken as many domestic animals as the original settlement could spare.

The land they entered was not uninhabited; it was just that it was inhabited at such a low density that the people living there were not strong enough to repel the newcomers. Much as Europeans moved west across the American prairies, only temporarily impeded by the hunter-gathering Native Americans, so these farming people gradually spread out from the Middle East. The people they met began to copy the ways of the incomers. The idea spread much more quickly than the people whose ancestors had developed it. The first signs of farming appear on the western seaboard of mainland Europe by 4500 BC, and there were farmers in Britain and Ireland by 4000 BC. Since pigs, quite literally, can't fly, the domestic animals had to be transferred to the offshore island by boat. So had the seeds needed for the cereals that appeared in the British Isles for the first time about then. Stacking barley in the bottom of a boat is one thing, but controlling animals as big as cattle is a lot more difficult, and would have taken a knowledge and expertise in handling large animals that could only be derived from long years of working with them. For this reason it was probably a new wave of colonisers that brought domestic animals.

The newcomers were searching out a different type of land than that used by the original inhabitants, which may have reduced any risk of conflict. They could not work the heavy soils and tangled woods of the river valleys. They looked instead for the lighter soils of the higher land. Stands of elm were a good indication of the right type of soil. This meant getting rid of the trees, but the new farmers were equal to this. Among their tools were polished stone axes easily capable of felling the smaller forest trees. The mature trees had a complete ring of bark removed from trunk. Sap was no longer able to flow and the crowns of the trees died. With no leaves to keep out the light, grass and other plants were able to grow.

To the natives, seeing ground cleared on a scale they had never dreamed of, and animals they had never seen before, like cattle and sheep and goats, the incomers must have seemed like wonder workers. Even to see the houses they built, so different from their own shelters that had changed little over two millennia, was to have eyes opened to a world of possibilities.

On the northern slopes of the Ballinderry Valley, in the townland of Ballynagilly, are the remains of one of the earliest houses discovered in the British Isles. The farmer who built it knew what he was doing. He chose the site carefully, at the top of a small hill of glacial debris which consisted mostly of gravel. In today's much wetter climate, it is almost the only dry spot on a wet mountainside. He cut and sank posts to mark out a shape that was almost square, the longer sides just over 21ft, the shorter sides just under 20ft. Along the longer sides he cut a trench into which he inserted the ends of oak planks that he had prepared to serve as walls. Halfway between the two walls he sank another series of posts, taller than the first series. These he used to support a pitched roof, of woven willow branches probably; a necessity even in those drier days to allow the rain to run off. He knew enough about engineering to know that the forces working on the gable walls would not be as complex as those on the walls supporting the roof, so there was no need to dig a trench to support those oak planks, while it would be safe to have a door here. Inside the house he built a hearth, and what might have been an oven. The site was reoccupied at some time in the Bronze Age, but before that, around 3700 BC, it caught fire. It is the charcoal that resulted from this blaze that allowed archaeologists to establish the early date of the building.

While it was lived in the owner would have had a very different kit of tools from those used in Ireland before. In addition to the polished stone axes, there would have been flint tools for harvesting crops, quern stones to grind cereals before cooking, and pots made from clay that could be used not only to cook the food, but to store the ingredients. In order that the farmer could supplement his diet with meat, he would have had arrowheads of flint and flint-tipped javelins, very different in design from those used by the Mesolithic hunters.

The pattern of settlement then seems to be much as it is now in rural Ulster, with farmhouses isolated from one another. Within the European context, such dispersed settlement is almost unique to Ireland. It was not till the Vikings introduced towns and the English introduced villages that the way of life changed. The Irish version of rural settlement can be seen in Gweedore, County Donegal, which has been described as a 'rural landscape verging on the urban'.

Even within Ulster, living places have been found at quite different extremes from the Ballynagilly house. Campsites of Neolithic groups that may not have been as stable or as large as the Ballynagilly community have been found in sand dunes near Dundrum in County Down, in sand dunes at White Park Bay in County Antrim, and along the coast near Glenarm. These may have been temporary places, where farmers worked much as the Mesolithic people had, collecting and working enough flint to last them the year. Near Carnlough in County Antrim there is evidence that Neolithic people worked flints on a site on the coast. Associated with this were the remains of farmsteads found on Windy Ridge, on the Antrim Plateau above the modern town. It is possible that the inhabitants of the farm in the hills went down to the coast on a regular basis to fashion new flint tools. It is also possible that some of the new settlers were primarily pastoralists, and that they had to move their herds to fresh grazing each season, in a practice that would come to be known to modern Irish farmers as booleying.

Not all settlements were small. On Lyles Hill and on Donegore Hill, also in County Antrim, there are the remains of huge hill-top enclosures dating from between 2000 BC and 3000 BC. Large numbers of people lived here. Ditches were dug around them, with red deer antlers used as picks. The enclosures were inhabited at the same time, although they were very close together. It is interesting to wonder what the relationship was between the two centres, and whether our farmer in Ballynagilly knew anything about them.

These are the only Neolithic settlements of this scale so far found in Ulster, indeed, the number of Neolithic settlements of any size discovered in Ireland falls far short of what might be expected from the rest of Europe. Where signs of settlement have been found, they are often associated with pits or ditches, and these are often filled with potsherds and flints. There is a debate among archaeologists as to whether the pits were filled in as part of a ritual offering, or simply dug as a handy way of getting rid of rubbish.

There is also a scarcity of evidence as to how Neolithic people lived in Ireland, what their economy was based on. In a large part, this is because most settlements were on what is now acid soil, which rots away animal and most plant remains. Plants which have been charred do not rot so easily, since the process of burning alters their chemistry and saves them from further decay. It occasionally happened that the clay used for pottery also contained some seeds from crop species. From this evidence we know that wheat and barley, at least, were grown. Among animals found around the settlements, the remains of cattle, sheep, goats, pigs and dogs have been identified.

We have evidence of the ways in which the Neolithic population altered their environment. One of the most enduring types of organic material is plant pollen. As sufferers from hay fever know, it gets everywhere, and the best thing to clear the air is a good shower of rain, which drives it down to the ground. In areas like lakes and peat bogs, it can build up as a record of the vegetation of an area at any given time, stretching back to the last Ice Age. Scientists have been examining the pollen remains from Neolithic sites like Ballynagilly and nearby Beaghmore. At both these sites any interesting change occurred around 3800 BC. At that time there was a significant drop in the amount of pollen from oak, pine, hazel and elm, with elm in particular suffering a spectacular decline. Any break in the forest canopy soon allows grasses to increase and, sure enough, there is a distinct increase in grass pollen. No natural process, however, can explain what appears along with the grass; quite large amounts of charcoal flecks, evidence of burning.

These first Irish farmers, with their efficient stone axes, cut down the trees. They then burnt out the stumps and planted their crops. Among the crops were weeds and flowers which were now seen for the first time in Ireland, such as fumitory. Pasture for their animals was easy to arrange, since it simply involved allowing the natural grasses to grow in newly opened spaces, a natural wood-land process, and allowing their livestock access to the forest, where they could browse on the fresh growth in the spring and grub for acorns and hazelnuts in the autumn. The opened patches need not be very large and their fertility could always be maintained by the manure of the domestic animals. If even this was not enough, there was always the option of moving on to a new area of forest. The old clearing might start to regenerate into secondary forest, but browsing by domestic stock and by red deer might convert it into a permanent glade in the forest, as happens even today in the wildwoods of central Europe.

We also have evidence that these early farmers had some sort of religious sensibility, at least in terms of their attitudes to their dead. They built elaborate tombs, many of which are now in plain view. Almost certainly others are still to be discovered, currently covered by layers of peat. These areas had a light, well-drained soil during Neolithic times. The better climate of the time meant that cereals could be grown at a much higher elevation than would be possible at present. One site showing evidence for cereal production has been excavated high on the slopes of Slieve Croob in County Down, over 1,500ft above sea level; this might have been at the upper extremity of cultivation, even then, and the evidence suggests that most farms were established somewhere between 400ft and 800ft above sea level.

The source of the Ballinderry.

Tombs were not the only structures that have survived to the present in a protective blanket of peat. Like his modern successor, the early farmer built stone walls to surround fields. These served the dual function of protecting growing crops from grazing animals and of clearing the fields of large stones, making the land easier to cultivate. The most extensive field system, at Céide Fields in County Mayo, would have taken a community of something like fifty families to carry out the project. Once again the question arises as to how these people lived; were their houses isolated, or gathered together into a village? Some sort of social organisation was involved, and it would have required more than a simple coming together of isolated farmers to get the work done.

In Ulster, the only remains of Neolithic field walls to be identified even tentatively are on the Antrim Plateau above Carnlough, but in County Tyrone walls disappearing into bogs is a phenomenon which has been recorded over many years, and it is quite possible that a Neolithic wall system will be discovered under the blanket bog that is still very extensive in the high ground on either side of the Ballinderry.

Neolithic tools were very effective. The tool we associate most often with these people is the axe. For some time after their arrival in Ireland, these first farmers still used flint axes. They soon discovered that a much better material was porcellanite. This is a stone that was formed when a laterite soil was baked by contact with lava. There are only two sources of this in Northern Ireland; one is on the side of Tievebulliagh Mountain, in County Antrim, while the other occurs on Rathlin Island. Who discovered these outcrops is unknown, but they were soon being exploited and were to form the basis of what may have been the first trading economy in Ulster. Weathering would have caused some broken fragments of the rock to be lying around, and it was probably these that were first exploited to make axes. When these ran out, the early miners began exploiting the outcrops themselves, building a fire on the surface that would cause the stone to crack. Using hammer-stones made from quartzite, the miners chipped the porcellanite stones so that they were roughly axe-shaped. These were then distributed to different workshops and here the final polishing would be done, using a sandstone grinding block. When the entire surface was polished, it was fitted to a wooden handle, and used like a modern axe. The resulting tool was extremely effective. Both Danish and Russian archaeologists have 'field tested' stone axes. In one case, three men cleared 500m^2 of birch forest in four hours; in another a man felled a pine tree which had a trunk 25cm in diameter in only twenty minutes.

Sometimes axe heads were manufactured that were so large, at up to 38cm long, and so heavy that it is impossible to believe that they were designed for practical use. These had a symbolic purpose, as expressions of wealth or power. Another stone product that reinforces the idea of a hierarchical society is the mace head, many of which date from around this time. They were made with a hole in the middle into which a wooden handle could be mounted. Because of the places in which they have been found, they seem to indicate high status and authority, perhaps as the modern mace symbolises the authority of the House of Commons.

Most tools were still made of flint, albeit of a standard of manufacture much more sophisticated than before. Better results were now being achieved in finishing these tools by the use of a technique known as pressure flaking. The flint was held in one hand, which was protected by a piece of durable leather. The other hand held the flaking tool, usually made from bone or antler tine. The tip would be placed against the edge of the flint and pressed hard. A small flake would come off the flint's lower side. Working carefully, the craftsman could produce a much sharper and more finely detailed tool than had been possible before.

Some of the most attractive tools of the period are the arrowheads and javelin heads that were being produced. Arrows were the main tool of the hunt, and could also be used in warfare. The heads used for javelins were much larger, up to about 25cm long, and much more robust. As well as being everyday objects, javelins were considered important enough to be left in tombs as grave goods. Flint knives were also used, but perhaps the most abundant tools remaining in Neolithic settlements are scrapers, designed to be used in preparing animal hides as clothes. Another form of scraper, known as the hollow scraper, with its blade like a concave bay, extended the possibility of the tool, and could have been used to prepare the shafts of arrows, or of putting feathers into those shafts, or even as a saw for bones. We can be certain that if we can think of different uses for the device, Neolithic man or woman could think of just as many, and probably a few more.

One of the major changes to everyday life that Neolithic settlers introduced to Ireland was the use of pottery, which could be used for storage or even for cooking. Archaeologists suggest that making pots was a task undertaken by the women of the group once or twice a year. Firstly, they would gather clay. After removing stones or any other impurities they would mix it with a little sand or crushed stone. This would minimise the amount of shrinking as the vessel cooled and meant that fewer pots would crack at that stage. It also meant that the pot could be heated in cooking food. The women would then coil the clay, in much the same way that children make 'snakes' out of Plasticine. The coils were then placed on top of one another and shaped so that the crude outline of a pot was formed. The women smoothed the outside and the inside of the pot and might even rub the outside with a bone or a smooth stone to give it a polished appearance. They put the pot on one side to dry, since the presence of any moisture in the clay left it liable to explode during firing. Kilns were not used, and the dry pots were fired directly in the fire. The women had some control over the final colour. If the pots were exposed to the air during firing, they took on an orange colour. If, on the other hand, the pots were completely buried in the hot ashes of a fire, they would end up as black, or a very dark brown. As the Neolithic age progressed, so did the designs in pottery, and later pots were often covered in intricate designs. They also developed different shapes, presumably for different purposes. This maybe showed an increased specialisation by some members of the community, the beginnings of a craft.

We know very little about the clothes worn by these early farmers, except in a negative sense. They cannot have been made from wool, since the sheep that they cared for did not have wool in the way that we imagine sheep nowadays. The other material that was commonly used to make clothes on mainland Europe, linen, was not available in Ireland, and there is no evidence of flax in the pollen record till much later in the island's history. We are left to presume that the clothes of the time were made from animal hide, and this presumption is supported by the great number of flint scrapers that have been found in Neolithic sites.

View from the cairn.

Court tomb.

The Neolithic was the time of megaliths. When we examined the remains of Mesolithic man in Ireland, we commented on his use of microliths, tiny stones, in his hunting tools. Megaliths are at the other end of the scale; huge boulders which were used to erect monuments and to build tombs. Some of these stones are so large that it strains credulity that early man could have moved them given the limitations of the technology available to him. Early modern man looked at these enormous structures and found them so amazing that he attached names to them like the Giant's Grave or Diarmuid and Grainne's bed, linking them to mythologies of his own time. One of the most remarkably well-preserved tombs, and one of the earliest, is in Creggandevesky, near the headwaters of the Ballinderry.

Creggandevesky is a court tomb, one of the earliest types. Court tombs have three basic components. There is a stone gallery which is usually divided into a number of burial chambers, from two to five, by the use of stone lintels or sills. At the entrance to the gallery is a sort of forecourt, formed by a crescent of upright stones. Finally, the gallery is covered by a long stone cairn which is broadest at the front or court end, and narrowest at the back, behind the gallery. There was very little of this showing when Creggandevesky was first examined. There were signs of a cairn, but only the ends of three stones could be seen and it seemed to have sunk into the bog. The owner of the land wanted to reclaim it as agricultural land, and wanted to know if there was any reason he should not remove the stones. A rescue excavation was launched and an oval cairn which was 22m long, 17m wide and 2m high was revealed. The three original stones turned out to be two kerb

A large stone from the court tomb.

stones and the entrance lintel to the gallery. The stones had collapsed, making the tomb appear wider and lower than it would have been originally. When the collapsed stones had been removed, the investigators found a court at the south-east end of the cairn, and a burial gallery that was divided into three chambers. In and around the cairn were found a fine leaf-shaped arrowhead, some Neolithic pottery and the remains of some cremated bones. They also found some flint scrapers and pieces of waste stone at the rear of the tomb, at what would have been the original ground level when the tomb was erected.

Pottery is found in most tombs, together with samples of most of the tools that were used at the time: hollow scrapers; end scrapers; javelin heads; arrowheads; porcellanite axes, and sometimes personal decoration, such as stone beads. The range of grave goods, in particular the pottery, tells us that the tombs were built in the early part of the Neolithic, but that they continued in use for a long time, maybe as long as a thousand years. The cremated bones at Creggandevesky are also typical, because cremation seems to have been part of the ritual of death. Quite often pieces of charcoal were picked up with the burnt bones as they were being transferred from the pyre to the burial chamber. If there is enough charcoal, this can be used in carbon dating the remains.

Given the amount of effort that was put into building these court cairns and the fact that they were in use for almost a millennium, it is surprising that there are so few actual human remains discovered in the burial chambers. This has led some archaeologists to question the assumption that they were built primarily as tombs. Most archaeologists agree that the courts themselves were used as ritual sites, but some go further and feel that the entire cairn was part of the ritual. To explain their reasoning, they look towards the different way that the Neolithic peoples used the land compared to the Mesolithic hunter-gatherers. The population of Ireland in Mesolithic times was small and nomadic, and there would have been little attachment to any particular piece of land. A farmer's relationship with the land is very different, since a farm represents a personal investment in time and effort. Perhaps the picture we should have of these megalithic structures is that they were claiming the landscape for the group; by burying remains of its ancestors in the cairn, the group was legitimising its claim to the land. The way that they are spread out, on average three miles or 4½km apart, fits in with this supposition. If one family group claimed each section of land, these territories in a way anticipate the later division of the countryside into townlands, a system unique to Ireland. The distribution of the court cairns themselves are not unique to Ulster, but are almost so. The only counties beyond those of modern Ulster where they are found in significant numbers are: Louth, in the Cooley Peninsula, which was considered part of Ulster in the sagas; Leitrim; Roscommon, and in great numbers in Sligo and Mayo.

View of inner chambers.

A wider view of the inner chambers.

A much simpler sort of tomb was the Portal Tomb. Until relatively recently, these were called 'Portal Dolmens', and the name persists in many tourist signs around the country. These consisted of three or four megaliths standing on end. The 'portal' part of the name comes from the gap or portal which is always found between the two highest standing stones, placed at what is presumed to be the entrance to the tomb. On them is suspended the wonder of these tombs, a huge capstone. The biggest of these, in County Carlow, is estimated to weigh 100 tons. Portal tombs are probably the Neolithic structures which best capture the romance of the Irish countryside, with their simplicity of line balancing the weight of the stones symbolising the foundations of Ireland. Where they occur, they are much loved by the local people. The simple burial chamber is situated within the uprights and protected by the capstone, which itself was protected by a small cairn.

The human remains and the grave goods found within these chambers are so similar to those in court tombs that it is obvious that both were being used at the same time. The openings of both sorts of tomb face east.

There are a few portal tombs along the Ballinderry Valley, such as the one near Cregganconroe, which was damaged at some time. There are none of the huge tombs found along the Bend of the Boyne at Newgrange or at Dowth and Knowth, which might be seen as the acme of Neolithic tomb building in Ireland. Less spectacular versions of these, known as passage tombs, are found in south and east Ulster. Possibly the nearest one to the Ballinderry was at Sess

Kilgreen, near Ballygawley. Although the tomb is damaged, and one of the roof stones has become separated from the tomb and is used by cattle as a scratching stone, the pattern of spirals and lozenges can still be made out, and there are some of the best rock engravings to be found in Ulster.

The most modern – if that word does not seem strange in the context – tomb from Neolithic times is the wedge tomb. Its name refers to its shape, narrowing as it does at the far end of the tomb from the entrance. It is a type of tomb that is associated mostly with the south and west of Ireland, but there is a concentration in the three counties of Donegal, Tyrone and Derry. Only a small number of the 465 wedge tombs known in Ireland have been excavated, and the limited data allow lots of views about their dates and origins. Some that have been excavated show the usual cremated remains of humans, but also a much later pottery than we have seen so far, and almost half even have remains which we associate with the Bronze Age, such as a mould for an axe, and a bronze blade, which were found in north Tyrone, near Claudy.

One type of megalithic remains that is certainly not limited to Ireland is the stone circle. In Britain and Ireland there are more than 900 of these enigmatic monuments. Within Ireland, there are two main clusters: one is in south Munster, at the other end of the country; the second is in mid-Ulster, almost centred on the Ballinderry Valley. There are of course other stone circles beyond these, such as the one at Ballynoe in County Down. The circles can be quite small, such as the one at Ballybriest on the southern slopes of Slieve Gallion, which is only 3.7m, or as large as the one at Aghalane, in Omagh District, which is 35m, but the average is about 11m, with more than twenty stones. Although we think of these as standing stones, in many circles the stones have fallen down, or perhaps have never been raised. The stones themselves are rarely more than ½m tall, though there is often one taller than the rest, more than 1m tall. There is a temptation to assume that there is some significance in the location and orientation of the taller stone, but detailed analysis of numerous sites has failed to provide any universal solution of the mystery of why they were raised in the first place.

Some of the most interesting stone circles in our study area are to be found in the Beaghmore complex on the southern end of the Sperrins near Davagh Forest, and close to the site of the Ballynagilly house. The stones were discovered in the 1930s, but excavation was not begun until after the war, in 1945. What was found was an amazingly interrelated arrangement of stone circles, stone alignments and small round cairns. The stones were quite small, and seemed to have been placed on the ground rather than sunk into the earth. There are seven circles altogether. That with the tallest stones, up to 1.2m high, has a cairn within it, and the rest of its interior is filled with close-set stones known locally as 'dragons' teeth'. Associated with each circle is at least one alignment of stones, the longest of which actually stretches for 88m beyond the boundary fence. All the cairns have kerbs of small boulders, and most of them had traces of cremated bone. In one there was a polished porcellanite axe head.

One of the first things to strike a visitor to the site is the amount of labour that must have been put into their construction. It is possible to surmise that most stone circles have been designed to indicate a particular part of the horizon, associated with the rising and setting sun, with the moon and even with some of the brighter stars. Four of the circles at Beaghmore seem to be aligned with sunrise in midsummer. The stone walls are less easy to explain, and it may be that they are simply the remains of the boundary walls of an earlier field system. Examining the pollen trapped in these walls allowed scientists to put together a history of the vegetation in the area going back 7,000 years. This field system is undoubtedly Neolithic, but the circles continued in use for many years, and many of them were not built until the Bronze Age.

It is worthwhile using the evidence we have to attempt to reconstruct a picture of farming life in mid-Ulster in Neolithic times. The first thing we have to say is that there was no Ulster, certainly not in the north–south relationship with the rest of the island that identifies Ulster nowadays. Examining patterns of tombs leads us to the conclusion that megaliths in Antrim have a closer connection with Louth and the east of Ireland, while those of Tyrone and the west are connected to Sligo and Mayo. The cultural division was east–west rather than north–south. A certain amount of this perception persists to the present day, when some residents of Belfast and the Lagan Valley are concerned that crossing west over the River Bann takes them 'beyond the Pale', into wild and unexplored territory.

All the same, there were more similarities than differences between east and west. Both peoples lived similar lives, in isolated farms that provided all that was needed for sustaining life. Families came together for religious ceremonies that were based around court or portal tombs. They probably came together to help in construction projects on individual farms, for the building of a new house. They certainly came together for public work projects; for the great enclosures at Donegore and at Lyles Hill, and for the walled landscape at Céide Fields. Archaeologists studying the work done think they know how it was organised. Groups of men took turns doing the work, whether it was digging ditches at Donegore or raising walls in Mayo. They would have worked for a specific length of time, then handed over to the next team and returned to their own farms. They would have been tough and hardy, and they would have needed to be, for even the hardiest of them lived no more than thirty or thirty-five years. In the next years, however, there was to be a change that was to bring great advances in society – the increasing use of metal.

THE MAGIC OF METAL

The people of mid-Ulster would have been aware of metals for some time. Gold was, after all, freely available in some of the rivers of the area, and continues to occur in these, although not in great quantities. Within living memory, some farmers along the upper Moyola, above Draperstown, used to stretch straw ropes across the river during the autumn floods. When the straw rope was retrieved, small grains of gold were sometimes found amongst the strands; not enough to make a living, perhaps, but enough to fill a tobacco tin in a lifetime's collecting. Gold has the advantage of being relatively malleable, and pieces can be joined together simply by hammering. Gold is too soft to be used as a tool, but another metal which could be shaped by hammering was copper, and this was the first metal to be used as a tool. In Egypt, copper was one of the first metals to be used in carving stone inscriptions. It is not normally found in nuggets, as gold can be, but as an ore. Someone, somewhere, had found that copper could be obtained from the ore if it was heated enough. When the copper melted, it was possible to pour the liquid into a mould, which meant that the tool-making process became both more technical and quicker. Metalworkers became a skilled and high-status class, capable, almost, of magic.

Copper is still relatively soft, however, and work would have had to be interrupted regularly so that tools could be re-sharpened. Someone discovered that a small amount of tin, added when the copper was molten, combined with the copper to form a new metal, much stronger than its component parts. The new metal was bronze, and it became so significant that its name was given to the next great age of mankind, the Bronze Age.

About 2500 BC, beakers, which are simply pots without handles, vaguely resembling modern beakers, began to appear all over Europe. They had a good deal of ornamentation and they were much better made than anything produced in the Neolithic. On the Continent and in Britain, the best examples were found in graves, usually with other artefacts and quite often with objects that identified the owner as an archer. There were enough similarities all over the beakers' range for archaeologists to speak of the 'Beaker Folk', whom they imagined as having a sort of gypsy lifestyle, wandering anywhere and everywhere. They even saw them as equivalent to modern Irish 'tinkers', dealing in metals as they moved around.

Most modern archaeologists see things differently. The beaker itself, they say, had some religious significance, perhaps some role in an important ritual. The explanation then would be that beakers were adopted by peoples as part of a religious package, just as the ciborium, chalice and paten are part of the religious package of the Catholic Church. Whichever explanation is true, the distribution of the few beaker remains in Ireland is concentrated in the northern half of the island. Whether by coincidence or because the site was still the most suitable in the area, one of the few Beaker habitations found was at Ballynagilly, where our first Neolithic house had been found. Here excavators found, in an area of roughly 60m², concentrations of beaker pottery, tools, pits and hearths, together with charcoal which allowed the occupation to be dated to about 2500 BC-2200 BC. The investigators obtained pollen samples from the surrounding bog which allowed them to reconstruct the landscape at the start of the Bronze Age. They found that the forest had grown back after the original trees had been cleared by the Neolithic farmers. Now it was cleared again, allowing them to speculate that these new people were also farmers who needed open ground.

There was a particular way in which the Irish of the early Bronze Age differed from those living over most of Europe. They recycled the monuments already in the landscape. I mean by this that rather than build new monuments in which to place their burials, they simply inserted them in tombs which already existed, so it is possible to find Bronze Age funerary goods in a Neolithic wedge tomb. It was a characteristic that they shared with the people of north-west Scotland. And it is a characteristic that survived in Ulster up to the present day; many abandoned churches in the area have quite modern graves within the standing walls.

Signs of 'Beaker Folk' habitation are rare on the ground, and once again it is through the discovery of their artefacts that we have been able to build up a picture of their lifestyle. In Beaker graves there are often items which are associated with archery; arrowheads and wrist-braces, for example, which were used to protect the hand holding the bow from being damaged by the released bowstring. There are signs of a second Bronze Age culture at this time. Another sort of grave, complete with its own form of grave good, began appearing in Ulster and Tyrone. The new graves were often simple holes in the ground, but more often flat stones were used to construct a box; these were cist burials. The grave goods were still containers, but of many different types. For all their variety, they had a number of things in common:

They are normally found in graves rather than settlements.

They are more often found in cist graves rather than megaliths.

They are more often found with cremated remains than with inhumation burials, where the remains are interred unburned.

Their form and decoration are closely related to similar wares from Britain.

Much of the variation in the vessels seems to be regional, and it may indicate tribal groupings. If this is true, one such group seems to have lived in the Foyle Valley–East Donegal region; another was found in Antrim–Down; while a third, known as the Hiberno/Scottish series, lived in Antrim and Tyrone and included the Ballinderry River Valley. From remains found on Coney Island, in the south-west corner of Lough Neagh, we can deduce that they lived in rectangular, sod-built houses, with wooden supports for the roof, and a hearth for cooking indoors. Near Gweedore in Donegal, archaeologists found the remains of food at a settlement: shellfish; dog; sheep; ox; red deer; pig, and horse.

Graves and cemeteries came in many forms. They could be completely flat, with nothing to mark the location of the graves. At other times graves were placed under a small cairn. Usually each cist grave contains only one body, but there are examples where the remains of five have been found in the one place. Usually one or two pots were buried with the remains, but in a good number of cases there is no pottery. On some occasions a bronze knife or a bronze bowl has been placed in the grave. Near Claudy, in the northern Sperrins, an attempt was made to 'reconstruct' a body from unburned remains. The body was that of a young man, 6ft 2in tall, with very robust bones in his right arm. It was deduced from this that he took part in some trade that involved the repetitive use of one arm, such as carpentry.

An interesting aspect of the new graves, whether they are solitary or together in cemeteries, is their location. Until now graves had been built rather than dug, and were found in the uplands. Cist graves are found in the sands and gravels of river valleys. Farms were being created in this new environment. A combination of upland degradation and the spread of blanket bog, perhaps caused by climate change, may have made this move necessary, but it was the introduction to Ireland of the plough at about this time that made it possible. The new environment meant changes in farming practice. The land was less suitable for cereals, and if the climate was deteriorating, there may not have been enough hours of sunshine to ripen the crop. It was probably at this stage in Irish history that cattle became such a dominant part of the Irish economy.

It is interesting to speculate where the metals were obtained to manufacture the bronze weapons and bowls that were found in these graves. The only mine that we now know that was producing copper in the Bronze Age is in County Cork. Gold was to be had in County Wicklow. As far as the evidence of mining is concerned, tin would have had to be brought from Cornwall. The truth is likely to be simpler than that. There are several copper deposits in Tyrone. Tin can be obtained from Slieve na miskin in the Mournes, and there is gold in several parts of the Sperrins, as well as in the Moyola Valley and at Slieveanorra in Antrim. Although we have no definite evidence that they were used in the

Bronze Age, they may well have been. Many moulds for casting have been found in Ulster, which would indicate that there was a well-established metal industry in the province.

The earliest metal tools were simple flat axes made of copper. These could easily be made using a single sandstone mould. The toolmakers were always striving for greater sophistication, and two-piece moulds began to appear, made of soapstone or chlorite schist. This allowed curved sides and surface decoration to be an integral part of the axe. Bronze is twice as efficient as polished stone, but the amount of decoration that appears on some of the axes suggests that they were used for social purpose, to indicate status. Some axes were too big to be handy tools, and were probably used as weapons. There were other weapons. As well as bows and arrows, there were simple bronze daggers, to be used when an enemy got too close. Later, these were attached at right angles to a wooden handle and formed a halberd. In spite of all the advances in metallurgy, flint arrowheads and knives continued to be used. There was also an extension in the uses of metal in everyday life. Moulds for metal sickles, as well as for razors, have been found among moulds for socket spearheads.

Around this time there seems to have been an increasing emphasis on personal ornamentation. One of the most common pieces of personal jewellery was the lunula, named after its likeness to the crescent moon. This was made of a thin sheet of gold, cut and beaten into shape before being decorated. It seems to have been worn round the neck and may have been a badge of rank or of office.

As the Bronze Age continued, we get further glimpses of everyday life. In Cullyhanna, County Armagh, about 1526 BC, another family group left signs of their domestic way of life. They had an enclosure that was about 20m across, surrounded by upright oak stakes. Within this was a timber-built house, about 6m across, with a hearth in the middle. Also within the enclosure were the remains of a flimsy structure which was probably a windbreak for an outdoor hearth. Another site, at Ballycroghan in County Down, shows us how they cooked their meat. A hole was dug in the ground and then lined with wood to make it waterproof. It was then partly filled with water. A fire was lit nearby and stones were heated in it. When the stones were hot enough, they were dropped in the water, which came to the boil. To keep the water boiling, the cook kept adding hot stones. A device like this could cook a 10lb leg of mutton in four hours. It was such an efficient piece of equipment that some were used right up to medieval times, although their heyday was the Bronze Age.

There continued to be advances in metallurgy, particularly in the matter of weapons. Large flanges were added to axe heads to give them a better grip on the handle. 'Stop' ridges were added to stop the axe riding up the handle and splitting it. This led to the invention of the palstave, which in turn allowed more sophisticated carpentry. Spearheads were now made with an inner cavity so that the shaft could go most of the way up the head. Loops on the head allowed it to be more securely fastened on the handle, meaning that it wouldn't pull out as a warrior tried to retrieve his weapon from an enemy's body. Lighter spearheads were designed for javelins, while larger heads were used in hand-to-hand thrusting weapons. Some daggers were lengthened into dirks or rapiers. Many of these have been found in the Bann, raising the question as to whether they are the souvenirs of long-ago battles along a natural frontier or were offerings made to the river goddess.

Another innovation was a different way of managing trees. Ash and hazel trees were no longer felled and cleared away. Instead they were coppiced, cut back to just above ground level. This produced a harvest of long, straight shoots which could be collected after a number of years and be used for posts, or handles for axes, or as shafts for spears and javelins.

It is possible, through the study of hoards found in different parts of Ireland, to put dates to some of these developments. Socketed axes, hammers and carpenters' tools such as the saw, the punch, the graver and the chisel appeared about 1200 BC. Among more personal possessions are gold bracelets, necklets and earrings. The first swords appeared about 1000 BC. By 900 BC swords were more sophisticated, and there were now metal buckets and cauldrons, horns and decorative shields.

These changes in tools and weaponry must have been accompanied by – or even caused by – changes in society. To keep trade moving and to keep order needed strong leadership. To enforce the leader's decisions, he would have brought together a group of enforcers; a warrior class. He would have sought to impress others by his wealth and prestige, often by displaying his metal weapons and ornaments. The rapid spread of metal razors not simply in Ireland but throughout Europe indicates that Middle-Bronze-Age Irishmen kept themselves clean shaven. The increasing elaboration of weapons indicates that there was, indeed, a growing warrior class. This concern with military display and warfare came to a peak in the Late Bronze Age, after about 1200 BC.

Because of the materials from which they were made, weapons and tools and ornaments of the Late Bronze Age have survived in great numbers, and the museums of Europe contain impressive quantities of bronze and gold objects, gleaming in the spotlights of their display cabinets. In spite of the fact that this holds just as true in Irish museums as elsewhere, we know remarkably little about those who lived through the 900 or so years of this period; remarkably, we are even ignorant about how they buried their dead. We do know that society was becoming very stratified, and we know this because of the greatest Bronze Age site in Ireland, some thirty miles south of the Ballinderry Valley, the complex at Navan Fort, outside Armagh. This area requires much more description than is possible here, but there are some aspects we must look at.

Firstly, it was a long-lasting site of great social importance. Its place in tradition as the Emain Macha of the ancient kings of Ulster is supported by many of the finds here. One find in particular is fascinating: the skull of a Barbary ape. This must have been brought all the way from southern Spain before being donated to the king as an especially regal present, rarer, and therefore more precious, than any ornament of gold or silver. Nearby, at the King's Stables, are the remains of an artificial pool, the only one in Europe surviving from prehistoric times. At its bottom was a great collection of animal remains, many that had been thrown into the water without being butchered or cooked. An exception was the front half of a man's skull, which had been cut away from the rest of his body. This was obviously a ritual pool, where people made offerings to a god. It is interesting to consider that, in many parts of Ulster, country people still visit small versions of such pools, albeit now called holy wells, and leave votive offerings for the patron saint in return for his or her intervention on behalf of the supplicant.

At another site near Clogher, in County Tyrone, there is another fortified structure of only slightly lower status. This was the hill-top capital of the Airgialla, who were the successors of the kings of Navan. Of special interest here is the nature of the defences, which are timber laced, and very similar in construction to those of Iron Age Celts in Europe or, closer to home, south-west Scotland. Another example has been found in Rallagh, near Banagher in County Derry. The important thing about these walls was that their stones made them safe from fire, while an inner core of earth, which was often turned into glass by intense heat, made the stonework safe from battering rams. This tells us that such walls were meant for serious warfare, rather than simply raid and counter-raid.

We can make a few guesses what the people living in these settlements would have looked like. Almost certainly the men would have been clean-shaven, since many examples of bronze razors have been found from that time. Although no actual clothes have been found in Ireland, complete suits of clothes dating from the Late Bronze Age have been found in bogs in Denmark. It is a leap of faith to assume that Irish men and women wore the same type of clothes, but a fragment of cloth found in a bog near Armoy, in County Antrim, had been made using the same weaving technique as the Danish cloth. As well as that, we can make educated guesses about how the clothes were worn by the type of ornamented fasteners that were used to hold them in place. Small sleeve fasteners were found near Ardboe, close to where the Ballinderry River empties into Lough Neagh.

War became a bit more personal about 1000 BC. Before that warriors fought with spears and with stabbing rapiers. New swords were made with heavy, leaf-shaped blades that were designed for slashing. To make sure that the blade was not twisted out of a warrior's hand by the force of his stroke, the blade was extended to form a full metal hilt, which was then covered by wood, bone or ivory to give a comfortable and secure grip. Because the edges had to be kept sharp, and to avoid accidents, the swords were carried in scabbards. The main part of the scabbard was made out of hide or some other perishable material, but the tip of the scabbard, the chape, was often made of metal and the remains of these are often found. In the case of spears, rivets had replaced the system of loops and tyings that had secured the head to the shaft.

The increase in the effectiveness of weapons encouraged warriors to carry shields to defend themselves. Many of these have been found in Ulster, made of bronze, leather and wood. A bronze shield might look good, but it could be destroyed by a single slash of a sharp, heavy sword. It was safer to use them only on ceremonial occasions. A leather shield, properly tanned and shaped over a wooden shield mould, was quite capable of deflecting even a heavy stroke. It is interesting to think that Zulu warriors carried similar shields when they defeated a nineteenth-century British expedition at the Battle of Isandlwana, in Natal.

Not everybody could afford the financial and labour investment that such defences required. Lakeside campsites had been used for some time, but from now on their inhabitants went to some effort to improve their defensibility. A small island or a relatively shallow part of a lake would be built up using wooden logs, stones and fill, contained within a ring of timber piles that had been joined together by wattle. An artificial surface of brushwood or peat would then be created. There was usually one dwelling, but some crannogs had more than one house. Large flat stones were used as hearths, since much of the foundation material was inflammable. In the earliest crannog settlements the inhabitants moved by canoe between dwelling and shore. Crannogs were used right into medieval times, however, and later lake-dwellers sometimes built a causeway joining the artificial island to the shore.

Not all Irish families of the Late Bronze Age felt the need to defend their property. In the uplands and along the coast, settlements were more open. It is tempting to think that these were the houses of poorer people, living on the margins, who did not have anything of worth and that, since they did not have much worth stealing, there was less need to protect their property.

Ancient pollen samples taken from Slieve Gallion, on the north of the Ballinderry River, and at other sites in north Ulster, tell a story of forest clearance and increased grasslands. This increase in agriculture provided the economic driving force that allowed the development of industry, the leisure that encouraged ornamentation, and the greed or fear that led to warfare. Yet life was not a straightforward graph of increasing wealth and sophistication. At some stage during the Late Bronze Age, about 3,000 years ago, the volcano of

Hekkla, on Iceland, suffered a major eruption. The modern study of vulcanology has shown how such giant eruptions can affect the weather in subsequent years; sometimes the effect lasts for decades. People in Caithness and North Uist had to leave their homes, sometimes leaving entire villages deserted. The eruption had caused what used to be called a nuclear winter, with a combination of increased rainfall and cold weather. People trying to make a living in marginal land would be faced with crop failure and the subsequent death of livestock. They might have been able to survive a year or two, but beyond that the very young and the old would have started dying of hunger and deprivation and families would have been driven to look for salvation elsewhere.

There is evidence that disaster hit Ireland at the same time; not in abandoned houses, but in the growth rings of trees. Every child knows how the age of a tree can be calculated by counting its annual rings and most of us, at some time or other, have tried to work out the age of a log or a stump when it was felled. What is not so well known is that these rings can also give an idea of the climate each year that the tree grew; in a good year there would be a broad ring, while in a cold, wet year, the ring would be much narrower. Trees of the same species in a given area will all follow the same pattern. Scientists have used this fact to study the climate in Ireland back beyond the Bronze Age and have found that, for a period of about eighteen years, the oak trees of Ireland went through a period of great stress, probably caused by a rise in the water table. This period corresponds neatly with the great Hekkla eruption. It was shortly after this that some of the major defensive sites in Ulster were erected, perhaps in an effort to protect those who had a little from those who had nothing. It was also the time that the ritual pool at the King's Stables at Navan was built, and it is tempting to imagine people desperate to appease the gods that seemed determined to make the waters rise until they drowned the earth. In bog near Killymoon, just outside Cookstown, diggers found a wooden box containing a gold dress fastener which may also have been an offering to the gods of water. Perhaps the wife of a wealthy local chieftain was prepared to sacrifice this for the good of the land. For the average farmer along the Ballinderry River, far from the centre of power and simply waiting for the floods to recede and hoping for enough warmth and sunshine for the grass to grow and his few crops to ripen, it must have seemed as if the gods had abandoned him already. The hungry crying of his children would have told him that. Death must have seemed very near.

Strangely, in the whole of Ireland only three or four burials can be assigned with confidence to the Late Bronze Age. In the few that have been discovered, the human remains have been cremated, and the ashes have sometimes been placed in a pot. There are few signs of any places of public ritual, such as the megaliths had provided for earlier people. The ritual pond at the King's Stables is an exception, and it may give us a clue as to what ritual did happen at that time. This is particularly true if we also consider the environments in which many swords from that period have been found. In both Britain and Ireland almost half of the prehistoric swords that have been found have been retrieved from rivers and bogs. At a somewhat later date, Roman authors noted that Celts in many parts of Europe made offerings of treasures in sacred lakes. It may have been that, in Ireland, surplus wealth was also ritually offered to gods by being 'buried' in bog or river. Such offerings, done on behalf of the clan, would certainly have impressed the neighbours and underlined the individual's social status. A modern version might be the endowment of a hospital ward by a wealthy family.

At about 600 BC, a new type of sword was beginning to appear in Ireland. The pattern was being made from iron on continental Europe, but in Ireland the swords were made from bronze. Perhaps they mean no more than the spread of a new fashion to Ireland, which in turn might mean that people were travelling about more, perhaps as traders. In any case, there is a period of several hundred years when little is known about Ireland, and our next bit of evidence comes from a strange source: Egypt.

Although traders had been visiting Ireland for hundreds of years, it was in their interest to keep their routes and destinations secret, in order to maintain their monopoly. When that supreme bureaucracy, the Roman Empire, conquered Britain, secrecy was not an option. From then on, the only monopoly was that of the Emperor. He allowed no one to control any material that was of strategic importance, whether corn from Egypt or lead from Britain. Details of Ireland's estuaries and of the tribes that lived near them were noted and then sent on to Rome. From there copies must have been sent to what was then the greatest collection of texts in the world, the Library of Alexandria. There, a Roman mathematician of Greek descent, Claudius Ptolemy, used these and other details to put together an atlas of the known world. Out in the Western Ocean is an island that the Romans had named Hibernia, the place of winter; a wry comment on the Atlantic climate. The map has only a superficial resemblance to Ireland, but there is enough information to recognise Ulster and some of the major estuaries. The river names are difficult to identify, since they had been written phonetically from a language that originally had no script and had to be transcribed to the Greek alphabet, since Ptolemy's book was written in Greek. In spite of the difficulty, scholars have been able to identify Belfast Lough, Rathlin Island, the River Boyne and, amazingly, Navan Fort.

Since the origin of the map lies in overseas trading, it shouldn't be surprising that the peoples or tribes shown are those whose territory abutted on the coast. They have been given Latinised names but it is possible to work backwards and

Dew on grass.

place them in the Irish tradition. Ptolemy calls the people who lived in Armagh and Louth the Voluntii. The Celtic name was probably Uluti, which became Ulaid in old Irish. Ulaid means Ulsterman, so we can see that the whole province gained its name from a tribe living in the second century AD. The map shows few details of Ulster's interior, not even Lough Neagh. The courses of rivers are shown as more or less straight lines flowing from the centre of the island. The truth of the matter is that probably few, if any, traders made their way to the interior. It would have meant meeting more chiefs who would have to be kept sweet with bribes disguised as gifts.

The people of Ireland by this time were Celts. That is not to say that there had been a fresh wave of invasion, bringing in an entirely new people. What had been imported was the language, and a Celtic way of live. One of the most beautiful hoards of gold to be found in Ireland was at Broighter, near Limavady. The best known item in the collection was a beautiful model of a boat, complete with oars. More important was a golden torc, or collar. This had designs made up of curling, abstract patterns that were typically Celtic. By the time the hoard had been offered to the gods, Ireland was Celtic. In later times *The Book of Invasions*, written by Christian monks, told of a bloody history of warfare involving Formorians, Fir Bolg and Tuatha De Danann. The heroes of this last, triumphant group were in fact the Celtic gods who were worshipped in Ireland just before the coming of Christ. They were beaten in their turn by a group from Spain led by the sons of Mil (or Milesians). Their descendants became known as Gaels. It is interesting that this story was considered as factual history as late as the nineteenth century, and that even today more conservative Irish scholars speak of the Milesians when referring to the early Irish. Even today, facts are not allowed to get in the way of a good story.

The interior was sustained by a pastoral economy. The cattle were small by modern standards, with a height at the shoulder of 115cm at the maximum. The grass was sweet and nutritious, however, and the fame of Irish beef spread far beyond the island. One Roman writer, in AD 43, solemnly wrote that the pasture in Ireland was so good that cattle had to be stopped from eating too much, or they would have burst. That is not to say that the Irish ate beef at every meal. In pastoral economies such as this, even at the present time in parts of Africa, the size of a man's herd was an indication of his wealth and, since wealth meant status and status was important in a warrior society, the animals would have been slaughtered only sparingly, or in a good cause. Their milk would have been important, and their blood would probably have been drawn off from time to time either to be drunk straight or mixed with gruel to form a basic black pudding.

The ard, the predecessor of the modern plough, was beginning to be used to cultivate ground. Its design allowed the sod to be turned over, rather than simply opened as had happened with the wooden plough. Pulled by two oxen it could cultivate ground to a depth of 20cm. Sickles were now being made of iron and were more efficient. Preparing cereal had become more efficient also. Before this, the grains of cereal had been rubbed between two flat stones to prepare them for cooking. The stones were known as saddle querns. These were now being replaced by much more efficient rotary querns, a style that had been used in Scotland and Northern England. Meals were probably boiled in large cauldrons, some made of iron but many still made of bronze, and washed down with drink taken from wooden tankards.

This was the time of the great heroes of Irish myth; of Conchobor and the Red Branch; of Cú Chullainn and his battle with the men of Connacht; of Deirdre and her sorrows. Their shadows, the shadows of giants, have hung over the stories that were written down a few centuries later by monks such as those who wrote *The Book of Invasions*. It was a time when hill forts made of stone, like Grianan of Aileach, were dotted around Ireland, the seats of petty kings. Over eighty of these have been found. In a time of constant strife, arms were more important than ever, and the makers of metal had discovered how to use clay as a mould which was more easily worked with than stone. Wooden swords were found in peat in the Moyola Valley. The craftsman would use these to make a mould from which a casting could be made. They were making advances in metallurgy as well. They had discovered that the more slowly and evenly a casting was allowed to cool, the more reliable the sword would be. To slow down the cooling, they added a little lead to the molten metal.

There is evidence that a Roman governor of Britain, Agricola, considered invading Ireland. A petty king, exiled from his Irish territories, came to him for help in regaining them. The governor considered that Ireland could be taken and controlled by one legion supported by a few auxiliaries. A mutiny in Galloway disrupted his preparations, however, and his great plan was never put to the test. There almost certainly were Romans, however, who did come to Ireland. There have been Roman remains found in the Clogher Valley and in other places in Ireland. The full-scale invasion which took place a few hundred years later was of a very different kind from the one envisaged by Agricola.

✣ 2 ✣

THE COMING OF CHRISTIANITY

AN ISLAND RACE

By the time of Christ the people of the island saw themselves as being a single race, different from the other peoples around them. They shared a language, a set of laws and a way of life, but they were not a single nation; they were uniform, but not united. It was an island of small kingdoms, and there were probably dozens of them. There were no towns or villages. People lived on family farms, spread out over the countryside. Each farm was centred on a rath, a circular area enclosed by one or more banks. There were thousands of these around the island, and many still exist in the Ballinderry Valley that are more or less intact. Many people call them ring-forts, pronounced 'forths' in the local area, but this is to misunderstand their purpose. The smallest of them were about 30ft in diameter. They were made simply enough, by digging a circular ditch and throwing the spoil on the inside so that it formed an embankment. On some of these there are traces of a palisade, which was probably intended to keep out animals rather than people. Inside the embankment were some basic buildings. Traditionally there were five of these; the farmer's dwelling and four shelters for animals. These were built of very simple materials; the walls of branches, which were plastered inside and out with mud, with roofs of peat or wooden shingles. In some raths there were underground storage areas known by the French term *souterrain*. If a farm was being raided, these could probably double up as a shelter. In areas where there was a lot of stone, the enclosure might be stone-built, in which case it became known as a cashel. Raths and cashels were a long-lasting

O'NEILL'S OWN COUNTRY: A HISTORY OF THE BALLINDERRY VALLEY

form of residence. Something like them had been used in the Bronze Age, while people went on living in them right up till the seventeenth century.

A final type of settlement was used in the north and west of the island. This was the crannog. The name comes from the Irish for 'tree' and they were situated in shallow areas on loughs. Trees were used as a foundation and on top of this an artificial island was constructed. This could be joined to the shore by a causeway, though in deeper loughs a small boat would have been used. Because these were more expensive to build, they may have been associated with richer farmers. A person's wealth was calculated from the number of cattle that he owned. Although the plough had reached Ireland by this time, only a very small proportion of agricultural land – possibly as little as 5 per cent – was arable. The remainder was used to graze cattle. Even the poorest farmer might expect to have five milk cows.

Groups of these farms would have constituted a kingdom. Modern views of royalty give an altogether unbalanced view of what they might have consisted of. These were very minor kingdoms. A king might have accommodation within his rath for ten or so nobles who would form the core of his bodyguard. The families whom he ruled were the tuath, his people. He was their guardian, but he did not govern in the conventional sense. The origins of kingship were religious, and the king was the embodiment of the tuath. When the tuath was at war, he led nobles and freemen into battle. If he died, the tuath was defeated. The poets sang of his beauty and strength. Within the tuath he presided over the people's assembly, although not everyone living within his borders had a right to attend. His people followed the law, and the people themselves were the enforcers of the law, carrying out decisions arrived at by legal scholars or judges. In the earliest times, the king, like the poet, was above the law. By the seventh or eighth centuries, however, the custom had arisen of 'fasting against the king'. In this, an aggrieved person might go on hunger strike because of a perceived wrong done to him by the king. If the person was allowed to die by the king, this put the king in the wrong and he had to pay compensation to the plaintiff's relatives.

The king did have privileges. The one official whom the law allowed him was his collector of tribute, an amount of wealth which his nobles contributed to the privy purse on a regular basis. To ensure wholehearted cooperation, the king, by tradition, took a boy from each noble household to be reared within his. To the cynical, this might seem a little like hostage-taking, but it was more than that. It was considered an honour to be part of the king's household and relationships built up here lasted for life. In many ways it could be considered an academy for warriors. The boy Setanta was brought up in the household of Conor MacNessa, and grew up to be the hero Cúchulainn.

From the earliest times there was pressure to concentrate political power. Groups of lesser kings made themselves subject to stronger ones, who became known as 'Kings of Kings' in law. The King of Kings did not rule each separate tuath, but all acknowledged themselves as being dependent on him. Once again, he accepted hostages into his household to cement this dependence, and was given tribute which helped to pay for the protection that he gave. There was one higher level of kingship, the King of a province, known as 'King of High Noblemen', which had the same relation of dependence with middle kings which they in turn had with the lesser kings.

The people had no tradition of primogeniture. The first-born son had no automatic right to succeed. The heir was chosen from those with royal blood, that is, those up to the great-grandchildren of a king. In an effort to minimise the chance of any dynastic struggle, the heir was chosen during the lifetime of the king, in an agreement between the king and the 'certain family'. The heir was known as the Tanaiste, meaning 'the awaited one'. He was probably chosen soon after the king's succession, and, at least in later days, had a specific role in the running of the kingdom. The transfer of power did not always go smoothly. If a family had not produced a king since their grandfather or great-grandfather, there was a danger of them passing out of the 'certain family' and losing their claim to royal blood as well as the right to own land. Such families had more than a passing interest in who was chosen as heir, so the king often had to deal with internal discord as well as external threats to the tuath. It was only after a potential king had dealt with these problems that he was confirmed by the assembly. Where details of the ceremony have come down to this day, in the great centres of Tara, Cruacha and Emhain Mhacha, the king is said to be married to the land, responsible for making it fertile.

A small but very important part of the tuath was made up of the learned classes; the poets, the druids and the scholars of the law, or brehons, and the scholars of genealogy and history. All of these had gone through long periods of study, because they were custodians of the oral tradition. It took a druid a minimum of seven years, and often as many as twelve, to complete his studies. He had to be able to 'sing' his knowledge, a combination of genealogies and prescribed stories, learned day after day in darkened rooms. The years of study brought their own rewards, and the learned classes were held in high esteem, not simply among their own people, but across the whole island.

The people of the tuath formed a strict hierarchy. Below the king's 'certain family' were the nobility. These formed the warrior class, who fought with spear and shield, carried into battle by chariots that were driven by one of the retinue that each noble was allowed to keep. Each warrior hoped that the hero within him might come to the fore in battle, for in that way he would become immortal in the tales of the poet and it would be his deeds that were recited in those darkened rooms. Equally, he feared that he might do something that shamed him or his people, because then it would be the sharp edge of the poet's tongue that would recite his actions. The most feared weapon that a poet had was his sarcasm. The stories that he told of others' failings have sometimes been called satires. This is much too tame a word; they were defamations at least, maledictions in most cases, and outright curses if the situation required it. The noble's retinue was made up of lesser freemen whose honour price he had paid; the larger the retinue the more credit he paid to the lord.

Most freemen were independent men who farmed their own land and who fought in their own right. They maintained households where each man was entitled to three 'wives'; the chief wife, the concubine and the mistress. Not even Christianity managed to wean the Irish off this tradition. When reproved by the priests, they simply quoted the example of the patriarchs to justify themselves. Equally, they refused to allow the Church to take control of marriage. As far as the Irish were concerned, it was a civil ceremony which could end in divorce with no harm done. The members of the household, even adult sons, were not in themselves fully free; their honour price was only a fraction of that of the head of the household.

Much of the servile work was done by slaves. These could be people who had committed a crime and had been unable to pay the honour price, or they could be captives taken on foreign raids. This was how Patrick was brought to Ireland, as we shall see later.

As we have already seen, there was a tendency towards concentrating political power. This made sense because the larger blocs of power made for greater stability, in much the way that the opposing blocs of communism and the democracies preserved a stability – not always comfortable – in the post-war world. The largest concentrations of power centred on the provinces. One of the first families to rise to prominence in these conflicts was founded by Niall of the Nine Hostages. He claimed descent from Cormac mac Airt, the mythical founder of Connacht. The nine hostages referred to were from the nine tuatha of the Airgialla; in other words, Niall had made the powerful Airgialla dependent upon him. After his death his descendants, now called the O'Neill, conquered Sligo and the western half of the land belonging to the Ulaid. At the Convention of Druim Cett in 575, the Northern O'Neills laid claim to the territory of Dal Riada, in the north-east of Ulster. By 637, they were the dominant power in Ulster, although the Ulaid persisted in the outlying areas. This way of gaining not simply sovereignty of the land but control of the actual territory was not covered in the ancient laws, but a phrase was soon applied to it; conquered territory was 'sword land'.

This gives a picture of Ireland in a great state of unrest, with kings fighting for their very existence. It is difficult, however, to estimate how much this affected the ordinary families who lived their subsistence lives. Fighting, remember, was primarily a matter for the king and his nobles. For example, one major cause of strife was the reluctance which a lesser king might show in paying his tribute in cattle and hostages on time. Faced with a situation like this, the greater king would show the lesser the value of a paid-up protection policy, while taking a little extra to cover his expenses. The remarkable thing is that such disruption was only relative. Writing of the year AD 664, the Venerable Bede said that there were many Englishmen, nobles and others, who went to Ireland to study for the priesthood or to lead holier lives. The Irish received these with great hospitality, feeding them as well as offering them free tuition and access to books. Other strangers, even those who were not studying religion, were made welcome. Dagobert II, the Merovingian King, spent some time in Ireland, as did Oswald and Aldfrith of Northumbria. But that was in the future, when Christianity had reached and spread across the island.

In modern mythology, St Patrick is the apostle to the Irish. In bishop's robes he is most often shown, crosier in hand, mitre on head, white-bearded but fierce, ready to fight for the God in whom he believes. Even through the pastel shades of his pictures, you can see the strength in his face, and you can imagine the lines that the struggle has etched in his soul. This is a man who has slept under thorn bushes too often to sing sentimental songs about them, who has longed, in the drought of summer mountains, for a drink of clear water. This is a man, in other words, who is far removed from the Patrick of the St Patrick's Day parades.

Yet there were Christians in Ireland before the days of Patrick. For a time, soon after the Romans had abandoned the island of Britain, a colony of the Laigins of Leinster was set up in Wales and remained for some time before being driven out. Equally, people from Munster had colonised parts of western Britain. When they set up their principal settlement at Cashel, it differed from all the other provincial settlements, Tara, Emhain Mhacha and Cruacha, in having no pagan connection. Even the name is a direct lift from the Latin for castle – Castellum. This was a likely entry point for Christianity to Ireland, and it was to this 'unadulterated' settlement that the Pope sent his first bishop to Ireland.

St Patrick was not the first Christian bishop in Ireland; that honour must go to the cultivated Palladius, who in AD 431, according to Prosper of Aquitaine, was sent by Pope Celestine as the first bishop to those Christians living in Ireland. He had been a deacon at Auxerre and was sent to Rome for special training. He had been chosen by Germanus, who was about to start a mission to the Christians in Britain, specifically to counter the Pelagian heresy. A thoroughly Romanised cleric, Palladius had been trained in the best colleges of Gaul. Gaul, unlike Britain, had become very closely associated with the Roman Empire. Its bishops spoke good Latin and had a recognised role in the administration, organisation and even the defence of their territories. They were the aristocrats of a contemporary world that was based on its Roman past. Celestine sent him to 'the Irish believing in Christ'. His task was to administer to the spiritual needs of those already within the Church; he had no brief to carry out missionary work but to ensure that his people were not seduced by the Pelagian heresy. His area of operations was the south, where most communication between Britain and Ireland had taken place and where, as we have seen, there may well have been the beginnings of a Christian dynasty. He brought with him relics of Peter and Paul. Germanus had used relics to win the propaganda war over Pelagius. If Palladius intended to use the same strategy, he must have taken for granted a high level of Christian understanding among the Irish to whom he ministered.

It is interesting that the date of Patrick's arrival in Ireland is given as AD 432, one year after Palladius. How accurate this is is open to debate, but he was certainly active in Ireland in the first half of the fifth century. He was the freeborn son of a minor civil servant. Though he says that he was not yet a Christian at the age of fifteen, that has to be taken carefully. He may simply mean that he had not yet been baptised or confirmed. At a time when the only sacrament guaranteed to forgive sins was Baptism, it was not something to hurry into. Many early Christians had the same prayer as St Augustine of Hippo, 'Lord make me chaste and continent, but not for a while yet!' Whatever the exact meaning of what he said, he was abducted at this age from his home and taken in captivity to Ireland, where he had to work as a herdsman. For the next six years he lived a hard and comfortless life. Northern tradition locates his captivity at Slemish, in County Antrim. This was his desert, where he spent his forty days over and over again. Faced with a hopeless future, he found his refuge in Christianity, praying often and being moved by visions. As he watched the sun go down on a winter evening, he would have looked across at the line of the Sperrin Hills, with Slieve Gallion standing out from them. They may even have taken on a special significance for him, because it was in this area that he was to spend many later years.

He escaped, and spent some time away from Ireland, but a sense of the spiritual need, as he saw it, of the Irish drew him back. He gloried in the fact that he had been chosen as a conduit of salvation to his old captors. Even given his studies for the priesthood, he could lay no claims to being a scholar. His Latin was very basic; it was the language of the self-taught, but was not needed for the people with whom he was dealing since they had never had any contact with Christianity. In his *Confession* and *Letter to Coroticus* he admits his difficulty with 'a foreign language'. Scholars have found traces of Irish and British syntax in both these writings. Incidentally, this would tend to disprove later stories that he had spent time in Gaul. His Latin would have been much more polished if this had been the case. Of necessity, he was a one-book man – the Bible. He worked for years before being made a bishop and baptised many thousands.

His work was among the Ulaid and the people of northern Connacht. Things did not always go easily, and he was made captive twice. On one occasion he was held for two months; on the other he was held in chains for fourteen days. It was, perhaps, these experiences that encouraged him to make gifts to kings, although this raises the question of where he got the money. He put his utmost trust in God. Although it was much later that a cathedral was built in Armagh, there is a tradition that this was where he established his diocesan seat. This made sense if he had put himself under the protection of the king of the Ulaid, who ruled from Emhain Mhacha (now called Navan Fort), which was only two miles away. As far as the centralised Church was concerned, however, he was working on the fringe of the world; that is, if they knew anything about him at all, since it was Palladius rather than Patrick who was in contact with Rome.

Slieve gallion.

Patrick's Church had bishops, priests and deacons, and they administered the sacraments of Baptism, Confirmation, Eucharist and Ordination. Lesser clergy were the readers, cantors and the humble doorkeeper. Clerics could be married, but they had to come together for matins and vespers. Monks and virgins took vows of asceticism and chastity, but they mainly remained in the world, rather than withdrawing from it. Although the Church was establishing its own aristocracy, the honour price of clerics derived from their worldly position. The canon laws of the first Christian Synod give us a picture of how the Church fitted into the pagan Gaelic world. They define, among others, the crimes of murder, theft, adultery and the refusal to pay debts. In all cases the punishment was excommunication. A Christian was forbidden to call a fellow Christian before the civil, or brehon courts. Christians were not even permitted to accept alms from pagans. The Church was a separate community within a pagan society.

That pagan society continued with its own priorities. We have seen previously that the O'Neill confederacy was putting pressure on the Ulaid for control of Ulster. The Ulaid were eventually driven from their capital of Emhain Mhacha. This may have happened during Patrick's lifetime; it is not possible to be at all exact about when Patrick's work flourished in Ireland. If he was in Emhain Mhacha during the O'Neill conquest, it would explain the tradition that he died at Downpatrick, since he would have fled there with the Ulaid.

Patrick recommended Christianity centred on the monastic life. It was a way of life that he encouraged people to follow, and he seems to have been much more interested in those who chose this path than in ordinary, baptised Christians. He saw as his finest achievement the fact that some of those who took to the monastery were the children of pagan kings. But Patrick's Church did not take on the monastic nature that was characteristic of later Irish Christianity. The diocesan system developed instead, each diocese based on a tuath, with its main church built close to the royal site. Indeed, the land given to the Church was often land that had been used previously for pagan ritual. The clergy from one diocese had no authority in another. The clergy administered by a bishop had taken vows and were in religious orders, but there was no vow of celibacy and they were permitted to marry. Patrick's chief heritage was to inspire further generations of evangelists so that even the most recalcitrant pagan leader eventually submitted to baptism. The last pagan inauguration of a king was in AD 558 and Ireland was formally Christian by the start of the seventh century.

By this time the monastic movement had gained strength. Two of its early supporters were Finnian of Clonard and Ciaran of Clonmacnoise. There was an early setback when Ireland was struck by a great plague in AD 548/549, and many of the monks died. However, the movement was too powerful to be stopped and the monasteries were soon full again. At first the abbot was responsible for the government of the monastery and the spiritual welfare of his monks. After the founder died, the abbot was seen as heir to the monastery's property, which was vested in him. It was his task to lead services, unless a bishop was present; to write; to pray alone; to receive visitors; to watch the brothers at work; to check the monastery's supplies; to visit any sub-houses the monastery might have; to baptise the laity; and to preach and to prophecy. As administrative duties increased, confessors were appointed to look after the monks' spiritual needs. An alternative title for these was 'soul friends'. The monks' physical health was almost a product of their lifestyle. They worked the fields, milked the cows, harvested and threshed the grain, gathered the wattle and timber for building and raised the monastery buildings. On top of this they were celibate. The land given to monasteries, in contrast to that given to bishops, was usually private land. Indeed, very often a family would establish a monastery, with the sons and daughters of the house living in a celibate community.

By the early seventh century the legend of St Patrick had gained prominence in Ireland, and Armagh started laying claim as the primal diocese. It became both chief church and chief monastery of Ireland. Prominent families claimed a role in its affairs. As the Church expanded, so that all the land was served by diocesan churches or monasteries, it had to come to terms with the lay authorities and in some way to reconcile brehon law and canon law. In the edition of canon law that was published by the Irish Church in the eighth century, the laws on evidence, surety and inheritance reflect brehon law. The significance of this is that the Church had abandoned Roman law in order to meet the sensitivities of its laity.

Monasteries had changed as well by this time. Instead of being introspective places where people strove to lead ascetic, religious lives, they were now centres of population, the nearest thing the Irish had to towns. There were markets and schools; there were even prisons. The abbot had become a prince in secular as well as religious terms. In many cases, the abbacy belonged to the family that had donated the land. That family had the right to dictate who should succeed. In some cases, even, the abbot was not a priest; he could marry and look forward to his own son and grandson succeeding him. This was not the only way that monasteries might differ from our idealised picture of them.

There were times that the relationship between the monastery and the tuath was so close that the monks went to war in support of the secular power. Indeed, it was sometimes the monastery, or someone within it, who instigated the fighting. When, in AD 759, the priest Airechtach was disappointed to be passed over as abbot of his monastery, near Emhain Mhacha, he got secular backing. So did his opponent, and there is record of a battle between the Northern O'Neill and the men of Ulster. Airechtach seems to have chosen the stronger side, because

Ardboe Abbey.

there is a record of an abbot of his name dying in Armagh in AD 794. At this time Armagh was a sub-kingdom of Airthir. The kingship was shared among a number of families, including O'Neill and O'Haughey. Many of the stewards were O'Neill and many of the abbots were O'Haughey.

In the late eighth century there was a growth of asceticism in Ireland. Unhappy that secular affairs were becoming so important in the established monasteries, bands of like-minded clerics joined together to raise new, reformed monasteries. They called themselves the vassals of God, and the name later became anglicised as Culdees. Interestingly, some Protestants later believed that the Culdees preserved an ancient Celtic Christianity free from the contamination of Rome. The new monastic houses were particularly strict about matters of sex. Any cleric who sinned against chastity lost his orders and could not regain them. Women were men's 'guardian devils'. Lay abbots and married priests were preached against. They lived as strictly as they preached. Two monks remained in the chapel, praying, all night. Praying between the periods of the daily office was encouraged. Learning was encouraged and books were highly valued. On Sunday there was no travelling, no work, food could not be gathered or prepared. In spite of all, none of these new monasteries committed their way of life to a written rule and after a period the early enthusiasm waned and there was a return to the old ways. What did persist, however, was the emphasis on learning.

Some of the priests who would have been ascetics under the old regime worked hard in the monastery libraries. Others, however, chose to become pilgrims for Christ. In Ireland the clergy had gained high status. The pilgrims chose to turn away from this. Once they had left Ireland they had lost their status and had to rely on the mercy of God, since they had cast off their secular protection. At first it was simply isolation they sought. St Cormac sailed from Iona, seeking the solitude of the ocean. By the end of the eighth century there were Irish hermits in Iceland. The European continent offered challenges much greater than those of the ocean.

Gaul was nominally Christian, but the writings of St Gregory of Tours described a barbaric society that had little political organisation. There was little comfort here, but that was no problem to Irish priests whose motto was, 'Naked you are born and you will be naked in the grave.' Confronted by the conditions in Gaul, St Columbanus saw that his task was to sow the seeds of salvation, and he made many converts to Christianity. He seems to have been almost deliberately provocative, preaching to condemned men in prison, destroying offerings to Woden, and always, always, keeping on the move. He taught, 'Understand creation if you wish to know the Creator.' He prayed, 'Let us adore the Lord, Maker of wondrous works; great bright heaven with its angels; the white-waved sea on earth.' He and other monks prayed to feel the presence of God. In the dangerous time of the Viking raids, when the perils of Europe were visited on Ireland, a monk prayed, 'Over me as I sit, over me as I lie, Christ's cross be all my strength till we reach the King of Heaven.'

Even among those who remained behind, penitential discipline was important. Recompense had to be made for sins of action and sins of omission; for actual sin and for sin in the mind; for deliberate sins and sins of carelessness; for sins of the flesh and for sins of the spirit. Penance was a medicine for souls. Private confession was an Irish innovation; before that confession had been a public matter. The confessor was seen as a doctor, judging the appropriate penance for any combination of sins. In his judgements he had to take into account the character of the penitent and whether any provocation had taken place.

There were bound to be problems when it was so difficult to maintain communication between Rome and the Church in Ireland. Probably the most famous one was centred on the date of Easter. The Council of Nicea had given a formula for determining when Easter Sunday fell and decreed that all Christians should celebrate Easter on this day. The Irish Church seems to have used a calculation based on St Jerome, which was in turn based on the Jewish Passover. The difference was that the Council decreed that if Passover fell on a Sunday, Easter should be delayed for a week. The Irish Church did not postpone Easter, even if Passover did fall on a Sunday. The result was that, every six or seven years, the Irish celebrated Easter a week before the Roman Church. Confident in their learning and their sources, the Irish were very reluctant to give up this practice.

THE VIKINGS IN IRELAND

The homeland of the Vikings, the countries we now call Scandinavia, was not overly endowed with land that was suitable for farming. Much of it was simply too cold, near or within the Arctic Circle, or too precipitous to allow agriculture as we think of it. Even Denmark was low-lying, with fen and marsh restricting the land available on which to make a living. By the 700s, pressure on land meant that many of the nobles, together with their personal warriors, began to gather in groups and go on pillaging expeditions along the coasts of better-off countries. These adventurers were mostly younger sons, with nothing to lose. They sold what they stole and many made a comfortable living, maintaining families in long-houses where they could spend the long winters in comfort, waiting for the calm weather of spring and summer, when they could go raiding again. At first they restricted their operations to the Baltic and the north-western shores of continental Europe, but as they gained skills and confidence they began to look over the seas to Britain and Ireland, and they had in the longboat a vessel that had no difficulty in dealing with all but the roughest seas. Their victims called them north-men, which became Norsemen. Later, they became known as Vikings, which came from a Norse word meaning 'people of the bay, or inlet'. It is, possibly, a name they called themselves, referring to the fact that they often sailed far up inlets on their raids. Their official name for themselves was Ostmen, meaning men from the east.

The first raiders in Ireland came from Norway. In 795 they attacked and burned a monastery on Rathlin Island. Being pagans they saw nothing to respect in Christian symbolism, but soon learned that churches and monasteries were fine spots in which to find treasure. For a period of some fifty years, monasteries all round the coasts of Britain and Ireland were attacked. The great foundation of Iona, Colmcille's own, was burnt in 802. The Viking technique was to raid a monastery with a small group of ships and stay for a few days, finding what they could of value and burning the rest. Monks had long made a practice of writing poems in the margins of the books they were copying, presumably to relieve boredom. It is not surprising that, at this time, some of them comment on how pleasant it is to listen to the stormy winds roar and realise that the Vikings could not land that night. Slaves were as important as goods, so even the houses of the commoners who lived around the monastery would be attacked. The brutality with which they treated their prisoners and the ruthlessness of their destruction inspired fear, but at this phase there was perhaps only one raid in Ireland per year. The main trouble that the defenders had was in concentrating their forces against the raiders; there were so many places where a landing might be made. It was not until 811 and 812 that the first successes were made by the Irish in beating off Viking bands.

It was this perhaps that persuaded the Vikings to change their tactics. Instead of raiding with three or four boats, they started to arrive with fifty or even one hundred. When they landed they set up a fortified camp. Using this as a base, they raided the countryside all about, secure in the knowledge that the Irish were unlikely to put together a big enough army to threaten them and that even if they did, the Vikings still had a defensive position to fall back on, and ships to escape on if it became really necessary. The Irish called these bases 'Longphorts', which means ship harbour. The situation of the town of Longford shows just how they penetrated inland. They often remained for a whole summer. One of these bases has been identified in Annagassan on the east coast. It was protected on three sides by the bend of the River Dee and on the fourth by an earthen wall. Now even the fortresses of Irish noblemen were no longer safe. In 839 Armagh was raided three times within a month. In 840 the Vikings rowed up the Lower Bann and spent a whole year camped on the western shore of Lough Neagh, near the mouth of the Ballinderry River. Their raids took them as far as the monasteries of

Armagh and Louth, capturing many of the monks and selling them into slavery. They did not abandon the camp on the Ballinderry till the late summer of 841. Armagh was visited again in 845 and this time the archbishop was carried into captivity. In the winter of 848/49, some Vikings overwintered in Lough Neagh. They were joined in the spring by 'seven score of ships'.

Of course the Vikings had losses. One of their most famous warrior kings, Turgesius, was captured by Mael Seachnaill of the Southern O'Neill later in the same year that the archbishop of Armagh was enslaved. 'The War of the Irish against the Pagans', written some 250 years later, claims that it was this same Turgesius that had actually taken the archbishop. It did him little good, because he was drowned in Lough Owell. Mael Seachnaill had just become King of Meath that year by the simple process of killing his brother. He now set about uniting the disputing factions of his clan, a task that was made slightly easier the following year, when he also became King of Tara. Shortly afterwards, he was acknowledged as High King of Ireland by his kinsmen, the Northern O'Neill, and by the Kingdom of the Ulaid. There was no major Viking attack on Ireland after 851. They had decided that there were richer pickings in Britain. This did not mean that Ireland had become a safe country; it was not only the Vikings that carried out raids. In the first twenty-five years of Viking raids they had attacked the country twenty-six times, but during the same time the Irish had carried out eighty-seven attacks among themselves. Mael Seachnaill raided Armagh shortly after the abbot had proclaimed him High King, and much of his life was spent fighting with his cousins, the Northern O'Neill.

Not all the Vikings had left Ireland. Many Irish kings had recognised the value of some Viking mercenaries in their war bands. Some of these intermarried with the Irish and some of the second generation Vikings even took Celtic names. Most even became Christian. Dublin, which had started as a raiding camp, was a thriving town by the second half of the century. In 853 Olaf the White, who was Norwegian, brought a fleet to Dublin and Ivar, who had arrived from Denmark two years previously, agreed to rule Dublin jointly with him. This was needed because of the tension between Norwegian and Dane. Olaf married an Irish wife. This intermarrying with the Irish did not stop the Vikings raiding the great tombs at the Bend of the Boyne and plundering their wealth in 863. The King of Tara and chief of the Northern O'Neill at that time was Aed Finnliath, Olaf's father-in-law. Aed and most of the Irish looked on this as sacrilege, but it was not till 866 that he was able to gather enough strength to drive the Vikings out of all their coastal settlements from Donegal to Antrim. This expulsion may explain why so few Viking place names exist along the Ulster coast. In spite of this it has to be pointed out that the name 'Ulster' is of Viking origin. The Vikings called the land at the north-east of Ireland 'Country of the Ulaidh', pronouncing the Irish 'Uladztir'; thence Ulster. At this time Ivar seems to have moved to the kingdom of York, where he stayed until 871. His great achievement when he was on the eastern island was to burn Dumbarton in 870.

Dublin's main export was Irish slaves, although there must have also been a trade in jewellery. Clasps and brooches of Irish design became fashionable in Scandinavia. Ivar died in 873 however, and after that date there was a lot of internal strife in the town. It managed to remain independent of the Irish until 902. In that year a coalition of Irish forces drove them out. Other Viking settlements went the same way: Cork in 848, Waterford in 864 and Youghal in 866. The expelled Vikings moved to the Isle of Man or on to the Danelaw of England.

They had not gone forever. In 914 a large fleet arrived in Waterford and the town was soon back in Viking control. When they were reinforced by a second fleet the following year they launched a number of raids deep into Munster and Leinster, going as far west as Cork and Lismore. This was followed in 917 by an attack which recaptured Dublin. Fleet after fleet arrived and, although they were separate groups acting in an uncoordinated way, they threatened to engulf the entire island. Most of them came, not from Scandinavia, but from the settlements around Britain and the Isle of Man. Population pressure had built up yet again and Ireland was one of the few areas of Europe still open to Viking exploitation. It was during this time that many monasteries were rebuilt in stone rather than the traditional timber. They also started constructing tall, thin, multi-purpose stone towers that could be used as belfries and store houses in time of peace, but strong enough to withstand all but the most determined attacks and fires in time of strife.

Niall Glundub (Black-knee) was chief of both Southern and Northern O'Neill at the time and the most powerful king in Ireland. His lands in what are now Meath and Westmeath were most directly threatened by the Viking presence in Dublin. He put together an army involving all the O'Neill septs and, with the support of the men of Leinster, advanced against the Vikings of Munster in 917. The Vikings routed the Leinstermen before they could unite with O'Neill, while O'Neill's own forces withdrew from Munster after a few indecisive skirmishes. It was a more determined Niall Glundub who led his men against Dublin two years later. Once again, however, the Vikings prevailed, this time managing to kill Niall and 'the cream of the O'Neill'. Thirteen Irish kings were killed that day.

The Vikings were now free to continue their raids, and felt confident enough to establish two new towns in the 920s, Wexford and Limerick. They invaded Tirconnell and thirty-two ships sailed up Lough Foyle, spreading panic as they went. Others penetrated Lough Erne, portaging around the waterfalls of Assaroe, and ravaged the islands. It was not until Muircertach of the Northern O'Neill, son of Niall Glundub, reached maturity that the Irish were able to strike back. He defeated the Vikings in a ship-to-ship battle on Strangford Lough in 926. In 939 he burnt Dublin and, two years later, reversed roles by raiding Viking settlements on the Hebrides. When he died in battle in 943, the fortunes of the Northern O'Neill declined, and a southern dynasty, the Dal Cais, was able to take advantage.

It was probably lucky for the Irish that much of the Vikings' effort during this period was expended in England, where the Norse were establishing a territory out of the old kingdoms of Northumbria, Mercia and East Anglia. It was an ambition of the Dublin kings to become kings of York. Since much of the cutting edge of the Irish Viking army was occupied in the eastern island, those remaining in Ireland concentrated on developing the towns which they had established. Pre-eminent among these was Dublin, and by 934 it exercised control of the other Viking towns in Ireland. Its prosperity as a trading and slaving centre grew and, in 952 Dublin split from the English Vikings and set up its own kingdom. By this time, also, Vikings had given up raiding and were more or less peaceful settlers and traders. Under King Olaf Cuaran (Sandal), Dublin controlled a considerable hinterland. The star of the Vikings was on the wane, however. In 980 Olaf was defeated and killed by Mael Seachnaill II, King of Meath, at the Battle of Tara, and Dublin lost its independence.

From then until the coming of the Normans, the Vikings were allowed to have their own kingdoms, but paid tribute to the Irish. They remained wealthy, because they still controlled international trade. Largely, they became integrated into the Irish community. Irishmen eventually became kings of Dublin in 1052 and some even lived there. Coins were introduced for the first time. There were interruptions to peaceful trade, but Dublin found that neutrality benefitted trade. They even held back during the Battle of Clontarf, in 1014, though the fighting took place just across the River Liffey and was probably clearly visible from the town's walls.

In 1005 Brian Boru came to Armagh with a huge force. He had gathered together the armies of Munster, Leinster, Meath, Connacht and Dublin. This was his third time north; on the previous occasions he had tried to coerce tribute from the northern kings. This time he used a more subtle approach. First of all he paid twenty ounces of gold into the Armagh Church and recognised Armagh as the ecclesiastical capital of Ireland. In the Book of Armagh he had himself named 'Emperor of the Irish'. The following year he went about establishing this in fact. He started at Sligo and, keeping the sea on his left, made a progression around the coast, visiting each kingdom in turn, until he reached Down in the autumn of the year. Like the Orange Order in later years, he had marched his boundaries and claimed ownership of what he had circumambulated. It took more than this to drag Tirconnell into the fold, however; it took several punitive expeditions and five years to gain their submission.

While Brian's attention was focused on the north, Leinster decided that it was an opportune time to withhold their tribute. Brian was having none of that, and on Good Friday 1014 the greatest battle that Ireland had seen until then was fought at Clontarf, near the mouth of the Liffey. The actuality of the Battle of Clontarf needs to be separated from the legend. It was a battle for supremacy between the dynasties of Munster and Leinster. Vikings fought on both sides and Munster, at least in theory, won, driving their enemies into the sea, although Brian Boru and his son were killed in his moment of victory. Their bodies were taken to Armagh for burial. It was probably the poignancy of death in victory that made the incident so attractive to Icelandic and Irish storytellers in years to come. It was they who changed the story into one where Brian destroyed Viking power in Ireland; unfortunately for Brian's renown, this had already been done at the Battle of Tara, thirty-four years previously.

In fact, Clontarf settled nothing. Brian had destroyed the power of the O'Neills. Now his own dynasty had been stubbed out. The vacuum that was left encouraged the ambitious to strive for the ultimate honour of the high kingship. It was a time of bloody contests between rivals. Although some of the provincial kings claimed to rule the land, there was always opposition somewhere on the island. That opposition most often came from the north, where many of the best fighting chiefs ruled. Ulster, however, lacked money, and it did not have the wealth-creating potential of Viking towns within its borders. Right up to Tudor times it was considered the poor country cousin; indeed, this was why it was able to maintain its Gaelic heritage. Ulster became more hemmed in as the Kingdom of Breifne became more powerful and blocked the route south through Cavan and Leitrim.

Autumn leaves.

Far away, on the north coast of France, another Viking army had landed many years previously. Rather than have to fight a costly war, the French king gave them lands at the mouth of the Seine on condition that they guarded the river and its hinterland from further depredations by pirates. Their chief, Rollo, accepted the French title Duc, or Duke, and the land which these North Men controlled became known as Normandy. The Irish were not yet safe from the descendants of Scandinavian raiders.

The Church in Ireland was coming closer to Rome and the Pope. Cellach, Abbot of Armagh, and more particularly his protégé, Malachy, were able to obtain the support of the Pope in reducing worldly abuses. Malachy was appointed Primate of Ireland in 1132, and almost immediately began to introduce new orders of monks to the country. In 1142 he founded the Cistercian Monastery of Mellifont, with the help of St Bernard's architect. The leading Gaelic monasteries of Bangor, Movilla, Nendrum and Derry had not recovered from the Viking years and were in no position to oppose this move. Armagh had no interest in maintaining Gaelic culture; the Church was more interested in importing Roman culture. From now on it was left to secular poets, bards and historians to carry on the tradition.

THE NORMAN INVASION

After the departure of the Romans from Britain, invasions by Germanic peoples from Europe pushed the native British tribes into the west, into Wales and Cornwall. Almost by default even closer trading links were established between the Welsh and the Irish, who shared a common culture. Welsh and Irish had joined in alliances that attempted to oppose the Norse raiders. When the Normans invaded England in 1066, the Welsh and Irish once again formed an alliance, this time with the Norse, in the hope of putting a limit on Norman expansion. Ever resourceful, Norman barons began intermarrying with the Welsh, and soon had a toehold in the south of the country.

As soon as the conquest of England was consolidated, Normans started looking across the narrow waters of the Irish Sea and considered the possibility of invasion. William had been very careful to establish a semi-legitimate claim on the throne of England before attacking, but there was no obvious way he could lay claim to Ireland. It was not until the reign of Henry II that an opportunity presented itself. When Dublin became a Christian city, it was inhabited by Norse. These were not on the best of terms with the native Irish so, instead of becoming a unit of the Church in Ireland, they had their first bishop consecrated by the Archbishop of Canterbury, and became a diocese of the English Church. In 1152, the diocese decided to become an Irish archbish-opric, rejecting the rule of Canterbury. Henry sent a mission to Rome, under the leadership of the Bishop of Lisieux. The Pope at that time was, fortunately for Henry, an Englishman, Pope Adrian. Not surprisingly, the Pope found in favour of Canterbury and went on to award Henry and his successors the right to rule Ireland in order to bring about religious reformation there. Henry was too busy establishing his control of England to take up the Irish option imme-diately, but it was something he could file away for use later.

He did not have very long to wait. While he was putting down opposition in England, there were the usual rival claims for the High Kingship of Ireland. At this time the chief contenders were the High King, Muirchertach MacLoughlin from Inishowen and Ruari O'Connor of Connacht. MacLoughlin was allied with Dermot MacMurrough, King of Leinster, while Tiernan O'Rourke, King of Breifne on the Connacht-Ulster border, supported O'Connor. MacMurrough and O'Rourke had their own quarrels anyway, since they both claimed the kingdom of Meath. The war became personal when MacMurrough abducted O'Rourke's wife, Dervorgilla. In 1166 MacLoughlin died, allowing O'Connor and O'Rourke to concentrate their forces against MacMurrough, who now found that even the Norse in Dublin had turned against him. Completely over-whelmed, he turned to the English Henry II and asked permission to recruit among his knights. Permission was granted, and MacMurrough started putting together his army of mercenaries. As their leader he chose Richard de Clare, who was in dispute with Henry about his claim to be Earl of Pembroke. In Irish history, he is better known as Strongbow. MacMurrough promised him land in Ireland and his daughter Aoife in marriage. As far as Strongbow was concerned, this would make him heir apparent to the kingdom of Leinster.

MacMurrough's first attempt to regain his kingdom, in 1168, was a failure. With a small force of Welsh and Flemish he linked up the O'Kinsellas of south-east Leinster, but was defeated by a joint army of the current High King, Ruairi O'Connor and Tiernan O'Rourke. The following year the Norman knights landed with three ships carrying 400 warriors on the southern coast of Wexford. Another 200 landed the following day and both forces then joined with MacMurrough, at the head of 500 Irishmen. Their first action was to attack the Norse town of Wexford. The 2,000 Norsemen defending the town were unhappy at the combi-nation of armoured knights and Welsh archers and retired behind the walls of the town. The Normans then demonstrated that they could attack a fortified town and the Norse sued for peace and accepted MacMurrough as their overlord.

It is of course important to reward success, and MacMurrough granted land which he confiscated from the Norsemen to several of the Norman knights. In this way he ensured that more Normans would hear that there was land to be won in Ireland. Then, further reinforced by the Norsemen of Wexford, he turned his attention to the King of Ossary, Donal MacKilpatrick, who had captured and blinded his eldest son, Eanna. In a hard-fought battle that stretched over three days, MacKilpatrick's forces were routed. So in turn were the armies of O'Byrne, O'Toole and O'Connor of Offaly. As the army of the High King marched back into Leinster to oppose the triumphant march, the Church authorities intervened in the hope of saving lives and arranged for negotiations at Ferns. In the Treaty of Ferns, 1169, MacMurrough was recognised as King of Leinster on two conditions: that he recognise Ruairi as High King and send his foreign allies back to Wales. To show his good intent, he also had to give his son as hostage to Ruairi. In his turn, Ruairi forced the Norsemen to submit to MacMurrough's authority.

The truce did not last very long. At the end of the year two shiploads of Normans and Welsh arrived in Leinster. Seeing this as a hint from Providence, MacMurrough sent a message to Strongbow asking for more troops. When he had considered the various possibilities of benefit to himself, Strongbow sent another party, under the command of Raymond le Gros, while at the same time starting to gather a larger landing party that he would command himself. Raymond landed near Waterford City in May 1170 and set about establishing a beachhead to await Strongbow. With hastily improvised defences, he beat off an attack by a Norse army from Waterford.

Strongbow himself landed towards the end of August, with a force of about 1,000 men. He came ashore at the Passage, close to Waterford and attacked immediately. At the third attempt his men found a weak point in the city walls and were able to enter the city and capture it. The Norman forces that were already in Ireland joined him here, as did MacMurrough, who brought with him his daughter Aoife. Here Strongbow and Aoife were married, and Strongbow was declared heir-in-succession to the kingdom of Leinster. It was obvious that war with the High King, Ruairi, was not far away.

Strongbow was anxious to secure his lines of communication with Wales and was determined to gain control of Dublin. News came that Ruairi was already getting together a large army with the intent of pre-empting the attack of the Normans on the city. Strongbow and MacMurrough force-marched their men, however, and arrived at the southern walls of Dublin. They made a great show of preparing to attack. The defenders, having heard of the fate of Waterford, sent envoys to ask for negotiations. While these talks were going on and everyone was concentrating on the southern defences, two parties of Normans under Raymond le Gros and Milo de Cogan managed to get into the city and put the Norse to flight. The King of Dublin, Asculf, was forced to escape by sea with such forces as he could get away. When Ruairi heard that the Norse had been prepared to negotiate, he marched his army away in disgust. MacMurrough responded by capturing the land of Meath.

Dermot MacMurrough was not to enjoy his expanded kingdom for long, since he died in May 1171. Strongbow now became King of Leinster. This was not a situation acceptable to most of the Irish kings. While they had been happy enough to see MacMurrough use all the help he could get in the battle against the High King, Ruairi, they were not prepared to see a Norman as King of Leinster. The Leinster kings rose in revolt and Ruairi, ever a one to spot an opportunity, called upon the other provincial kings to help him drive the foreigners out of Ireland. At first things seemed to go well for the Irish and their Norse allies. Waterford and Wexford were both captured and the Irish set a tight siege around Dublin, with 60,000 Irish on land and the ousted King of Dublin, Asculf, guarding the sea with a large fleet. The siege lasted for two months until the Normans, in desperation, sallied against the Irish. Showing a knowledge of modern tactics that the Irish were unable to match, Strongbow took the day and Ruairi was forced to withdraw to Connacht, beyond the reaches of the Norman war machine. Strongbow then set about retaking Leinster and was soon in control of what he saw as his patrimony.

None of this was missed by King Henry, back in England. He was pleased at the success of the Norman forces, but concerned in case Strongbow set up a state in Ireland that would rival England. Given the ravages that Strongbow's followers were bringing to Ireland, Henry was able to portray himself as the protector of the Irish, and, landing in Ireland in October 1171, he soon brought the barons to heel. Strongbow accepted Henry as his liege lord and was given the kingdom of Leinster for his pains. Henry kept the key ports of Dublin, Wexford and Waterford for himself. As a bonus, most of the Irish kingdoms accepted the authority that the Pope had given Henry to rule Ireland. This may seem remarkable, given the way that they reacted when Strongbow had declared himself King of Leinster, but they were used to being under the nominal authority of a high king. Even better, as far as they were concerned, was the fact that this overlord would spend most of his time on another island. Not all of Ireland submitted, however, and most of Ulster, together with Connacht, resisted the change. These, of course, had been the areas from which most of the recent high kings had come.

Those kings – now to be thought of as chiefs by Henry – who had submitted were soon to find that the old ways were changing. Henry spent the winter in Ireland and, before leaving in April 1172, granted the province of Meath, consisting of the present counties of Meath and Westmeath, to Hugh de Lacy. He also made Hugh Constable of Dublin and Justiciar, or Viceroy. Within a few months Hugh had murdered Tiernan O'Rourke, King of Breifne. He and Strongbow then set about destroying Irish resistance in the lands they controlled by the relatively cheap means of sharing it out among their chief vassals, to whom they left the task of pacification.

Henry extended his control over Ireland by the Treaty of Windsor in 1175. By this he promised to recognise Ruairi as High King of all Ireland except Leinster, but since the Irish chiefs of Connacht were now required to pay tribute, it was simply another way of dressing up the submission of an Irish king. Henry got a tighter grip on Leinster after Strongbow's death. He already had taken Dublin for himself, to be colonised by men of unswerving loyalty. Here was established a central administration which kept a tight grip on the Norman barons as well as the Irish who lived in those places he controlled. In 1177 he transferred the Lordship of Ireland to his son John, villain of so many stories in English folklore. This left only parts of Ulster free from the Normans.

That same year another player arrived on the scene. John de Courcy was newly arrived in Ireland and, seeing that most of the land had already been allocated, he mounted an expedition into north-east Ulster. He arrived at Downpatrick so unexpectedly that the King of the Ulaidh, Rory MacDonleavy, fled, taking his people with him. A week later he returned, having gathered the full might of the Ulaidh to support him. The Irish had no match for the military technology of the Normans. Against armoured knights whose whole mode of life was dominated by tournaments and jousting, they fought with no stirrups. The Irish technique was to ride close to the enemy and throw their spears. They were easily unhorsed in the first clash of arms and then had to fight on foot with their Viking-style battleaxes. Gerald of Wales, chronicler of the Norman invasion, wrote that the Irish warriors would continue to fight even when all they had left was stones. However, the Normans had brought men-at-arms who fought with crossbow or longbow, and these killed many of the Irish before they had got near enough even to throw their spears.

The Irish were not finished, however. The following year the Normans camped in a glen near Newry, secure in the knowledge that they had just beaten an Irish army. A force of the Ulaidh, supported by the King of Oriel, attacked them during the night and won a victory. Shortly after this, de Courcy was beaten by the forces of the Ui Tuirtre, and was lucky to escape on foot with eleven of his knights. The reason that he was able to survive this attack was that the Normans had started building the defensive positions known as mottes and baileys, whose design they had brought with them from France. The motte was an artificial hill some 30 to 40ft high. On top of this they built a defensive keep from roughly dressed local timber. There was also an outer defensive palisade that enclosed a larger area known as a bailey, which could be equipped as a living area for men and horses. They could be thought of as the medieval equivalent of the modern aircraft carrier, able to project force upon an enemy while able to give shelter to friends. They are found in what were frontier areas. Many of those in Ulster lacked a bailey, so they may not have had a permanent garrison.

On Carrickfergus, a tongue of rock which stuck out into Belfast Lough, de Courcy built his major castle. The central keep was built of stone, with basalt walls 9ft thick and 90ft high. He built another at the Castle of Rath, a rocky outcrop above Dundrum. This sent a message to the natives; the Normans were here to stay. De Courcy did stay, and for twenty-five years ruled Ulster as an independent principality. He even minted his own coinage and appointed his own steward, chamberlain and constable. Although he had many barons with their soldiers to support him, this was not a colonisation in the sense that was happening elsewhere in Ireland. The change was only at the top level; the natives still remained to do the dirty work of tilling the soil. De Courcy had a reputation for meanness and for being unreliable, but he also gave money to the Church. This was in keeping with the Norman belief, firmly held by them since Rollo became a Christian, that God was on their side. He allowed a cathedral to be built at Downpatrick on what would have been an excellent site for a castle. In the tradition of the old Irish chiefs he founded several monasteries; although, unlike them, he imported orders from England and the Continent. Cistercians came to Inch, Benedictines to Black Abbey on the Ards Peninsula, Augustinians to Muckamore and Downpatrick, the White Canons to White Abbey and Cistercians to Grey Abbey. He also restored Nendrum and transferred the reputed remains of Patrick, Brigid and Colmcille to Downpatrick.

Henry II had named his son John 'Lord of Ireland', and the latter confirmed de Courcy as his chief governor of Ireland in 1185. Things seemed to be going well for the adventurer. However, when John became king in 1199, de Courcy must have done something to annoy his master because John authorised Hugh de Lacy, Lord of Meath, to make war on the erstwhile governor. The campaign lasted five years, and it was not until 1205 that de Lacy was made Earl of those parts of Ulster that de Courcy had held. In spite of attempts to regain his territory, de Courcy was reduced to being a knight merely, though he did become reconciled to John. This enabled him to witness the downfall of his tormentor, Hugh de Lacy.

It was the fault of William de Braose, Lord of Limerick, who was de Lacy's cousin. He had fallen behind with his payments to the king. When King John demanded his son as hostage, de Braose's wife had refused to hand him over, since John had scandalously killed his nephew, Arthur of Brittany. John was not a man to permit impudence and he gathered a huge force which he took to Waterford. Under his command were 7,000 knights, together with archers and bowmen. Suitably alarmed, de Braose sought refuge with his cousin. Foolishly, de Lacy took him in. Soon afterwards, he discovered that John was also coming north. By July the king was in Carlingford. De Lacy moved to the Moyry Pass, trying to block this gap into the north. King John simply transferred his army across Carlingford Lough by a bridge made of boats. Dundrum Castle was his first target. Although this was a formidable obstacle, the royal army had brought such a collection of siege engines that the castle's garrison simply abandoned it. John had the defences put in order and then went on to Downpatrick. While de Braose and de Lacy were able to escape to France, Matilda de Braose and her son William were captured. They were brought to John by none other than John de Courcy, now restored to the king's good favours (though not yet to his land). King John ordered the captives thrown into a dungeon, where they were left to starve to death.

John stayed in Carrickfergus Castle for a time, distributing money to those barons who had helped him. While he was there Aed O'Neill, King of Tír Eoghain and the Northern O'Neill, came to pay him homage. Perhaps it was to ensure the permanence of this homage that John ordered the warrior Bishop of Norwich to have built a number of galleys which were to be based at Antrim with the intention of controlling Lough Neagh. The ruthless manner in which John had dealt with trouble in Ireland meant that he had greater control over the island than any king before him. When he left for the Isle of Man in August 1210, no threat remained behind him. His Norman vassals in Ireland were so cowed that none joined the English barons who forced John to sign the Great Charter at Runnymede in 1215.

John was careful to reward those Norman Scots who had helped him in his Irish wars. The Glens of Antrim, from Larne to Glenarm, went to Duncan of Carrick. The lands from the Glens to Lough Foyle were granted to Alan of Galloway and to Thomas of Atholl. This was a more dubious gift, since this land had not been conquered before, and the two grandees had to strive hard to get even a toehold on the coast. They got little support from the king. Those close to him noticed that he was getting very fat, though he retained his power as a warrior. He died suddenly in 1216, to be succeeded by Henry III, who was still only a child. This seemed to be a golden opportunity for Hugh de Lacy, who was fighting in the crusade against the Cathars in the south of France. The young king tried to be conciliatory, and sent a letter to de Lacy offering to compensate for any wrong his father, King John, might have done. The only compensation de Lacy would accept was the return of his earldom of Ulster, and he was prepared to defy his rightful king to get it. When this became obvious King Henry ordered that the royal castles of Ireland be prepared against siege. The Pope, Innocent III, excommunicated de Lacy, but even that was not enough to stop the exile returning to Ireland in 1223, prepared, obviously, to sin now and repent later.

Ireland was thrown into confusion. De Lacy and his allies attacked castle after castle, at first taking them all. The greatest warrior in England, William, the Marshal of the king's army, came to Ireland and put together a force of Normans and of Irish with the intention of causing de Lacy to repent sooner rather than later. This great force moved northward, retaking the Leinster castles one after the other. Trim was taken after a siege lasting six weeks, and Carrickfergus, which was holding out against the rebels, was relieved from the sea. De Lacy withdrew to Tir Eoghain, where he persuaded Aed O'Neill to join him in an alliance. His first target was the Earl of Atholl's castle at Coleraine, which was a threat to their rear. When they had destroyed this, they sent parties to guard all the passes into the north and invited the Marshal and his men to come and get them. The Normans, according to the Annals, were not prepared to take on what would have been a protracted and bloody struggle on the borderlands of Ulster, and an armistice was agreed. De Lacy was confirmed as Earl of Ulster, although he had to forego the land which had been granted to the Scots Normans. In return he gave two sons as hostage to the Marshal. The powerbase of the native Irish in Cenel Eoghain and Cenel Conaill meant that any Norman expansion could only be along the coast, and it was here that Hugh de Lacy focused his greedy eyes. The king averted his royal eyes as de Lacy now ejected the Scots. This land along the coast became known by the Normans as Twescard, a word taken from the Irish for north. This became one of the most prosperous parts of the earldom, and remained so when de Lacy died in 1243 and it passed back into the ownership of the crown.

This flanking move along the coast put pressure on the remaining Gaelic kingdoms of Cenel Eoghain and Cenel Conaill. Their defensive capacity was weakened when Aed O'Neill died in 1230 and there was the usual struggle to succeed him. Donal Mac Lochlainn was able to hold the crown until 1241, when he was killed in battle by Brian O'Neill. The Normans were able to take advantage of these internal divisions to establish castles on the west of the River Bann and from these to conquer parts of Ulster as far as Armagh. With various alliances, Brian O'Neill tried to push the invaders back, mounting campaigns again and again until he was killed outside Downpatrick in 1260. He had proved himself such a thorn in the side of the Normans that his head was sent to London.

Henry III is often seen as a weak king, easily manipulated by his council. The same could not be said of his son, Edward, one of the most war-loving kings that England has ever known. Edward spent a lot of money on his wars, and he had a particular antipathy to the Scots. He saw an opportunity to pay off one of his major debts while at the same time ridding himself of the expense of guarding the vulnerable Twescard. One of his largest creditors was Walter de Burgo, and it was to him that Edward granted the land and the title. This meant that there were three great lordships in the north of the island: de Burgo ruled in Antrim, Down and along the north of Derry; Cenel Eoghain held the rest of Derry and Tyrone, while Cenel Conaill held Donegal and Fermanagh. To ensure that the Gaelic lordships did not combine against him, de Burgo established an alliance with Aed Buidhe O'Neill against the O'Donnells of Cenel Conaill. He even persuaded Aed to accept him as his overlord, and Aed sent him four hostages as tokens of his good faith. As a final cement in the relationship, de Burgo's cousin Aleanor was betrothed to Aed, who promised 'to treat her honourably' – an unlikely prospect given the Irish approach to matrimony. Walter de Burgo died in 1271, potentially a disaster in terms of building a dynasty, since his son Richard was only twelve years old. Sure enough, as soon as the funeral was over there were squabbles among Walter's vassals as to who would act as regent. These did not die away completely till 1280, when Richard was deemed capable of coming into his inheritance. Since much of the bickering among the Normans had been for extra land, Richard turned his power against Gaelic Ulster, a reliable source of fresh land. He extended his territory as far as Limavady, at the expense of the O'Cahan clan. In 1305 he started building the castle, the dramatic remains of which still command the narrows at the mouth of Lough Foyle.

His exploits were not confined to Ireland. He fought with Edward in his devastating wars against the Scots. To reinforce the power of his sword, he made sure that his daughters married well; all four of them married Earls. One, however, married Robert the Bruce; this matching was fated to bring the ruin of the earldom of Ulster. For the time being, however, there seemed to be no flies in the ointment. The Gaelic lordships, particularly Cenel Eoghain, were constantly under pressure. For some families the pressure was too great; some simply upped sticks and left, looking for safer pastures in the service of an over-lord in a less exposed part of the country. In the countryside that they left small towns, known as boroughs, were established. One, le Roo, was built on the site of Limavady, deep in the heart of O'Cahan country. This was a direct challenge to the king of the O'Neills, who was O'Cahan's overlord. It was not until the Irish started to imitate some of the tactics of the Normans, using some old stone forts as defences and building stone keeps and mottes in disputed territory, that they began to hold their own and to stabilise their frontiers. Then something happened which promised to change the fortunes of Cenel Eoghain.

When the Normans conquered Scotland they had defied the king of England and chose their own king. This was a source of ongoing strife, since the English believed that Scotland was theirs by right of conquest. It was to claim his lost land that King Edward had expended so much blood in war, and his son, Edward II, was still trying to do what his father could not. The Scottish king Robert Bruce had had to shelter in Ireland on at least two occasions, the most recent in 1302. In 1314, Robert inflicted a crushing defeat on the English at Bannockburn, but the victory had not been as decisive as he had hoped and it looked as if the English armies would attack yet again. He decided to outflank the English by launching an attack on the English colony in Ireland, a colony which had supplied many recruits to the English army in Scotland. Stretching reality slightly, he claimed a shared heritage with the Gaelic Irish and called on them to support him.

Robert's brother Edward Bruce landed near Larne with a large army in May 1315 and Domnall O'Neill, King of Tir Eoghain, marched to join him. Their united armies ravaged the lands of the Earl of Ulster, striking as far south as Dundalk and Ardee. In the latter town, the attackers burned the church, although it was full of women and children seeking sanctuary. This lightning campaign was so unexpected that de Burgo was in Connacht, while the new Royal Governor, Edmund Butler, was even further away, in Munster. Both men gathered forces and marched north. De Burgo assembled his army at Roscommon and then marched to Athlone and on to Meath and the land around Tara, which had been the territory of the Southern O'Neills. He destroyed buildings and slaughtered people as he marched, making no difference between clergy and laity. So determined was he on personal vengeance that he refused to allow the army of Edmund Butler to join him, claiming that he was strong enough to drive the Scots out of the country without the need for any more help.

Edward, meanwhile, had withdrawn north on the advice of his Gaelic ally and attacked the earl's lands around Limavady and Inishowen. The earl brought his army north on the Antrim shore of the River Bann, but by the time he got to Coleraine, the Scots had demolished the bridge and were camped on the opposite shore. At this key moment, Felim O'Connor, who had been fighting on the de Burgo side, was persuaded to transfer his allegiance by the promise of the entire province of Connacht. Edward now had his army taken across the Bann by boat and marched towards de Burgo's camp. After an initial, inconclusive skirmish, the earl fell back to the heart of his territory, and took a final stand at the Kellswater at Connor. Here the Irish and Scottish army completely routed the defenders. Sir William de Burgo was captured, while Earl Richard was lucky to escape, having lost power and lordship in one afternoon.

What remained of the army took refuge in Carrickfergus Castle. Edward II, dismayed by the possibility of losing Ireland entirely, ordered that the castle be supplied with stores sufficient to withstand a long siege. The ships carrying these provisions were caught in a great storm, however, and had to return to England. Edward Bruce, meanwhile, left enough soldiers to keep the Carrickfergus garrison bottled up, while he took the rest of the army to dispose of the English supporters in the rest of Ireland. The main force of the Scottish army was made up of spearsmen, fighting on foot. Winter warfare was to their advantage, since the colonists fought as mounted knights, and their heavily loaded horses sank deep into the winter mud in Ireland's damp climate. All that winter the Scots prevailed in battle after battle. What prevented their total success was the fact that there had been a bad harvest in Ireland that year. Used to living off the countryside, hunger eventually defeated them and they had to fall back to Ulster.

In Carrickfergus the hunger was even greater, and no attempt was made to relieve the garrison until Easter 1316. When a relieving force from Dundalk landed, they were caught in the streets of Carrickfergus by the Scots and Irish and defeated, in spite of an attempt by the garrison of the castle to reinforce them. Disheartened, the defenders of the castle inevitably surrendered, although not till September of that year. Reports said that hunger had reduced them so much that they had killed and eaten some of their Scottish prisoners.

Edward Bruce now held all the important castles of Ulster, from Lough Foyle to Carlingford, and had the support of many clans in Connacht and Leinster. In May he had been crowned King of Ireland in Dundalk. Now, at Christmas, Robert Bruce joined his brother at Carrickfergus, bringing a large army with him. Early the next year the brothers marched south with their O'Neill allies. Pausing only to defeat Richard de Burgo in Meath, they went on towards Dublin. De Burgo had fled there from the battlefield, only to find that the Mayor of Dublin suspected him of being a spy in the service of his Scottish son-in-law. In a twelvemonth that had seen one humiliation after another, the Earl of Ulster now found himself thrown in prison. His captor, meanwhile, ordered the citizens of Dublin to repair the city's walls and to burn all those houses which were outside the city's defences. His preparations were not needed, because the Bruce army now turned away and started to plunder the countryside, going as far as Limerick. Like Napoleon in Russia, centuries later, the brothers found that their greatest enemy was the winter itself. The harvest had been even worse than that of the previous year and the winter even colder and wetter. The men were soon starving, and the annals have gruesome accounts of soldiers digging bodies out of cemeteries to eat and of mothers devouring their own children. Once again, hunger brought what remained of the army back to Ulster. In May Robert returned to Scotland, leaving Edward and the O'Neills to face the vengeance of the English.

At first there was a stalemate brought on by the continuing famine. Edward II's governor in Ireland, Roger de Mortimer, arrived from England with a large army, but he was reluctant to go on campaign until he was sure of his supplies. He remained in Dublin, his only positive act being to release the Earl of Ulster from prison. The crucial action did not occur till 1318, when an English fleet captured the Bruce ships so that Edward was cut off from his Scottish supplies. Luckily for him, that year's harvest was both early and plentiful, and Edward's army was soon ready to march south. Any optimism was premature, however, because they were met and utterly defeated by an English army north of Dundalk, near Faughart. Edward was killed, with many of his leading allies. Richard de Burgo was able to take possession of his lands once again.

He lived for another eight years, and recruited an army of Irishmen to protect his interests. He owned half the land of Ireland and was connected by marriage to many of the great families on both islands. When he died, however, his heir, William, was only fourteen. Edward III, who was now King of England, knighted him anyway, and he was confirmed in his inheritance and became known as the Brown Earl. Unfortunately, he was no match for his grandfather, except in cruelty. He was challenged by his cousin Walter. With the help of King Edward, William captured Walter and locked him in the great castle of Northburgh, at the mouth of the Foyle. Here the unfortunate Walter was left to starve to death. The deed is commemorated in the coat of arms of the City of Derry, for it is Walter's skeleton that contemplates the viewer, and the tower in the background represents Northburgh.

It seems that William had been elevated to greatness before he was ready for it, because he developed a great knack of making enemies. In 1333 he was waylaid near Carrickfergus and killed by two of his own tenants. His only child was a daughter of two, and her mother fled with her to England. Without a figurehead, the earldom began to collapse almost immediately. O'Cahan seized the land west of the Bann and, although it took nearly a century, the entire province eventually reverted to Gaelic land. The Gaelic resurgence was helped by a number of things. In the first case, many of the colonists simply gave up being English. The de Burgos of Connacht, for example, changed their name to Burke and took up the Irish language, lived by Irish custom and law, and intermarried with the native Irish. A set of laws, known as the Statutes of Kilkenny, proved powerless to prevent this. Secondly, the weather conspired against the colonists. This was a cold wet period, when the climate deteriorated to the extent that the Norse had to abandon their settlements in Greenland. The Normans in Ireland depended on corn and sheep for their staple food and it was these that suffered the greatest losses. The native Irish, more used to the country, were better able to ride out the storm. When the Black Death struck, once again it was the colonists, used to living in the squalid, cramped conditions of towns, who suffered most; they had lost almost half their numbers by the end of the century. It was hard to attract new settlers, especially to the disputed lands of Ulster. Most importantly of all, the English kings turned their attention elsewhere; firstly to the wars in France and then to the dynastic struggle that became known as the Wars of the Roses.

The Gaelic lords of Ulster were not slow to take advantage. To help them, they imported gallowglasses (from an Irish phrase meaning foreign warriors) from Scotland, mercenaries of partly Norse blood who were famed for their fighting ability. Whole clans settled in the north, the most numerous being MacSweeny of Doe. They fought as the Vikings had, using battleaxes, and had a reputation for not giving up, but fighting to the death. The fiercest fighters were the MacDonnells,

Carndaisy Glen.

who became firm allies of the O'Neills and settled around Ballygawley. Their fighting ability helped the O'Neills to make Tir Eoghain the centre of Gaelic Ireland. The area around it became known to the English as the 'Great Irishry'. The English gone, the clans were able to go back to the struggle for domination.

The longest, least conclusive struggle was between Cenel Conaill and Cenel Eoghain. The O'Neills lost part of their territory to the O'Dohertys, allies of the O'Donnells of Cenel Conaill. The O'Neills expanded south and east. Niall Mor O'Neill broke off this search for living room, since Richard II of England had landed with the largest army yet seen in Ireland and was holding his grandsons as hostages. He went south and made his submission, among eighty chiefs who did so. Turlough O'Donnell was the only chief from the north who felt strong enough to decline the royal invitation. Niall was forced to promise tribute to the descendant of de Burgo's heiress, Roger de Mortimer, who now claimed to act as Earl of Ulster. In a letter to King Richard, Niall predicted that de Mortimer would attack Tir Eoghain after the king had sailed back to England. This proved to be true, but the English force was badly mauled when it marched into Ulster, and the Leinster Irish, who had no love for de Mortimer, killed him as he tried to return to Dublin. Richard II returned on a punitive expedition, but it also proved disastrous and he was forced to return to England, where he was imprisoned and murdered by the Lancastrian faction, the bloody deed which began the Wars of the Roses.

Life in a Gaelic lordship is illustrated by an account left by Ramon, Viscount of Perellos and Roda. His king, John of Aragon, had died in a hunting accident and Ramon was concerned that, as the king had not made Confession, the regal soul would now be suffering the pangs of hell. As a good courtier, the viscount decided to undertake a pilgrimage to St Patrick's Purgatory at Lough Derg. It was believed at the time that a soul might be released from hell if the pilgrim survived the terrors of the pilgrimage. Pope Benedict III tried to discourage him, but eventually gave his blessing, and the Catalan gentleman set off on his journey to the edge of Europe.

The Pope was living in Avignon at the time, so it was here the pilgrim left, making his way through Paris to Calais and on to England. Here he was entertained by no less a being than King Richard, but after a week he set off to Chester, where he charted a ship to Dublin. Roger de Mortimer met him there, and added his warnings to the others that had been freely given to Perellos all along his route. As we have already seen, Roger should have heeded his own warnings, but he was unable to dissuade the Catalan from the last stage of the journey. Perellos was given an escort to the Ulster border, but the soldiers would go no further. In spite of all that had been said, Niall Mor O'Neill bade him welcome, treating him to a meal of beef while impressing him by the size and demeanour of his armoured escort. Perellos was also impressed by the weapons that the Irish wore, but found them very reminiscent of Saracens. Prepared in body, he then made the hard journey the length of Lough Erne and over the hills to Lough Derg itself. The monks there were uneasy about his chances of surviving the ordeal, and sang a Requiem Mass before he crossed to Saint's Island, just in case. In the pit on the island, he claimed, he was able to make the journey to Purgatory, where he met with his late master and was delighted to find that the royal soul was already on the way to salvation. He spent Christmas with O'Neill, and was back in Rheims by March.

In spite of the roast ox donated by O'Neill, Perellos was not impressed by the Irish diet. Noting that there was no wine to be drunk, since the country produced none, he said that the great lords drank cows' milk to show their wealth, or a meat broth, a sort of Gaelic Bovril. Ordinary people washed down their meals of wheat with water, but showed great ingenuity in the ways they used butter, which was plentiful, to vary their diet. Other observers commented on the amount of butter that was used by the Irish. It was kept in hollowed-out wooden containers, which were sometimes buried in bogs to preserve them. The English were not fond of the resulting flavour. A simple meal was uncooked oatmeal with butter stirred through it. Whole milk was too valuable simply to be drunk, but the Irish enjoyed buttermilk and clotted milk. Blood might be drawn from a vein on a living cow and mixed with butter to form a nutritious cream. Alternatively, it could be mixed with oatmeal to form black pudding. These recipes had the advantage that they were high in protein, while the beast survived to be milked on another day. Their favourite meat, when they could get it, was pork, from as fat a pig as could be found. All this meat was supplemented by plants taken from the woods, the favourites being mushrooms, wood sorrel and watercress. Until recently, rural women in Ireland referred to these edible plants as 'kitchen'. In spite of what Perellos said, wine was imported into Ireland, either paid for in hides or in the right to fish in Irish waters. It was still restricted to the gentry; the commonality preferred ale or whiskey.

One thing that Perellos noted without enthusiasm was the style of Irish clothing. Both men and women, he thought, were well built and handsome, but the effect was lost in the clothes they chose to wear. Even nobles went barefoot and trouserless, wearing only a long, low-cut tunic and an exaggerated hood. They even wore spurs on their bare heels. The poor were worse, showing their shameful parts without shame, even the handmaids of O'Neill's wife. Not just the poor; a Bohemian count met sixteen women near Limavady who, he said, were naked, yet who could converse with him in Latin. He accepted their invitation into their house, unsurprisingly. They were joined by the O'Cahan himself, who made himself comfortable by removing all his clothes, commenting all the while on his Bohemian guest's excessive modesty in refusing to do likewise. It is interesting to wonder whether these accounts are true or if they were written to confirm widely held beliefs about the Irish, just as Perellos wrote his story of his journey into Purgatory.

Because of the basic nature of the Irish houses, and because the Irish spent so much time out of doors, Perellos made the assumption that they were nomads, following their herds from pasture to pasture. What he possibly witnessed, or heard of, was the removal of the herds to high pasture during the summer, only to be returned to the arable land as winter set in, to graze among the stubble; this practice was continued well into modern times and came to be known as booleying. While some of the younger members of the family went into the hills to milk the cows and churn butter, the older men took charge of the ploughing, such as it was. If they were opening new ground the work was done with a spade, because they did not have proper harness for a plough horse. For re-ploughing land that had been already dug a light plough was tied to the horse's tail. As well as being unpleasant for the horse, this was inefficient in the extreme, since it depended on the strength of horsehair rather than on the power of the animal itself. Temporary fences were built around these fields to protect the grain that was being grown from stray animals. The fences were used as fuel during the winter, a practice that could be sustained while Irish woods were plentiful, but which was very wasteful in later years, when most of the woodland had been cleared.

Niall's ambition to expand his borders was enthusiastically supported by his sons. Niall Og succeeded him, Cu Ulaidh plundered the church in Armagh, while a third son Henry, known to posterity as Harry Avery, whose castle's remains are found near Newtownstewart, held off the O'Donnells at the frontier around Raphoe. The next generation of O'Neills fought among one another, however, and left the borders open to opportunistic enemies. Luckily for Tir Eoghain, the O'Donnells were so busy with their own disputes that they were unable to take advantage of this. In the end it was England that rebuilt the reputation and power of the O'Neills of Tir Eoghain. The Wars of the Roses were occupying English minds and Edward, Duke of York, who inherited the earldom of Ulster after the Mortimer family died out, did not want to be troubled by his Irish possessions. His father, Henry VI, authorised his chief representative in Ireland, the Earl of Ormond, to meet with Henry O'Neill in August 1449. On behalf of his father, who was still living, Henry recognised the English king as his liege lord, promising to support the crown with armed men when required. In return the O'Neills of Tir Eoghain were recognised as overlords of Ulster. Henry O'Neill delivered on his side of the bargain immediately, bringing to heel those Ulster clans which had been raiding the area around Dublin known as the Pale, and who had even forced the Norman manors in County Louth to pay them protection money (known at the time as black rent). As a reward, Henry VI sent him a collar of gold.

For most of his reign as Lord of Tir Eoghain, Henry maintained a constant war to keep the O'Donnells and the Clandeboye O'Neills in their place. It was a long war of attrition, but by 1483 all the Gaelic lords in Ulster recognised his authority and accepted his right to billet soldiers in their lands. He was recognised by the English as the Great O'Neill. He retired that year, unfortunately, and the O'Donnells soon began to test the strength and resolve of the new chief. While this was happening, something truly momentous in its implications for Ulster was happening in England. Henry, Duke of Richmond, brought together a confederacy of the great lords of England and defeated Richard III, the last Yorkist king of England. The House of Tudor now reigned in England, and the newly crowned Henry VII set about reducing the power of the barons in order to reinforce the strength of his hold on England.

As far as Ireland was concerned, for the time being King Henry was prepared to leave its governance to his main supporter in Ireland, the Earl of Kildare, Garret Mor Fitzgerald. The latter was concerned that the Great O'Neill was becoming an over-mighty subject and he joined his army with the O'Donnells and the Maguires and attacked Dungannon, where the castle was taken by assault. From here they went on to attack Omagh, but the people of that district submitted to Kildare, giving hostages as token of their peaceful intent. King Henry's only real interest in Ireland was the Pale around Dublin, and he was happy to allow his loyal followers to pursue their own agenda, as long as they did not interfere with the crown's strategic priorities.

It was a dangerous policy, and it came back to bite Henry VIII, who retained the services of the Earl of Kildare. Kildare's own son, known as Silken Thomas, rose in rebellion. The rising was easily quashed. Henry decided that he needed his own man in Dublin and appointed a Lord Deputy. Many people advised him to conquer Ulster, since they believed only areas which had felt the sharp edge of English swords would be truly loyal. The Ulster chiefs were aware of this, and were also aware of the guns that the Lord Deputy was bringing to Ireland. Now the great stone tower-houses that the Irish had built in imitation of the Normans were no longer safe. On the grounds that if you have the power you should use it, the Lord Deputy, Lionel Grey, launched several attacks against Ulster, culminating in the laying waste of the land around Dungannon, where his army burnt crops and slaughtered cattle. In the end, it wasn't the Irish who defeated him, but Henry's distrust of anyone who seemed to be getting above his station. Grey was summoned back to London, where he was tried on corruption charges and beheaded.

His replacement, Sir Anthony St Leger, was of a liberal mind. Anticipating Terence O'Neill by several centuries, he maintained that if you treated the Irish as you would treat the English, they would see the error of their ways and behave as Englishmen, obeying English law and showing loyalty to the crown. This could not happen overnight. Firstly, Henry would have to take the title of King of Ireland; before this he had been content to be Lord of Ireland. Then the key Ulster chieftains, O'Donnell and O'Neill, would require a demonstration of the power of the king's men. If they submitted, the lesser chiefs would follow. When confronted by the size of the Lord Deputy's army, Manus O'Donnell submitted readily. There then followed a dreadful three weeks around Dungannon, when all the winter victuals were destroyed, even the butter. Conn Bacach O'Neill had no choice but to follow the example of Manus.

The next step was to alter the way in which the chief held his land. Up till now, in theory at least, each chief held the land in trust for the clan. This was not how things worked in England, where the king held all the land and granted it at his pleasure to barons who had served him well. The corollary of this was that he could confiscate land from those barons who did not please him. St Leger wanted to introduce this system to Ireland. To achieve this aim, he wanted each Irish chief to surrender his lands to the king, who would immediately grant them back to the chief. To reinforce the change in status, the chief would also renounce the Gaelic title under which he had ruled and accept a title granted by the king. This would mean that Conn Bacach would no longer be the Great O'Neill, but would be entitled the Earl of Tyrone.

Having seen at first hand the might of a king's army, Conn Bacach was perfectly prepared to go along with this. He was created Earl of Tyrone in October 1542. He spoke to Henry in Irish, which was translated into English by a priest. To ensure the succession, his son Matthew, considered by many to be illegitimate, was made Baron of Dungannon. The thorny problem of who controlled Inishowen was resolved when Conn agreed to renounce his claim on the peninsula in return for an annual tribute of sixty cows. This was never paid, but it gave Conn an excuse to concentrate on the affairs of Tyrone. Things seemed to promise well, but there was a new element that threatened future peace. Henry VIII was having problems with the Pope, and seemed determined to impose the religious changes already taking place in England upon an Irish population, the largest part of which turned out to be unwilling to countenance them. Worse, there were those at court who were more determined to subjugate the Irish than to 'civilise' them.

Renouncing the Pope, as Conn Bacach did in 1542, was not the main problem. The Pope had been a distant figure to the Irish. The first Irish monasteries had already been dissolved in 1539 without any great disturbance. These had been in the Pale and in County Down, and the monasteries concerned had long given up their charitable connections with the local community. The destruction of relics was taken more seriously, and there was great dismay when the Staff of Jesus, which had been taken to Dublin from Armagh, was smashed.

It is probable that Henry was so caught up in English opposition to his reforms – it was only by trickery that he survived the Pilgrimage of Grace – that he was not more forceful in Ireland. His reforms, anyway, were not altogether whole-hearted; it is likely that he simply wanted a Catholic Church with himself at its head, whatever his Protestant advisers might have aspired to.

When his sickly son, Edward VI, ascended the throne, matters were different. This was a determinedly Protestant reign, and it would have been interesting to see what would have developed if the king had survived in power longer than the six years he managed. During this time Dublin began to accept the Reformed Church, but there were no Irish martyrs to the Protestant cause when Mary assumed the throne in 1553. When Mary in her turn died, the throne came to Elizabeth. The new queen was not in a position to push through reforms, especially in Ireland, even if she had wished to do so. She seems to have been a very pragmatic young woman, although later generations have tried to put an idealist twist on her decisions. One of the most prominent of her court musicians until his (natural) death was the Catholic Thomas Tallis. William Shakespeare's father was also a Catholic, yet he was able to be Mayor of Stratford on several occasions. Elizabeth asked only that Catholics did not flaunt their difference; if they conformed to the requirements of the Established Church, they could do what they liked privately. It was the Pope who made the difference. In two rulings, he condemned the Catholics of England to a second-class existence. Firstly, he declared that attendance at a Protestant service – a legal requirement in England – was a mortal sin, potentially a ticket to hell. This made those who wanted to retain the old religion stand out like sore thumbs; all the enforcers had to do was to check who had not attended on Sunday.

The second ruling of the Pope was a personal attack on the Queen herself. He said that anyone who killed her would not be guilty of sin. From then on anyone who maintained a loyalty to the Pope could be deemed a traitor, wishing Queen Elizabeth dead.

This is not to say that Elizabeth had it in mind to subjugate Catholic Ireland. Many of her representatives in Ireland, however, saw the opportunity of enriching themselves in the lands of Ulster. It was a time, after all, when the younger sons of Europe were scattering around the globe, seeking riches where they could find them, showing little respect for the current owners. They looked for territories that could not protect themselves and then exploited weakness. For those who did not care for the long transatlantic crossing, Ulster seemed an easier choice. They thought they had found their excuse when, in 1559, Shane O'Neill killed his brother and drove his father, Conn Bacach, out of Ulster. The war which followed continued, on and off, for well over one hundred years, only ending with the Treaty of Limerick in 1691. It resulted in the total collapse of the Gaelic system in Ulster.

THE LONG WAR: SUBDUING ULSTER

THE PRIDE OF SHANE O'NEILL

Shane O'Neill gathered the opprobrium of the English and of most of the Irish clans. Stories are told of him that chill the soul, yet it is difficult to see through the myth and legend and to find the truth of all that has been said about him. Stories of how he treated women have obviously been elaborated, even if there is a grain of truth in them. Other stories imply that he lacked courage in battle, but it is unlikely that he could have mobilised the resources not simply of his own clan, but of the greater part of Ulster, if he had not shown himself an adequate warrior and a more than competent captain. Winners write history, and it was the English who won the Long War.

Shane was born in 1530, the year his mother died. He was fostered by the O'Donnellys, hereditary marshals of the O'Neills. He first came to prominence in 1548, when he led an attack on Clandeboye, during which a son of the MacNeill of Clandeboye was killed. Three years later, civil war broke out in Tyrone and Conn Bacach survived only with the help of Shane. By the following year Shane was the dominant force in Tyrone. His brothers were dead or dispersed. He moved quickly to remind the other chiefs of Ulster of his power, driving Felim Rua O'Neill of the Fews to take refuge in the Pale and demanding tribute from Maguire, O'Reilly and McMahon. Meanwhile, he tightened his grip on Dungannon and on Conn. When Shane had his half-brother, the Baron of Dungannon, killed in 1558, Conn decided that it was time to flee. He found refuge with the Bishop of Meath, but only survived another year.

Shane was able to carry out these plans because the two forces which he had to keep an eye on were otherwise engaged. Calvagh O'Donnell had usurped his father with the help of Campbell mercenaries. Sir Henry Sidney, Elizabeth's Lord Justice in Ireland, brought an army north to settle the dynastic squabble that followed. Playing his cards carefully, Shane had guided Sidney through Tyrone, but had excused himself from taking part in the actual fighting. Sidney showed his displeasure by laying waste to Armagh and by looting churches and removing their treasures. This operation, meant to cow Shane into submission at the spectacle of English power, resulted instead in the young lord developing a hatred for Sidney which lasted the rest of his days.

Another development that helped Shane was the death of Hugh MacNeill of Clandeboye. Hugh had been a close ally of the MacDonnells. Now Shane was free to deal directly with the Scots, and began to recruit large numbers of them in his army, so much so that the authorities in Dublin requested reinforcements. Shane wanted to be recognised as Earl of Tyrone. In 1559 Sussex, the Lord Lieutenant, had come to Dungannon for talks, but there was no meeting of minds. Shane demanded restitution for the destruction of Armagh. Sussex insisted that any complaints that Shane had against his neighbours should be settled by English arbitration. When Sussex reported back to Elizabeth, he used the opportunity to persuade her that war was her best option. With her permission, he put together a great army and created an alliance of the Ulster chiefs. Shane responded by a sweep in a huge arc through south Ulster, and the alliance melted away. He used his enlarged army to attack the O'Reillys and raid the Pale, before turning west and attacking Calvagh O'Donnell. He seems to have been in contact with Calvagh's wife, Catherine, because she led her husband into a trap where he was captured by Shane's men. Calvagh was kept in Dungannon in chains, while Catherine became Shane's mistress, and the focus for many salacious stories. Meanwhile, the alliance melted away.

It was not until June 1561 that Sussex was able to set out for Armagh. The expedition was not a success. Shane had removed all his cattle to west Tyrone and the River Blackwater was so badly in flood that the English could not cross it. Their supplies ran out and they had to retire to Newry. Sussex even considered poisoning Shane. Instead, with more reinforcements and extra money, he made another attempt on Tyrone. This time he captured horses and cattle *en route* to Omagh, but Shane refused battle with such a great host. Sussex was forced to kill the animals, since he could not manage them, before marching to Derry, where he was due to be supplied by sea. When the ships did not appear – a personal humiliation to Sussex, since he had the army of the O'Donnells with him – once again the English were forced into a long cross-country retreat. To try to salvage his reputation, Sussex claimed that the power of the O'Neills had been broken. Shane demonstrated the truth of the matter by launching a devastating raid on Meath. Queen Elizabeth, as careful in money matters as her grandfather, decided it was cheaper to negotiate.

Shane came to London in January 1562, with an exotic escort of gallowglasses. These were bare-headed, with shoulder-length hair with short tunics, linen vests and heavy cloaks. He had been reluctant to leave the safety of Tyrone, but a gift of £2,000 and the promise that the Earls of Kildare and Ormond would not leave his side had been enough to persuade him. At Greenwich Palace, in the presence of all the court and of several ambassadors, he prostrated himself in front of the Queen and submitted – in Irish. Kildare translated.

The matter was not yet decided, and when Sussex arrived on the scene, Shane's manner lost any servility. Elizabeth could not make up her mind. She decided that she would have to talk to Shane's nephew Brian, the young Earl of Dungannon, whose father had been murdered on Shane's orders. She sent for Brian but he was murdered at Carlingford on his way to London. There was no proof of who carried out this act, and Shane claimed that it had been done by rebels who supported Turlough O'Neill. (And, in fact, Turlough O'Neill tried to seize the leadership of the clan just before Shane got back to Ireland.) In the event, Elizabeth decided to go part of the way to meet Shane's claims. He was to be recognised as Captain of Tyrone, O'Cahan's country and much of Antrim. He was not to be granted the title Earl of Tyrone. This was something that Shane resented, and he saw it as a petty revenge from someone – Sussex – he had thrashed in battle. Nevertheless, he signed the terms, even undertaking to live in peace with his Irish neighbours for a minimum of six months.

He did not feel himself bound by these restrictions, however, and prepared to get his revenge for the pettiness of Sussex. Dealing with Turlough was no problem, but there were other pressing issues. The English garrison in Armagh was feeding itself at the expense of Shane's people, while some of the English lords were conducting raids into Tyrone and taking off cattle. Rather than try to do everything at once, he decided on his priorities. The first thing he wanted to show the Irish chiefs was that they could not rely on the English for protection. He mounted an all-out attack against Maguire, who was the chief ally of the English in Ulster. The soldiers of Tyrone crossed the Erne at Belleek and devastated the country beyond just as the people were gathering the harvest. So successful was this attack that Hugh Maguire had to take refuge on the islands of Lough Erne, where he prepared to make a last stand. Next Shane raided Tirconnell, taking 30,000 cattle in recompense for those Sussex had destroyed. All the while he kept up raids on the garrison at Armagh and on the border villages of the Pale. At an assembly of the O'Neills he boasted, 'I went to England not to keep [my possessions] but to win [more].'

Sussex was running out of time. Elizabeth's cousin Lord Cecil was the Queen's closest adviser and was also one of Sussex's most powerful supporters. Cecil, however, was being replaced in the Queen's affections by the Earl of Leicester. Some say that she considered marrying him, but there was a scandal concerning the death of his first wife, who had died from a fall down stairs. When Queen Elizabeth in turn developed smallpox in the autumn of 1562, Leicester was in France, but his sister nursed her back to health. Weakened more than she was prepared to admit by her illness, Elizabeth was reluctant to fund a war in Ireland while she was still paying for an expedition in France which was aimed at protecting the rights of French Protestants. It was precisely at this time that Shane sent messages to England, with presents for Elizabeth, Leicester and even Cecil. He had been wronged, he said, and attacked when he had done no offence. His loyalty to Elizabeth was undiluted and he only asked that she recognise this by creating him Earl of Tyrone. Hesitant about committing herself, Elizabeth replied that this was a decision that would have to be made by Sussex.

Sussex, however, was seeing his power drain away from him. For some years Leicester had been gathering complaints made about the Lord Lieutenant. He was accused by certain of his captains of withholding some of their pay. It was recommended that a full audit be held before the next pay distribution. The people of the Pale refused to give him supplies or to allow soldiers to be billeted on their property. As a result, Sussex had no army to meet Shane's attacks except for some Irish mercenaries. Shane's attacks became more blatant. It was not until early 1563 that Sussex was ready to move north. Even then things were not as they should have been. His protector, Cecil, seeing the way the wind was blowing, sent neither munitions nor reinforcements. The Pale provided the most meagre of supplies. Kildare sent word that he was 'ill', and the Irish troops that he was to lead never appeared.

Desperate, Sussex went ahead anyway. He conducted some raids into Tyrone and took some cattle but, once again, Shane refused to make an appearance. Feeling the need to show some result for all his endeavours, Sussex paid a man called Smith to assassinate Shane by poisoning his wine. To the horror of the Lord Lieutenant – and his agent – Shane woke the next morning with nothing worse than a hangover. The army had lost heart and by this stage even English soldiers were defecting. Sussex's last chance was gone.

Elizabeth once again sought advice. This time she turned to a former Lord Chancellor of Ireland, Sir Thomas Cusack. His belief was that the only way to a lasting peace was through negotiation. She agreed, writing to Sussex that he must stop the war and adding, rather gratuitously, that the Lord Lieutenant's humiliation was a price she was quite happy to pay. She then authorised Cusack to initiate talks with Shane.

These took place at Drumcree, near Portadown, in September 1563. From Shane's point of view they seemed to go very well. Almost everything that he asked was either granted or promised in the medium term. It was even agreed that the Queen would try to find a suitable English noblewoman as Shane's wife. When it came to implementing the treaty, however, things did not go so well. Shane had been promised safeguards before any meeting with the Lord Lieutenant, but Elizabeth herself threw this out, arguing that to allow this would be to treat Tyrone as an independent principality. Since this is what Shane considered it to be, he was very annoyed about this. His annoyance was aggravated when the Queen seemed to be dragging her feet on the matter of finding him a wife. Worst of all, he had been promised that he would be made Earl of Tyrone as soon as the Barony of Dungannon was extinguished; there was no sign of this happening. There was no sign even of Smith, the man who had tried to poison Shane, being brought to trial.

There was actually a reason for this, but Shane was unaware of it. The Queen had determined to call an Irish Parliament, but she was reluctant to do this until she had appointed a Lord Lieutenant powerful enough to control it. Behind the throne there was a web of intrigue as powerful lords tried to get their own clients chosen. Tired of waiting, Shane attacked and captured Lifford Castle, one of the O'Donnell strongholds. He was promised a ransom for the release of Calvagh. When this was not paid, he launched an invasion of Tirconnell which did much to establish his reputation for merciless ferocity. His men took away hundreds of thousands of cattle and killed an estimated 4,500 of the population. Shane placed garrisons in all the chief castles and set up Calvagh's brother Hugh Dubh, as a puppet chief before returning to Dungannon that autumn.

This had been done without the sanction of Dublin, so Shane quickly acted to negate any displeasure that the English might have. Early the following year, 1565, the Antrim MacDonnells, with reinforcements from Scotland, began a major push south through County Down. To show that his heart was in the right place, Shane cut off the raiding parties in Down, leaving them to be dealt with by the local Irish. He took his own army across the hills to besiege the MacDonnell fortress at Red Bay. Having destroyed that, he marched on to besiege Ballycastle. The Scots army came out to meet him and they clashed in Glenshesk. After a bloody battle, in which more than 600 Scots were killed and many taken prisoner, Shane prevailed. Among those he had captured were the MacDonnell chief, Sorley Boy, and his brother James. Only Dunluce Castle held out against him but it too surrendered when he threatened to kill Sorley Boy beneath its walls. To ensure that there would be no more trouble from this quarter Shane placed garrisons in all the castles, as he had done in Tirconnell, and began to move some of his own people into the area as colonists.

Although he now controlled Ulster from Slieve League in the west to Red Bay in the east Shane was not yet satisfied. Late that same year he invaded Breifne, supporting Cahir O'Reilly against his brother Hugh, who had just become chief. Using this as a springboard, he went on to invade Connacht, where he took away 4,000 cattle from the O'Rourkes which, he claimed, was ancient tribute. In the east he expelled the English garrisons from Dundrum and Newry. A year that had begun with a war fought to show his loyalty to the English throne had ended with an action which seemed to show his independence of England. He even entered into negotiations with the Duke of Argyll, hoping to find in the Campbells an ally to counter the power of the MacDonnells.

Elizabeth and her council decided that Shane could not be controlled, nor would he be satisfied with a subordinate position; he had to be destroyed. They appointed Sir Henry Sidney to carry out this task, a man who had fought against Shane before. Before he could proceed, however, the Queen changed her mind again. It was until mid-June of 1566 that she finally decided on war, and it was not until September that troops and supplies began to arrive in Dublin. It was almost October before Sidney was ready to move. This gave time for Shane to raid and burn all that summer, and to move all his valuables to safe locations.

When Sidney eventually came north he found only burnt earth; there was nothing to destroy. Once again, Shane refused to meet him in battle. The English army crossed Tyrone and linked up with a force that he had sent separately to Derry. When the two forces were united, it became obvious that there was not enough forage in the country round to support both of them. Sidney decided to return to Dublin via Sligo and Roscommon, leaving Colonel Randolph to face the winter on the Foyle. When Shane saw that the English had divided their forces, he attacked what he thought was the weaker group, that of Colonel Randolph. Unfortunately for him, it was not weak enough, and the Irish were routed. The only fatality that the English suffered was the good colonel himself. It was the beginning of the end for Shane, although he did not know it.

Against expectation, Sidney launched a mid-winter raid into Tyrone, surprising Shane so much that it was said that he had to flee from his Christmas dinner. Shocked, Shane tried to reopen negotiations on the basis of the Treaty of Drumcree. Sidney, however, had been watching the signs and saw no reason to placate his Irish opponent. Rumours had been reaching Dublin that Shane's main supporters, O'Hanlon and O'Cahan, were showing signs of increasing disaffection with his adventurist policies. Cahir O'Reilly had regained Breifne and was so incensed against Shane that he swore to defend the Pale from an O'Neill attack. The MacDonnells wanted revenge for the massacre of

Glenshesk. Even Hugh O'Donnell repudiated him, since he was now undisputed chief of Tirconnell since the death of Calvagh, his brother and no longer needed O'Neill support. Even his own people were beginning to complain of the ongoing cost of the wars. It was possible that a rival might appear.

None of this had any effect on Shane's aggression. His intention, once the campaigning season of 1567 had begun, was to punish his erstwhile ally, Hugh O'Donnell. This seemed an easy task, since Hugh was not popular with his people, who still remembered the devastation that Shane had inflicted on them. Hugh found no volunteers coming to help him. The Tyrone army of 2,000 men marched unopposed to the great ford of Farsetmore, on the Swilly, and here it camped, on the western shore of the lough. It looked as if they were settling down for a long stay. This changed the equation. Although Tirconnell was O'Donnell territory, a number of lesser clans, O'Doherty and the various MacSweeny clans, occupied the peninsulas on the north coast. These also felt threatened by the Tyrone army and they made common cause with dissident O'Donnells to oppose it. They even joined up with Hugh's soldiery. The united forces were too much for Shane's men. Their line broke and, with the tide at the full, there was nowhere to run. Six hundred died on the field; more than double that drowned trying to escape. Although Shane and a small force did manage to escape, many of his most competent officers were left to feed the Tirconnell ravens.

Around Dungannon, it was not ravens that began to close in. Turlough restarted his rebellion and the illegitimate son of the dead Baron of Dungannon, Art, also laid a claim to the chieftainship. Reports came in that Sidney was preparing another army to bring north. It was now that Shane decided on the most desperate gamble of all. He would go to the MacDonnells for help.

It is hard to work out his thought processes. It was as if each year was a fresh start and nobody carried any resentment forward. To be fair, he had made his peace with some of the MacDonnells, and had even employed some as mercenaries in his latest invasion of Tirconnell. He still had some cards; Sorley Boy was still his hostage. What he did not know was that Sidney had been trying to tempt the MacDonnells with the promise of a permanent settlement in Ulster, being very careful not to let slip the fact that Elizabeth would almost certainly veto the initiative. Whether the MacDonnells valued this offer is debatable, but one fact that did enter their calculations was that Shane was now weak and vulnerable. If he survived the current crisis he might become strong again. It was better not to take a chance.

Shane arrived in Cushendun on 31 May. The negotiations were held in an open field, each leader with only five followers. They continued each day till 2 June, when Alexander MacDonnell decided that Shane had nothing of value to offer. He reached across the table and cut the throat of the Great O'Neill. Shane's followers met the same fate. The story was put about that Shane had been killed during a drunken argument, but that was for the Irish market. The Gaelic tradition of hospitality would have taken a serious dent if it got about that a host had killed his guest of honour.

There is a curious postscript to the incident. The MacDonnells buried Shane, but an Englishman, Captain William Piers from Carrickfergus, dug up the body and removed the head. This he sent to Dublin, thus being able to claim the thousand marks that the Government had offered as a reward. The head was placed on a spike over the gateway of Dublin Castle, where it remained until it had rotted enough to fall off.

BETWEEN ACTS

The death of Shane did not bring about the collapse of the O'Neill clan. Turlough, who now took on himself the title of the Great O'Neill, was himself a great warrior, and was not ruled by impulse or emotion. He soon had his people united behind him and made up with the O'Donnells. He even hired soldiers from them as he set about regaining control of 'greater' Tyrone. Once again there was a block of Gaelic power in the north of Ireland. An untimely rebellion in Munster meant that the English had no soldiers to spare for the purpose of containing it.

Nor did Shane's murder bring peace to the MacDonnells. All the time that Sidney had been hinting to them that they could have an Ulster homeland, he had been planning to establish a colony in Antrim, at the expense of the MacDonnells. He was unable to persuade any English gentlemen to take up the challenge. A later attempt was made to colonise Clandeboye, but Sir Brian O'Neill, Lord of Clandeboye and supporter of the English against Shane O'Neill, took exception to this and wiped out the settlement.

In 1573 Walter Devereux, Earl of Essex, another favourite at the court of the Faery Queen, landed at Carrickfergus after a stormy passage from Liverpool. He met with Sir Brian and shook his hand as a gesture of reconciliation between the Ulsterman and the Crown. He then went on to requisition 10,000 head of Sir Brian's cattle, a hostile act that came to no account, since Sir Brian bribed the guards at Carrickfergus to let them go again. Essex had no more success with his colony, since most of his gentlemen returned to England as soon as they could. The following year he was made Governor of Ulster, and there was no more Mr Nice Guy. He hanged some of the colonists for trying to leave Ireland, to make sure that the colony remained true to its purpose while he was away. He then set about teaching Turlough O'Neill a lesson. The first to die were some of Turlough's men who were trapped on an island on the Blackwater. Thereafter the English force made its way through the river valleys of Turlough's territory, taking cattle where they found them, but they were unable to bring the Irishmen to battle. Frustrated, Essex took the cattle with him, but left some 200 men to build a fortress on the Blackwater. In October he invited himself to Sir Brian O'Neill's castle beside the ford at Belfast where, after a few days of civilised conviviality, he killed all of Sir Brian's followers and sent the Lord of Clandeboye himself, together with his wife and brother, to Dublin, where all three were quartered as traitors.

The following year Essex launched an attack on Rathlin Island, in the course of which all the inhabitants were killed. Sorley Boy MacDonnell witnessed this from the Antrim shore and swore to have his revenge. Yet not even the burning of Carrickfergus gave him satisfaction for the despicable massacre. Nor did Essex get much satisfaction. Although Elizabeth approved of his actions, she lost heart in his ability to carry things through. Sidney, still on the scene, was serving another term as Lord Deputy. He came to Ulster in the year of the Rathlin killings to discover that the fort on the Blackwater had not been completed and, because of its location, was not worth finishing. Clandeboye had been so despoiled that it was deserted, while Rathlin was so vulnerable that it could be retaken by the Scots at any time. He came to the conclusion that no private individual could afford to establish a colony in Ireland; it would require the resources of the Crown. Essex was given the title of Marshall of Ireland and retired to Dublin. There he died of dysentery, aged only thirty-six.

One result of the English concern with a Scottish clan settling in Antrim and Down was that it took some of the pressure off the O'Neills of Tyrone. It was not that the administration thought that Turlough was no longer dangerous, simply the worry that Catholic subjects of the Catholic Mary, Queen of Scots, might cause untold mischief if they were part of a larger plot involving Scotland and France. When, in fact, the MacDonnells were reconciled to the Crown, in 1586, it was Spain that was causing Elizabeth concern. Two years later the Spanish Armada was blown past England in a fierce gale and the scattered ships found themselves trying to make their way against the prevailing winds southwards past the west coast of Ireland. Many ships were wrecked, of course, and very many of their soldiers and sailors were drowned. Others reached the shore, and the fate of these men depended on who they met. Most of the Irish clans gave what help they could to the distressed mariners, even though the MacSweenys, who received many of them, were concerned that they would incur the displeasure of the English. The English, on the other hand, were concerned that even a small band of Spanish soldiers, if they combined with the native Irish, could cause great mischief throughout the island. They were under orders to kill every Spaniard they came across. Since many of the Lord Deputy's soldiers were Irish, it became possible for the Council in London to deny any involvement in the slaughter. The killings had been done by the uncouth Irish.

One incident is worth noting for this story. In the townland of Galliagh, just north of Derry, a group of Irish soldiers in English pay came across a large group of survivors from *La Trinidad Valencera*, which had been wrecked on the north coast of Inishowen. The Spanish were told that they would be escorted to Dublin. When they surrendered their weapons, however, they were stripped of their clothes and murdered. Over 200 died and, although about 100 got away, most of them died of hunger and exposure before they could be smuggled to Scotland by the MacDonnells and O'Cahans. The significance of this incident was that the Irish troops were probably under the orders of Hugh O'Neill, who had been made Earl of Tyrone in 1585. It is worth examining how he came into this inheritance.

Hugh was the brother of Brian, that Baron of Dungannon who had been murdered in mysterious circumstances while on the way to the court of Queen Elizabeth. The Queen herself had affirmed him in his brother's title before setting about having him reared as an English gentleman. It seemed that Elizabeth had chosen well. He had campaigned on the side of Essex, had lent military aid to the Lord Deputy and had, as we have seen, tendered no help to the Spanish. Given the ferocity with which he turned against the English in later life, it is worth speculating as to the reason for his close cooperation with them at this time. Probably, it was simply a matter of survival. Hugh was not universally welcomed in Tyrone; Turlough was still alive, though his base was in Omagh, on the other side of the Sperrins, and the sons of Shane were still after Hugh's blood. A close relationship with the most powerful authority on the island was a good safeguard. The English could only be discarded when a more powerful ally offered, and the only force in Ulster powerful enough was the O'Donnell clan, the traditional enemy and rival of O'Neill. Only the most unusual of circumstances would make allies of these two clans. Typically, the chain of circumstances which led to this situation was initiated by the Lord Deputy himself, to whom it may have seemed a good idea at the time.

Red Hugh O'Donnell was the stuff of which *Boy's Own* adventures are made. While still only sixteen years old, in 1587, he was already the favoured heir to Tirconnell and son-in-law to Hugh O'Neill. Using the network of spies that has always been Ireland's curse, the Lord Deputy, Perrott, discovered that Red Hugh was staying as guest of the MacSweenys in Rathmullan, beside the shores of Lough Swilly. Seeing the opportunity to obtain a hostage who would guarantee the good behaviour of the O'Donnells, Perrott sent a ship straightaway to Rathmullan. The captain invited Red Hugh on board to sample some wine that was worth drinking. Red Hugh, nothing loath, drank rather more than was good for him and woke to find himself a captive, and on the way to Dublin Castle. There, although he was given a certain amount of liberty each day, he spent every night in a 'closely secured apartment' in the castle; the castle itself was surrounded by a wide, deep moat.

There was one attempt to escape, after Christmas 1590, and Hugh made his way to Phelim O'Toole in the Wicklow Hills, looking for refuge. Phelim considered him too dangerous, however, and returned him to the English. It was a full year later before Red Hugh had another opportunity, on Christmas Day 1591. This time two other prisoners got away with him, Art and Henry, the sons of Shane O'Neill. They made their way through the snows of winter to the fastnesses of Glenmalure, headquarters of the O'Byrne clan. The trials were too much for Art, who died of hypothermia. When they had recovered their strength, the two survivors made their way north to Ulster, guided by Turlough O'Hagan. They arrived safely in Dungannon. Henry stayed with his cousin, but Red Hugh was hurried by boat to Ballyshannon, where his father had a castle. There the young man, still not twenty, had his frostbitten toes amputated. In May of that year, 1592, his father stood down as the O'Donnell, and Red Hugh took his place.

The two Hughs may have discussed the future during their short time together in Dungannon. It must have seen that the world they saw as their own, the aristocratic life of the semi-independent Gaelic lords, was threatened with extinction. The massacres on Rathlin and in Belfast had been repeated more recently in Connacht. Not even a 'civilised' chieftain could be sure of the future, when English policy seemed so fickle. Some of O'Neill's own actions may have seemed less than civilised; in 1591, when he was already fifty years old, he eloped with the twenty-four-year-old sister of Sir Henry Bagenal, marshal of the Queen's Army in Ireland. Sir Henry never forgave O'Neill, especially when his sister died after only five years of marriage. His antagonism to the Earl of Tyrone showed itself in 1593, when the two campaigned together for the last time. They were fighting Hugh Maguire, who was concerned that he might lose land in Fermanagh. The combined forces of Bagenal and O'Neill routed Maguire at Belleek, but the Fermanagh man retreated to Enniskillen and prepared to withstand a siege. The island castle was duly invested by Bagenal's troops, but without the help of O'Neill. Although the castle was stormed in February 1594, Maguire and many of his men escaped and continued the fight, now with the help of Red Hugh O'Donnell. The castle of Enniskillen was left dangerously exposed, and Bagenal sent to O'Neill for help. For the first time O'Neill risked open defiance and sent nothing. When a relief force was sent to

Bagenal, commanded by Sir Henry Duke, it was overwhelmed by the Irish as it tried to cross the Arney River. As well as arms and horses, the Irish captured the supplies that were being sent to the garrison at Enniskillen.

UNITED AGAINST THE ENGLISH

The most important step that Hugh O'Neill took in his defiance was a symbolic one, but one which had a strong resonance with his people. After the death of Turlough, he had himself inaugurated at the fort of Tullahogue as The O'Neill. By doing this he renounced his previous connections with the English and the English claim that he held his lands from the Queen. As far as the English were concerned, he had gone native.

His first overt act of war was to attack the fort that had been built on the Blackwater by Essex. Enniskillen had already demonstrated the vulnerability of these isolated outposts to attack, but to abandon them was to abandon any hold on Gaelic territory. Rather than do this, the Irish Council was prepared to lose men and supplies in order to maintain their presence. Ironically, Hugh had helped Essex to raise the walls and fortifications that he was now levelling. The result of the action was that the most forward outpost the English had in Ulster was in Monaghan, since Enniskillen had also fallen by this time. Almost all of the Ulster clans were in arms by now and the McMahons now surrounded the castle at Monaghan. Sir Henry Bagenal led a relief column, but it was ambushed by O'Neill's men near its destination and much of the powder and ammunition that Sir Henry was bringing to the fort was expended in fighting a way through.

Having delivered his supplies, Sir Henry took his men homewards by a route along Lough Muckno, through very rough country. O'Neill harried them all the way, before making an all-out attack near Clontibret, while the English were crossing a stream. Here O'Neill had rather more of an adventure than he might have wanted. He was identified by a man called Seagrave, who immediately led a group of forty horsemen charging against him and his escort. At the time men still wore body armour and carried lances. Seagrave and O'Neill shattered their lances on one another. Seagrave then threw O'Neill to the ground, but became somewhat handicapped when O'Cahan's son cut off his arm. O'Neill then finished off the unfortunate man with his knife. Around them the battle was continuing, and did so till nightfall. The English used so much ammunition that their first line of defence was their pikemen. Darkness separated the two sides, and the English spent the night melting down their pewter for musket balls. Dawn brought relief, however. The Irish had gone. They, too, had run out of powder.

Sir Henry was lucky to get back to Newry. He knew that he had lost more men than he could afford, and that he was facing an opponent as shrewd and professional as any leader in the English army, who was leading soldiers at least as good as the English they opposed. The difference in the Irish ranks was that there were fewer Scottish mercenaries; the Scottish clans were caught up in their own troubles with Clan Campbell. The men who fought were not fighting for money, but for what they saw as their own. For them there was no retreat across the North Channel if things turned against them. They had to win, and were prepared to show the discipline necessary to do so. It was not only the land-owners that fought alongside Hugh O'Neill, but the common people. They were armed and trained. They were formed into closely related companies. The arms they carried were the most modern, and they were confident in their use of them. Even the long-settled gallowglasses from the Blackwater Valley, the MacDonnells, were prepared to give up their battleaxes for a musket or an arquebus. Even the poorest woodmen and servants had a place, as light soldiers who could move quickly and sting quietly. The Ulster nation was in arms.

The war spread, and the last few routes into Ulster were being blocked to the English one after the other. Sligo was taken, and now only the dangerous pas-sage into Armagh was left open. Seeing the importance of this, the Lord Deputy, Sir William Russell, brought the army north. Although he was shadowed all the way by O'Neill, no attempt was made to impede him and he reached Armagh safely in June. Here he reinforced the cathedral as a fortress. O'Neill thought that his intention was to go on and capture the castle at Dungannon, now only fourteen miles away. Rather than see the English win an easy propaganda victory, he had his own castle demolished, with the stones being carried away and hidden for later use. Nonplussed, Sir William offered a truce, which was gratefully accepted by the Irish. They needed time to plan for the future. They needed international help if there was to be any possibility of matching the resources of the English. The offer came from Spain. Phillip II was prepared to offer help to the Irish in their ongoing battles against the heretic English. In fact, two expeditions were equipped and sent towards Ireland, but both were caught in Atlantic gales and scattered with great loss of life. The Irish were on their own for the time being.

The latest Lord Deputy, Lord Thomas Burgh, was determined to pressu-rise Hugh O'Neill. He planned a joint attack on Ulster, with the Governor of Connacht attacking Tirconnell, while he himself would attack through the tra-ditional route of Armagh and the Blackwater. This plan was disrupted when the army of Red Hugh defeated the Governor at Belleek, and drove the Connacht army down along the Erne to Ballyshannon. An absolute downpour saved the English, because the rain prevented the Irish from lighting the slow fuses of their firearms. Nothing daunted, Burgh built another fort at the Blackwater. Since he abandoned Armagh to do this, the men in the new fort were more isolated than ever from support. The supplies of the district were soon used up, between the attackers and the defenders, and a localised famine developed. Soldiers and civilians both suffered, and Burgh himself died of famine fever in October.

The isolated nature of the Blackwater was reinforced by events that happened in County Antrim. Burgh had intended to supply his fort from Belfast and across Lough Neagh; hence his willingness to abandon Armagh. This plan was thwarted when the O'Neill Lord of Clandeboye captured Belfast Castle and slaughtered the defenders. Sir John Chichester, Governor of Carrickfergus, recaptured the place easily and went on to capture Edenduffcarrick on the shores of Lough Neagh. In doing this, however, he neglected to guard his flanks. One of his officers, Captain Maunsell, drove off a huge herd of cattle belonging to Sir James MacDonnell, now leader of the MacDonnells. Sir James took a large escort and rode to Carrickfergus to get the matter sorted out. At a parley outside the walls of the castle, Sir John, rashly as it turned out, chose to attack the MacDonnells. He was shot through the head and nearly two hundred of his men were killed. Sir James protested to the Queen that he had only wanted to discuss the return of his cattle. Whether or not this was true, the MacDonnells were now part of the Gaelic confederacy against the English. The garrison on the Blackwater was completely surrounded.

Practical voices advised that the troops be withdrawn, but even the fact that they seemed only to be holding on by the skin of their teeth was not enough to shake the confidence of the Irish Council. Fresh troops arrived from England in July 1598, and Sir Henry Bagenal set off to relieve the fort with a force of 300 horse and 4,000 foot. He was in Armagh by 13 August, with the fort only a few miles away. Hugh O'Neill was ready. He had gathered the full strength of his forces, and was waiting. The two Hughs commanded the front, O'Neill on the left, Red Hugh O'Donnell on the right. Randall MacDonnell held his men in reserve, as did Sir Hugh Maguire, who commanded the Irish horse. When Bagenal left Armagh the next morning, he soon found himself under constant fire from nearby woods. The English cavalry, whose task would normally have been to clear away these skirmishers, were useless in woods and were unable to do anything.

The key fact was that the pack convoy and the column's cannon were in the centre of the English line. On the narrow trail they impeded the regiments following behind them. This allowed the front of the column, commanded by Sir Richard Percy, to become separated. This was made worse when one of the heavy cannon got stuck in a bog stream. Bagenal came forward to clear the obstacle and was shot dead. Meanwhile Percy's men, finding themselves overwhelmed, began to retreat. In the melee around the supplies, a burning match from a musket fell into some gunpowder, and two barrels exploded. The Irish took this opportunity to charge and the English retreat became a rout. There is no doubt that the Irish could have killed or captured the entire force, since they had no refuge nearer than Newry, but O'Neill chose not to press home his advantage; he even allowed the garrison from the fort to withdraw unhindered. Perhaps he was reluctant to carry out an act so ruthless that it would rule out any possibility of future negotiations. On the other hand, he may simply have wanted to send the message: stay out of Ulster and you'll have no trouble from me.

Two things militated against this. First, the scale of the English disaster – 800 killed, 400 wounded and 300 defected to O'Neill – was such that it put all thought of talks out of Elizabeth's mind. Only the defeat of O'Neill would satisfy her. Second, whether he willed it or not, the rebellion was spreading to parts of Ireland that had been thought safe. Connacht was taken by Red Hugh, the O'Mores attacked the English settlements in the Midlands and the colony in Munster was wiped out completely, the only survivors being those who left their land and fled to Dublin. This would have been the moment to go for the all-out expulsion of the English, but O'Neill hesitated, possibly hoping that the Queen would recognise his position as ruler of Ulster, and the moment passed. It is unlikely, even if the English had been expelled, that any amity among the Irish clans would have lasted for long.

In London, the entire winter was spent in preparation. More troops were levied than ever before; others were transferred from the ongoing war in the Netherlands. London merchants were made rich on the contracts for food, munitions, camp supplies and medicines. The leader chosen for this huge enterprise was another Devereux, the second Earl of Essex. This was a gamble. His father had been a ruthless man who saw things through. This Essex was a courtier, and it was whispered even at the time that the Queen might have favoured his looks and courtly manners over the proven experience of other men. She even gave him the exalted title of Lord Lieutenant.

It was April 1599 before he left for Dublin. A vessel that sailed from Dublin to meet him foundered in a storm, and nineteen loyal noblemen, including the Earl of Kildare, were drowned. The English army landed without loss and were soon ready for action. It was the largest army that Ireland had seen, it was reported, yet it was not used against Ulster. Essex spent that summer in a series of inconsequential expeditions and sieges, as he tried to eliminate allies of O'Neill's in Leinster and Munster. Perhaps he wanted to secure his rear before advancing north, but his lack of decisive action was annoying Elizabeth, who complained that he was costing her £1,000 a day. She took to hacking at the wall-hangings in her private chamber with an old sword she kept. It would be interesting to know if her imagined opponent was Essex or O'Neill.

Things only seemed to get worse. A force led by Sir Conyers Clifford was wiped out in the Curlew Mountains by the O'Rourkes, and the head of the unfortunate Sir Conyers was sent as a present to Red Hugh. Then Essex brought his army, at last, against the Ulster forces. The two sides met at Ardee. The leaders, Essex and O'Neill, met in the middle of the River Lagan and talked together for half an hour. They then called witnesses and, before them, they agreed to a six-week truce. When Elizabeth heard that Essex had agreed to this without concessions or guarantees, she was almost in despair. Essex relieved her of the trouble of recalling him by abandoning his post and fleeing to London, where he was put in the care of the Keeper of the Tower of London.

Elizabeth allowed the truce to be extended, because it gave her time to make her preparations. Time was not on the side of O'Neill. Already his coalition was beginning to show weaknesses at the joins. In January 1600 he burned land belonging to the O'Carrolls because they were not showing sufficient loyalty to his cause. In Munster, he burned the land of the Barrys and took hostages from the other clans. He was being forced to think in all-Ireland terms, no matter how much he wanted to consolidate in Ulster. Now he was to be confronted by his most ruthless opponent yet: Charles Blount, Lord Mountjoy.

To those who did not know Mountjoy, he would have seemed an unlikely general officer of an army. He was convinced that his well-being was on a knife edge and that he was vulnerable to all sorts of illnesses. To guard against the damp Irish climate, he smoked heavily. To guard against cold he wore three pairs of silk stockings, with a pair of woollen stockings over them, and wrapped himself up in three warm waistcoats under his coat. He could do nothing about his headaches, but he managed to have an afternoon nap most days. Terrified of disease, he was, however, fearless in battle and easily inspired his men by his bravery and by the fact that he gave them more success than any other leader.

One of the reasons for his success was that he made his preparations carefully. He planned to use his army to break O'Neill's resistance by a war of attrition. He was determined to be more ruthless than his predecessors, if that was possible. There was to be no break for bad weather; the Irish would get no rest in the winter. In fact the war would be taken to them at that time of year, when leafless trees could give them no cover, when stores of grain could be found and burned, when hungry cattle could be stampeded to exhaustion. This plan, however, depended on getting men into the right positions. In particular it meant that the English had to open a second front. Previous attempts to do this had involved trying to bring a Connacht army north, which had to meet the power of the O'Donnells head-on. This time, Mountjoy sent Sir Henry Dowcra to the mouth of the River Foyle. This area was a borderland between O'Doherty, O'Cahan, O'Donnell and O'Neill clans, and the junctions between armies tend to be their weakest points. Dowcra landed a few miles north of Derry, where the river opens into the lough at Culmore. There were the remains of an old castle here and the soldiers set about restoring it to a defensible position. When Dowcra was satisfied, he left a small force at Culmore and marched the rest to the island of Derry. He liked what he saw here. Although it was not strictly speaking an island, Derry was surrounded on three sides by the broad River Foyle. The only access was across a boggy stretch of ground – still known as the Bogside – where a few tracks allowed the traveller to arrive dry shod. Derry towered steeply over this approach and so was easily defended. Dowcra set about establishing his base as a strong point, prepared to remain there all winter.

The wait was not uneventful. Some of the Irish forces joined them. Art O'Neill, son of Turlough, joined the English on a raid across the narrows between Greencastle and Magilligan which allowed them to make off with some hundred of O'Cahan's cattle, while they slaughtered many of the rest. On their way back towards Derry, the Lord of Inishowen, O'Doherty, attacked them, and Dowcra's horse was shot dead from under him. He had a closer shave in August, when Red Hugh captured 200 of the English horses, which had been grazing outside the defences of Derry. Dowcra led the unsuccessful pursuit when he was struck in the head by an Irish spear. For almost a month it looked as if he was dying, and by the time he was on his feet again, the position of the English did not seem too secure. Once again they had not allowed for Irish weather and, although it was still only September, many of the men were sick and unable to do their duty. Since there were not enough men to forage for supplies, Dowcra estimated that they had provisions for only six days.

It was now that O'Neill joined Red Hugh and launched a night attack across the bog. Unfortunately for the Irish, someone fired a musket at too great a range and alerted the English. Foiled, the Irish withdrew. The English luck held the next day, when fresh supplies and reinforcements arrived. It continued to hold, for in October, Niall Garbh O'Donnell, who had been given command of Tirconnell by Red Hugh, arrived in Derry and offered his services to Dowcra. This allowed Dowcra to capture Lifford Castle, using Niall Garbh's men, thus making his position very secure. The only way to oust him now would be for O'Neill to defeat Mountjoy so that O'Neill and O'Donnell could meet along the Foyle.

Yet defeating Mountjoy was not going to be easy. Although the autumn gales must have made the Lord Deputy concerned about his health – his tent was blown over on numerous occasions and he was continually wet – he pressed forward with his army until he came to the formidable defences of the Moyry Pass. This was where O'Neill had expected to meet an invasion of Ulster and he had prepared accordingly. Even Mountjoy commented on the professionalism of the defences. Rather than stand on the defensive, however, O'Neill attacked down the pass and threw back the advancing English. The English counter-attacked a few days later, but the result for them was no better. Reports came in from spies that the Irish were improving their defences all along the Ulster frontier. To make matters worse, dysentery broke out among the Lord Deputy's men. Then, when it looked as if the mighty army was going to have to return to Dublin, O'Neill abandoned his defensive positions and allowed clear passage to Mountjoy. It was the first of several strategic blunders that O'Neill made, and it is hard to fathom his purpose. It allowed Mountjoy to press forward to the gap at Mountnorris, where he built another fort. O'Neill's men harassed the work, but to no avail. Mountjoy left 400 men there and retired towards Carlingford. On the way he was ambushed by O'Neill and lost many men, but the ring was tightening around Ulster, and the seemingly endless resources of the Crown began to tell.

Some Spanish help did arrive. A load of guns and munitions from Spain arrived in Donegal Bay and King Phillip insisted that another expedition be sent to Ireland as soon as it could be assembled. He changed his mind later and sent the ships elsewhere. By the time another armada had been brought together, the Ulster lords were in a perilous position. The English had managed, through a burnt-earth policy, to suppress opposition outside Ulster. In Ulster itself, they did everything they could to kill O'Neill's soldiers and to starve his people. Niall Garbh acted as guide to Dowcra's men and his knowledge of the country meant that time and again they were able to make off with large numbers of O'Cahan's cattle. Art O'Neill, son of Turlough, 'died of drink', but a new recruit more than made up for this. Cahir O'Doherty became Lord of Inishowen on the death of his father in 1601. He brought his clan to the sup-port of Dowcra. Immediately, Dowcra marched against the MacSweenys, who submitted by March 1601. When MacSweeny later showed signs of breaking his parole, Dowcra marched against him again and burned houses and stores. The resulting famine took north Tirconnell out of the war.

This burning of winter stores and killing of cattle was also carried out in the Fews of south Armagh and in Monaghan. Woods were cut down to deny the Irish cover, and stronghold after stronghold was taken, with the joint pur-poses of pressing the Irish closely and separating O'Neill's from O'Donnell's armies. Sir Arthur Chichester was strong enough to keep the MacDonnells at bay while sailing across Lough Neagh and burning houses and stores to within a few miles of Dungannon. From the south, Mountjoy had recaptured the fort on the Blackwater and was holding Armagh with a strong force. Using these as bases, he destroyed as much corn as he could reach, considering that only a catastrophic famine would bring the Irish to their knees. While he was engaged on this task, he received word that the Spanish were on the seas.

Not all the Spanish were happy to be there. It is obvious from the place where they chose to land – Kinsale was the nearest point to Spain though it was at the opposite end of the country from those they were supposed to be helping – that the captains of the ships were nervous of being intercepted by the English fleet. Indeed, the naval commander ordered that supplies simply be dumped on the tidal mud, to be picked up when the soldiers got round to it. To be fair, the Spanish general Aguila had wanted to land in Tirconnell, but had no control of the ships. He was left on a peninsula, with only 3,500 men, in a part of the country that was under the absolute control of the English. Since he was in the relative safety of a walled town, he decided to stay where he was and invite the Ulster lords to come and help him.

There were good arguments for leaving the Spanish to their own devices. Mountjoy was bound to march against them and this would have given O'Neill and O'Donnell time to regroup and re-establish control of Ulster. It was actually O'Donnell who persuaded the others to take the long trail south, which was ironic, given what happened when they got there.

As expected, Mountjoy set out almost immediately, with a force that outnumbered the Spanish by more than three to one. When he got there, he invested the town closely and destroyed any food resources in the area to ensure that the Spanish could see that they could not expect to replenish their supplies. This was not to be a gentle siege, no sitting and waiting for something to happen. The English attacked the walls constantly, giving the Spaniards no rest.

Both Hughs set out in early November. O'Donnell took a western route, but O'Neill took a diversion through the Pale, destroying what he could to weaken Mountjoy's supply lines. It was a long and arduous trek, in the coldest time of the year, but both groups arrived near Kinsale in good order. Even with the arrival of the Irish, Mountjoy had superiority in numbers, and O'Neill wanted to avoid a precipitate battle. He felt that the best hope for success was to surround Mountjoy's besieging force and to besiege them in turn. For a while it looked as if this tactic was going to work; at the very least the English were dying more quickly than the Irish and Spanish and would soon lose their advantage in numbers. In the English camp, people spoke as if they had been stricken by the plague.

Neither Red Hugh nor Aguila had patience for this. Both of them begged O'Neill to attack and, on Christmas morning 1601, he agreed to move. Mountjoy may have had an inkling, because he had not gone to bed that night. Alert English sentries spotted the flames as the Irish prepared their matches in the dark. There is some controversy over what happened next. Some say that some of the Irish bumped into an English patrol and that a battle of encounter, where neither general had any control of what was happening, developed. Admirers of Mountjoy say that he launched a cavalry charge on the Irish infantry as they manoeuvred in the dark and that he pinned them till morning, when they were caught in the open as they had never been before. Within two hours of dawn O'Neill's forces were routed. Red Hugh did not even commit his troops to the conflict, while Aguila's foray from the town was too little and too late, more a gesture towards military honour that a manoeuvre of military effectiveness.

It was the end of Gaelic Ulster, for those that had eyes to see. O'Neill came north again, as did O'Donnell's shamed army. Red Hugh himself sailed to Spain; there he met the new King Phillip III, but got no promise of help. He died within a year, in Salamanca. O'Neill offered to submit, but Elizabeth was cautious, and anxious to continue her Lord Deputy's policy until there was no hope of an O'Neill resurrection. Mountjoy was nothing loath. He made his way north at his leisure, and built yet another fort on the Blackwater, at Charlemont. Meanwhile, Dowcra had extended his control as far as Ballyshannon, killing those he found in arms; even if they tried to surrender, he ordered his men to hack them to pieces. In July, O'Cahan submitted. O'Neill was now left with a few hundred men. They hid out in the woods of Glenconkeyne and Killetra, around the slopes of Slieve Gallion and down to the shores of Lough Neagh. If the pursuit got too close, they moved to the woods of Fermanagh.

The pitiless task of starving the Irish went on apace. According to English reports, in the ditches around towns it was common to find corpses with their mouths stained green from trying to live on nettles and other vegetation. Having driven the people to extremes, Mountjoy claimed to be shocked that some of them resorted to cannibalism. He was disappointed when Elizabeth ordered him to offer O'Neill a pardon, since he was sure that he was near to capturing the fugitive anyway. He was annoyed when he saw the terms of the Queen's pardon. They seemed to him excessively generous: if Hugh ceased to call himself The O'Neill, he would be confirmed in all his previous privileges, even as overlord of O'Cahan. Elizabeth died before the negotiations were completed, a fact that was kept from Hugh. When he heard the news, it is said that he wept. Did he weep for a lady who had been generous to him in his younger days, or was he thinking that he could have got even better terms from the newly crowned James I?

ETHNIC CLEANSING

The terms satisfied very few of the belligerents. Particularly annoyed were the men who had come from England to fight against the Irish in the hope of amassing their share of the spoils. Now it looked as if there were going to be no spoils; the Gaelic lords that they had fought, some of them for nine years, were back in their positions of power. The subsidiary chiefs were also discontented. O'Cahan had submitted because he had been told that in future he would be his own man; he would no longer have to pay tribute to O'Neill. Now that promise had been broken and he was in effect under the control of a man he had abandoned during the war. Even the great lords themselves were unhappy because, although Hugh O'Neill had been confirmed as Earl of Tyrone, and Red Hugh's successor Rory O'Donnell had been given the title of Earl of Tirconnell, there was the humiliation of knowing that these titles were held by the grace of James II, and the knowledge that the English did not have a great history of honouring promises.

Sir Arthur Chichester, who was made Lord Deputy in 1605, was one of the most aggrieved. He had helped to beat O'Neill and now he saw his erstwhile opponent controlling three counties, while he had to make do with a bit of land around Belfast. He and other officers of the Crown put continuous pressure on the Ulster lords, accusing them of plotting against the King. Their task was made easier when Mountjoy died in 1606, because Mountjoy had been a member of the Privy Council and had been most insistent that all the terms of the peace settlement should be met. A Commission was set up to 'divide and bind' the land held by the chiefs.

It was Cuchonnacht Maguire who cracked first, certain that the Crown was out to make beggars of the Ulster chiefs. The Commission had removed half of his lands, dividing the confiscated portion among 200 freeholders. Rory O'Donnell was also concerned. Inishowen had been granted to Cahir O'Doherty, and the MacSweenys and O'Boyles were no longer required to pay tribute to Tirconnell. Niall Garbh had been granted the best land in Tirconnell, the fertile country around Lifford. Even the land owned by the Irish Church was now in the hands of Bishop Montgomery, the Anglican incumbent of Derry, Clogher and Raphoe. The Earl began to consider that a military career under Phillip of Spain would pay better.

Hugh O'Neill was determined to stick it out. He insisted on exercising his control over his client chieftains. The English worked at whittling away his authority. Bishop Montgomery, in particular, claimed that some of the land O'Neill held was in fact Church land and should be his. At the same time, the English encouraged Donal O'Cahan to repudiate the traditional overlordship of Tyrone. Matters got really bad when O'Cahan set aside his wife, who was Hugh's daughter. In the end, King James called them both to London, where he, James, would decide the matter. Some of the foreign ambassadors to the English court thought that Hugh would be imprisoned or even poisoned if he went to London.

A message from Lough Swilly made up Hugh's mind. If he stayed he might be accused of fomenting trouble. He took his leave of Chichester, with whom he had been working in Slane, and made his way quickly to Dungannon. Here he gathered together the people and accoutrements he thought he needed before pushing on across the Sperrins to Rathmullan. Over one hundred people clambered into the boat, the cream of Ulster's nobility. Their horses were left behind, and so, by accident, was Hugh's son Conn, when they set sail at noon on Friday, 4 September 1617. Old decency had gone and so, with it, had gone the protection of the clan that was the only justification for their existence. The poor people of Ireland were on their own.

The lesser lords were in little better position. The example of Sir Cahir O'Doherty can stand for most of them. Sir Cahir had fought at the side of Dowcra and had saved the Englishman's life at least once. He had even served as foreman of the grand jury which had found the flown earls guilty of treason, allowing their lands to be forfeited to King James. Dowcra had been replaced as governor of Derry by Sir George Paulet. The latter contrived an argument with Sir Cahir and punched him in the face. This was too much for the young man and he withdrew to plan his revenge. He captured Culmore by a ruse and on 19 April 1608, he attacked Derry with a force of seventy men. The city was taken and Paulet killed. The uprising spread over much of mid–Ulster and involved some of O'Cahans and of O'Hanlons. Chichester put this rising down with great brutality, hanging by the dozen any he thought involved in it. The last rebels took refuge in the still-wooded barony of Loughinsholin. Even before this, Sir Cahir had been killed near Kilmacrennan in Tirconnell. Chichester had promised that Niall Garbh would be rewarded for his loyalty, but instead he and his son, together with Donal O'Cahan, were accused of withholding information about the O'Doherty rebellion. They were arrested, charged with treason and left to die in the Tower of London. In Tirconnell the last of the rebellion stuttered on, involving flights to Tory Island, the taking of the castle at Glenveagh, and final, pointless pursuits into the glens around Errigal, Muckish and Glenveagh. In the end the last of the rebels were left to fend for themselves, while the Lord Deputy, Chichester, petitioned successfully for a grant of Inishowen. At the same time he suggested that there was no real possibility of a peaceful Ulster until there were more settlers in the country than there were native Irish. All the land west of the Bann was declared forfeit to King James, whether or not the landowners had been loyal.

King James saw in the suggested Plantation two advantages: he would have the opportunity to reward all those who had shown him service; and he would establish the true religion of Christ in Ulster, among men 'almost lost in superstition'. As a first step, Chichester rounded up as many men of military age as he could find in the woods of Ulster. He classified almost 1,000 of them as 'swordsmen' and, in effect, sold them for service in the Swedish army. Those to whom lands were to be granted, called undertakers, were to clear their land of the native Irish. The land had already been shired (divided into counties). Each county was now divided into baronies and each barony was further divided into 'proportions', which could be large (3,000 acres), medium (2,000 acres) or small (1,000 acres). Protestant Scots and English had to undertake to plant at least ten English or Scottish families for every thousand acres. If he did this the rent was £5 6s 8d per thousand acres. If he did not, the rent jumped to £8 0s 0d for the same area. Ex-officers, called servitors, and loyal Irish were able to rent smaller allocations, but the Irish had to pay £10 13s 4d and adopt English farming methods. All Planters were obliged to build stone houses and a defended area, known as a bawn, where a market could be held. There were supposed to be strict timetables for each stage of the Plantation, but it was found difficult to meet these. There were only a few Irish whose lands were exempted from the Plantation; in Tyrone the most prominent of these were the descendants of Sir Henry Óg O'Neill, who had been killed while helping to put down O'Doherty's rebellion.

Chichester was concerned about the breakdown of the allocations. Too much land was being assigned to rich undertakers who might have no experience if Irish conditions. Too little was being allocated to servitors who, knowing the land, would be best placed to carry out the defensive role assigned to them. With the amount of land available for them, there would be too few of them to make a difference. He also felt that the loyal Irish chiefs had been harshly treated, and suspected that this was going to build up a store of resentment that would explode in the future.

There was a general belief that England was overpopulated and needed to export its surplus mouths. One of the most attractive features of Ulster was the amount of quality woodland that was available. From the east of the Sperrins, Glenconkeyne and the lower wood at Killetra held fine stands of sessile oak, ash, elm, willow and alder, and this at a time when England and Scotland were running out of useable timber. The fisheries were scarcely touched; even in the 1960s the Foyle system was declared to be the most productive salmon fishery in Europe. There were even iron and coal deposits on the west of Lough Neagh, including the banks of the Ballinderry.

Many came to take advantage of this, some from the highest levels of society. The Earl of Abercorn, for example, took over much of the rich land along the River Mourne, where O'Donnells and O'Neills had long fought to try to establish their sway. Most of the wealth probably came from England, but the most determined of the small tenants came from Scotland. Many of these were people who had been evicted from Scottish holdings. Others came from the Border Country between Scotland and England, declared outlaws because they were reluctant to give up the practice of reaving – stealing cattle from their English neighbours. Some were given the choice of Ulster or the gallows; the Johnston clan figured prominently in this case. Others simply thought that the game was no longer worth the candle, and relocated themselves voluntarily. Not all of them actually rented land in Ulster, and there were complaints about the number of 'vagrant Scots' – again the Johnstons figured prominently – who pestered the Ulster Plantations. King James believed that many of the goods still being stolen in the border counties were sent to Ulster to be disposed of. Things got so bad that in 1622 the Irish Council issued an order that Scottish vagrants should be arrested.

But Scottish tinkers were not the only problem. In the baronies of Dungannon and Loughinsholin the woods were still thick and the hills were wild. Within their shadows were the wood-kernes, landless men who had fought with O'Neill and knew how to live rough. Each evening Planters had to bring their cattle into the shelter of the settlement and guard against the depredations of these night raiders. Tyrone was the first county to be planted with settlers, and things were not going well; too few people of wealth were being attracted to the interior of the province. Antrim and Down had many advantages, including having an easy means of escape if things turned rough. Tyrone seemed less safe than the recently established colony of Virginia, and the climate was worse.

It was at this stage that Sir Thomas Phillips travelled to London to suggest that the rich merchants of that city would find a good investment. He had been granted land at Coleraine, and had leased another section near Toome, but he felt that his investment was exposed and vulnerable unless other settlements were begun. Although the king liked the idea, since it would lessen the drain on the Privy Purse if somebody else would take responsibility for the infrastructure that the new colony would require, the City of London was less enthusiastic. To help sweeten the pill, the barony of Loughinsholin was transferred from County Tyrone to County Coleraine and the latter was to be re-named Londonderry. A deputation which visited the area in the autumn of 1609 was impressed by the amount of quality woodland there was, which would be easily transformed into valuable timber. The wooded area had two good-sized rivers, the Ballinderry and the Moyola, so that tree trunks could be floated to Lough Neagh and on through the Lower Bann to Coleraine. The ready cash this would earn would help to defray the costs of setting up the towns that would be required.

The new colony, which promised so much and delivered so little, was to be administered by the group which came to be known as The Honourable Irish Society. Because city merchants had a propensity to keep excellent records we tend to have a much more detailed account of the problems faced by the tenants of the Irish Society than we do of most of the private enterprises. One settlement has a particularly good account of its early days. Moneymore, which is on the banks of the Ballymully River, one of the major tributaries of the Ballinderry, owes its existence to the London Guild of Drapers. Theirs was one of the most southerly allocations in County Londonderry, stretching along the slopes of Slieve Gallion and reaching round into the valley of Ballinascreen, in the depths of the great wood of Glenconkeyne. The Drapers chose to build their castle and bawn near the southern boundary of their portion at a place where the woods were so deep that it was named the big thicket, or Moneymore.

Their big mistake was in their choice of agents. The opportunity to make good money at other people's expense was too much for some of them. A man called Robert Russell offered himself for employment to the Drapers, and was appointed assistant to their chief agent, John Rowley. This was in spite of the fact that Russell had already been discredited as an agent of the Irish Society. Rowley got the job started, with twelve houses built by 1616, but he died the following year. This gave Russell his chance. He took over as agent and the expenditure of the Drapers began to go up immediately. The walls of the bawn fell down. Russell had set up a brewery, and he paid his workers with beer. Not content with this monopoly, he set about establishing another. Although there was adequate water at little depth below the town, he decided that the town should have a piped water supply. This he brought from Lough Lug, on the escarpment above the town, and brought it through wooden pipes to each house in the growing town. Having the monopoly, he could charge as much as he liked. He also encouraged settlers from outlying areas to come to Moneymore on Saturday evenings to sample his ale, and the town got a name for rowdiness and drunkenness that annoyed more staid citizens.

This was not a situation likely to encourage immigration. The entire portion of the Drapers consisted of sixty-four townlands, yet only sixteen had British tenants by 1622. Irish tenants had the rest, paying a rent much higher than any Englishman would pay. This was still a hostile territory; there was more killing of Planters by kernes in East Tyrone and South Londonderry (at least more hanging of kernes for murder) than in any other part of Ireland. Until his death in 1616 there were constant rumours that Hugh O'Neill was going to return to reclaim his own, maintaining the motivation of the Irish in the woods. There were accusations that the native Irish lords O'Cahan, O'Neill and O'Mullan were planning an uprising in 1615. It was not pleasant to have to be on guard all the time that you are trying to work your farm, with a sword in one hand and an axe on the other, as one report had it. Another large part of the problem was that much of the land was of poor quality. The native Irish were pastoralists rather than farmers and had done little to improve the soil. In basalt and sandstone areas there would have been little fertility left in the soil after the forests had been cleared. Potential Planters were reluctant to invest heavily in improving and stocking farms which they might not live long enough to enjoy.

King James complained that the problem would be eased if the undertakers would fulfil the conditions of their lease, and remove the Irish from their land. The undertakers replied that they could not afford to do this, because the rent from the Irish was the only return they were getting on their investment. The Irish would pay almost any rent to stay. It was their land, they knew how to get the best of it and they were used to subsisting at a more basic level than their English counterparts. The Irish also had the advantage that soldiers would not be billeted on them. Most important of all, the fact that no one had ever done an accurate survey of the land confiscated meant that the individual companies were given far more land than was estimated. Companies needed tenants from anywhere they could get them. The Drapers felt that they could not let land at less than 1s per acre, to cover the great expense they had already undergone. Potential settlers felt they could not make a living on poor land if they had to pay so much. In fact, many of those settlers who did take up land simply didn't pay their rent. The City of London paid out £40,500 in the first twenty years of the Plantation. If that were not bad enough, when King James died and King Charles came to the throne, they found themselves liable for a great deal more.

Charles claimed that the Plantation was not being pursued with sufficient vigour. Continuing unrest meant that he had to maintain soldiers in Ireland. Since this was the fault of the City, the City would pay. After a show trial in 1635 lasting two weeks, the City was fined £70,000, payable to the Privy Purse, and the rents payable to the City were now to be paid to the Crown. Possibly for the first time, but certainly not for the last, Ulster became the cockpit in which many of the political struggles of England were worked out. This struggle between an autocratic ruler and a merchant class increasingly aware of its power was one of the early steps in the process that climaxed in the English Civil War. The City of London appealed to Parliament against the decision and their appeal was upheld in 1640; it was King Charles against the City and Parliament.

It was not only in England that trouble was brewing. Although in many ways the most pragmatic of the lords deputy, in that he advocated the allocation of land to those Irish who had proved themselves to be loyal, predicting that there would be trouble if their loyalty was not recognised, Chichester was still a Protestant at heart and he put into practice a vigorous anti-Catholic policy from 1611. This had an effect on the wealthier Catholics in the main and on the 'Old English', who had been integrated into the Government of Ireland, in particular. The penalties that were imposed were made at Chichester's discretion and did not derive from any Act of Parliament. Catholics could be deprived of office, be imprisoned or receive heavy fines; Catholic lawyers were no longer allowed to practise; Catholic wards of court were assigned to Protestants. The Old English began to wonder where their future lay, if indeed they had a future. When the Catholic Bishop of Down and Connor, a man in his eighties whose only crime was to have been chaplain to O'Neill, was executed for treason in 1612 there were riots in Dublin, and it is probable that the horror of the occasion made it certain that native Irish and Old English would resist any attempt to force them into the Protestant faith. They were confirmed in their opposition when Chichester so arranged the next Irish Parliament that it was bound to have a permanent Protestant majority. There was a moment of farce when the Parliament eventually convened. The man chosen by the Catholic members as Speaker tried to pre-empt a vote by occupying the Speaker's chair. The Protestant candidate for the position immediately sat on his lap and showed that the weight of a majority could be expressed literally – he weighed several times more than his opponent. The unfortunate Catholic had to be rescued by his colleagues before they staged what was to be a recurring theme in Irish politics, the walk-out.

When Charles assumed the throne in 1625, much of his Irish kingdom was characterised by the resentment of the remaining Catholics. He then set about, with some ingenuity, alienating the affections of many of his Protestant subjects. The similarity in titles of 'The Church of England' and 'The Church of Ireland' might lead a casual observer to assume that the only differences between the two are geographical. In fact, there have been great differences between the two since the very beginning. As far back as 1567 it was decided that the Church of Ireland should follow the Twelve Articles of Religion rather than the Thirty-Nine Articles of the Church of England. Partly, also, it was a matter of personnel. As we have seen, a substantial proportion of the most determined settlers were Scottish in origin. This was particularly true in the area of the Ballinderry Valley. Their religious practice in Scotland would have been Presbyterian and their outlook on the world more Puritanical than would have sat comfortably with the Church of England. Further, they brought many of their own clergymen with them. Other Scottish clergymen arrived after 1617, when King James imposed articles on the Scottish Church that many of them could not tolerate. Some of these became integrated into the Established Church of Ireland, but even these maintained their fundamental beliefs and attitudes. It was easier for the Irish Church to accommodate them than it would have been for the English Church, because even by the time of the Plantation, there was a very great distinction between the two. In particular, the fact that the Church of

Ireland had not thrived, that its smaller parishes were islands in a sea of Irish Catholicism, encouraged the sense that its members were the chosen ones, the elect. The first professors appointed to Trinity College in Dublin were Calvinist and Puritan and when the Church drew up its own articles in the Convocation of 1613-1615 they echoed this.

The matter might well have simmered on to its own resolution if it had not been for the intervention of King Charles's minister, Wentworth. He was sent to Dublin as Lord Deputy in 1633 with instructions to fill the royal coffers and to ensure that the Church of Ireland was uniformly 'High Church'. He started, appropriately enough, with the drive for finances. He let it be known that he was examining grants of land which were considered defective. The landowners concerned were forced to pay large fines to ensure the security of their tenure. It was this process that led to the conflict between the City of London and the Throne mentioned previously. The result was that rents at all levels were raised and the poor, as usual, were made to pay.

Many of the Irish lords who had been granted land during the Plantation were already finding it difficult to make ends meet. There had been a series of bad harvests during the early 1630s. Attendance at court was expensive in itself and also opened other opportunities to squander cash. Many of them became very fond of gambling. Wentworth chose this moment to enforce what were known as recusancy fines, which had to be paid out of a dwindling income for non-attendance at the services of the Established Church (this attendance the Pope had already declared to be a mortal sin for Catholics).

Having established an adequate flow of money, Wentworth proceeded to matters of the Church. A key difference between the Scottish Church and the English was the authority of the bishops. Charles appointed an authoritarian bishop, Henry Leslie, to the Diocese of Down. Bishop Leslie summoned a meeting of his clergy and attacked those who had become most like the Presbyterians and who were attempting to bring down the 'goodly orders of our Church'. The next day he deprived any who refused to recant of their living. The newly unemployed clergymen, together with over one hundred followers, tried to leave for America on the *Eagle Wind,* possibly the first ocean-going ship built in Belfast. Contrary winds drove them back, and many of them took refuge in Scotland. As the bishops in Ireland forced conformity on the clergy, more and more took the road to Scotland.

Here they found a welcome, because opposition to Charles and to the new prayer book that he was introducing was growing in Scotland and eventually led to the Covenant, a bond which united the king's enemies in Scotland. Even before it was signed, several of the leaders were exiles from County Down. Back in Ulster, many of those of Scottish origin were motivated to sign the

Covenant. Wentworth's reaction was to issue a decree that all over sixteen years of age would have to abjure the Covenant under oath. This became known as the Black Oath. He had already raised an army in the south of Ireland to fight for the king, and half of this, over 1,500 men, was sent north to oversee the taking of the oath. The oath itself had to be taken kneeling (an insult in itself to a Presbyterian), and any who refused to take it could be fined or imprisoned. Large numbers of Planters returned to Scotland to avoid this.

Charles found himself outmanoeuvred in Parliament, which alone had the power to raise taxes, and was obliged to offer Wentworth as a sacrificial victim. His absolute loyalty to the king's authority and his determination to carry out the king's wishes meant that he had no friends left to speak for him when he was impeached and executed in 1641.

THE COMING OF CROMWELL

There are few historical incidents in Ireland about which there is more controversy than the Rising of 1641. Reports of massacres on an enormous scale are still part of the Protestant world view in Ulster and events such as the drowning at Portadown and at Bloody Bridge are still used by some to argue that the Catholic Irish are always prepared to tear out an unprotected Protestant throat. The sheer volume of propaganda together with the vast number of victims claimed have led many Catholics to question whether the massacres took place at all.

The motivation behind the Rising has been touched on, but it seems to have been more than a group of impecunious Irish noblemen becoming frustrated as they saw themselves being bled dry. The initial actions were done courteously enough, as befitted landowning gentlemen who had contrived to hold on to their land for the thirty or so years since the Plantation. Sir Phelim O'Neill engineered to have himself invited to dinner at the home of Lady Caulfield and her son on 23 October 1641. He and his followers seized Castlecaulfield, imprisoned the family and then went on to take Mountjoy Castle, near Washing Bay, by a similar ruse. This was a signal for a general rising of the remaining Gaelic clans in Ulster. On the same night there was to be an attack on Dublin Castle, but this was foiled when a convert to Protestantism overheard a conversation and passed on the information. Those attacks which did take place were widely scattered, but so were the Planters, many of them in small groups of two or three houses incapable of self-defence. These Gaelic lords chose their targets carefully, and ordered their followers not to interfere with any Scottish settlers. They may have done this in order to keep their objectives clearly in focus, and bringing Scots into the equation risked complicating matters into a Gordian knot. Dealing with a Royal army in Ireland was going to be difficult enough; if an army arrived from Scotland to protect the Scots of Ulster, the rebel army would be squeezed between them. The Rebel leaders even gave it about that they were allied to the Covenanters and that they had documents to prove it. In actual fact, they may have been in contact with King Charles, since they claimed that they had his support.

The area around Moneymore and Lissan was recognised as an important focus for the insurgents. This was because of the mineral resources available on the slopes of Slieve Gallion. Once Castlecaulfield had been secured, a detachment of troops under the O'Quinn marched to Lissan House, the home of Thomas Staples, the first Baronet Lissan. He had come to Ireland in 1610 as one of the early enthusiasts for the Plantation of Ulster. He settled in Moneymore at first, living in the centre of the town, near the market square. He had the good fortune to marry the only child of a rich man, Sir Baptist Jones, in 1620, and was able to buy an estate which included the town of Cookstown. A key part of the new estate was a forge for producing iron, and it was this that the insurgents had as their target. Because they had this facility, they were able to produce pikes and other weapons throughout the Rising. Sir Thomas was away when the Irish arrived, but O'Quinn seized Lady Staples and their four children; these were made prisoners in Moneymore Castle, and remained there for almost two years. Also captured at the time were Desertmartin and Magherafelt. The whole area was then defended by the O'Cahans and the O'Hagans and remained a rebel strong point for a long time. Sir Thomas raised a group of one hundred soldiers on King Charles's commission and was later able to rescue his family. It may have been some comfort to him that the Irish spared the buildings on his estate while they destroyed the estate that was then Ballydrum (now known as Springhill). The new house built by Robert Lindesay at Loughrey was also destroyed while Robert was away at Newtownstewart, making sure that the women and children were safe. When he came home to find the devastation he rode to Antrim, where he joined Clotworthy's band and took part in the massacre of Irish in Templepatrick; indeed there are those who say he was responsible for the massacre, in revenge for what had happened to his home. He later went to England and joined the Royalist army.

Much of the early success achieved by the Irish was so much smoke and mirrors. They had few arms and the men were mostly untrained. The leaders themselves had little military experience; those with a hankering after an exciting life had long before taken service in the armies of continental kings. After the initial surprise that enabled them to take several towns they dominated the open ground of the province, but seemed unable to capture any more towns. Moreover, they had not the military skills to deal with their opponents even in the open. Sir Robert Stewart, from north Donegal, was a veteran of the Thirty Years War. The force that he assembled was so effective that it was able to relieve some of the besieged garrisons in County Tyrone.

The attempt to spare the Scots did not survive the situation on the ground. From a Scottish settler's point of view, it took a great deal of trust to assume that the Irish who were burning down English houses would take the trouble to enquire about his ethnic origins before they burned down his. For his family's sake as much as anything, he took his people and what animals and property they could move and made for shelter in the major settlements, such as Carrickfergus, Coleraine and Londonderry. Irish soldiers arriving at empty farmsteads presumed that they were English and burned them. Soon another element exacerbated the situation. For forty years the undeserving Irish – the poor and the outlawed – had been scraping a living in a land many of them still thought of as their own. To maintain their place in the countryside they had had to abase themselves, to accept humiliation at the hands of incomers, and always they knew how tenuous their hold on their hovels was. When the lid was lifted off this pressure it boiled over. Gangs roamed the country. Some attached themselves to an army. Others went reiving on their own account. Although at this time most of the troublemakers were looking for spoils rather than blood, a man who tried to defend his property was shown little patience. Much of the initial slaughter was carried out by groups such as these.

There was slaughter, and it does historians of a nationalist slant no credit to deny it. There was not as much killing as was recounted in the thirty-three volumes of depositions recorded afterwards, in themselves an extended pornography of brutality. The numbers involved in these allegations probably exceeded the number of settlers in Ulster at the time. There may not even have been as many as estimated by Lecky, who was a historian without separatist ambitions, and the figure must include a large number who were not killed directly by the Irish, but who died of exposure, hunger or disease. But there certainly were thousands killed, and death at the hand of mobs armed with improvised weapons is a cruel fate. A key moment seems to have been the attack on Lisnagarvey, which took place in November 1641. The attackers were repulsed and several hundred of them were captured. The settlers killed all of them. It was after this incident that the notorious massacre of the Portadown Settlers on the Bann Bridge took place. The atrocities occurred towards the beginning of a war that lasted many years, but the record of them was of considerable importance at the end of it, when they were used to justify the mass removal of Irish from their lands. Even before that, it justified the massacre of Catholic Irish prisoners.

These were as well attested as the killing of Protestants, but have come to be less well remembered, so it is perhaps as well to list some of them here.

The Ballroom, Lissan House.

After Newry had capitulated the captured soldiers were lined up with local merchants along the bank of the river and all were butchered. On the island of Rathlin a regiment of Argyll soldiers, under the command of Sir Duncan Campbell, found only MacDonnell women and children. These were driven ruthlessly over the cliffs to die on the rocks below; the number who died here was never recorded. In fact, there are no reliable estimates of the number of Catholic Irish who died in the war. Estimates of the death toll among settlers in Ulster range between 2,000 and 12,000; that is, between 5 per cent and 30 per cent of the settler population.

Accounts written by Protestants at the time emphasise the absolute shock of the outbreak. One wrote that it was like a woman having a child without knowing that she was pregnant and without feeling the pains of childbirth. Most took this to be proof that you could never trust the Irish; they were so good at dissembling that you could never know what they were prepared to do. To ensure that this was remembered, for over 200 years the Protestant population commemorated 23 October as a 'holy day', sacred to the memory of the Protestant martyrs of that time.

The war itself was of a strange nature. Usually a war is thought of as two opponents struggling for supremacy. In this case there were many parties, all of whom had different aims. The Gaelic lords claimed to be protecting the king's prerogatives against the encroachment of Parliament. The Old English, descendants of the Norman invaders, wanted freedom to practise their Catholic religion and the restoration of their position of power in the Irish Parliament. The Royalist army, under the control of the Duke of Ormond, largely raised from refugees in Dublin, was for some time an unknown force which could have aligned with either side. Parliament in London distrusted Charles, and would not vote the funds necessary to reinforce an English army in Ireland. The lord justices in Ireland did not trust the Old English, because of the fact that they were Catholics.

The religious element was important, because native Protestants, especially those who had profited by the Plantation, were attacked, while settlers who happened to be Catholic joined in on the rebel side. Initial opposition to the rising came, in fact, from the New English, those who had arrived in Ireland during or after the Tudor wars. Later, a Scottish army under General Munro arrived in Ulster and was based in Carrickfergus and Belfast. Before that, many of the landowners of north-west Ulster brought men together to form an army, the Laggan Army, which was one of the most effective units in fighting against the Irish. Parliament in London decided to finance the war by drawing loans from the business community, offering Irish land, which would be confiscated when the war was over, as collateral. Those who invested in the project were known as 'adventurers'.

The first year of the war reflected these mutual animosities. Marauding bands attacked civilians of opposing religious and ethnic groups, while at the same time taking care to avoid one another. With the sort of gravitation that makes snowballs bigger as they move around, these bands grew in size and it became obvious on both sides that unless the natural leaders – the upper classes – took a hand, Ireland would descend into pandemonium, a word used at the time by Milton to describe the hall in hell in which the devils convened. At first, landowners raised units of militia to control the violence and to protect their own. There was always the danger that the ordinary Irish, if they succeeded in getting rid of the settlers, might turn on them next. This sense of vulnerability was increased when King Charles, Parliament and the Irish administration, in a rare show of unity, let it be known that the landowners and nobility would be held responsible for the killing of settlers and that their lands might be liable to confiscation if they did not show sufficient energy in upholding law and order. Then the rebels defeated a government force of 600 men near Julianstown and it looked as if they might win. The Old English lords of the Pale marched to join them, only to fail when the united army tried to capture Drogheda. By now it was too late, and they were committed.

By the early part of 1642, the insurgent forces had resolved themselves into four main groups. In Ulster, the leader was Phelim O'Neill; near Dublin the commander was Viscount Gormanstown; the Butler family controlled the forces near their centre of power, Kilkenny; the Irishman Donagh McCarthy, Viscount Muskerry, led the forces in the south-west. British settlers led a crowded existence in Cork, Dublin, Carrickfergus and Derry. King Charles sent an army from England to put down the rebels, but trust between him and Parliament no longer existed. Parliament refused to pay for an army that might eventually be used against them, and the English soldiers were withdrawn. The rebels were not united enough to wipe out the British enclaves that still existed; the British had no intention of leaving their fortified positions. The resulting stalemate allowed the Irish, encouraged by their clergy, who approved of the war at a Synod in Kells, to come together and form a confederation. This was in place by the autumn of 1642.

The unity that the word confederation implies was never there. There were too many cracks in the structure: between province and province; between Old English and Native Irish; between townsmen and countrymen. Even if there had been greater unity, the lack of supplies, lack of training and lack of leadership put them at a disadvantage in the years to come. The result was a stalemate in the southern provinces, with each party reluctant to expose itself by taking the initiative.

In the north things were more in flux. Munro had landed at Carrickfergus in April with a Scottish army. He went on the offensive in June and soon had recaptured Newry, Mountjoy and Dungannon. The native insurgents were so discouraged that they were considering giving up the struggle. They were given heart when Owen Roe O'Neill arrived in Lough Swilly in July. His uncle was Hugh O'Neill, who had fled from the same lough almost thirty-five years earlier. More importantly, he had established a reputation as a fighting general in the Spanish Netherlands and the people of Ulster had for some time hoped that he would come to take their part. Although he was appointed leader of the Confederate army in Ulster, he was not in a position to make instant improvement to the situation; he lacked trained men and equipment. At a slightly later date another soldier with continental experience arrived at Waterford. His name was Thomas Preston and he was brother of Lord Gormanstown. He took charge of the Confederate forces in Leinster. He and O'Neill had been bitter enemies while abroad, and their enmity persisted. Neither would serve under the other, so there was no possibility of the Irish fighting under unified command.

This disunity could have been fatal in a very short time if it had not been matched by faults in the opposing forces. The government troops, too, were split, echoing the growing schism in the British population. Ormond was a Royalist before all, while most of the other leaders were sympathetic to the Parliamentary cause. King Charles wanted to make peace with the Confederates because he wanted to bring his Dublin army back to England, where he had more need of it. He used as an excuse the fact that Parliament would not reinforce these troops to justify his orders to Ormond to look for a ceasefire lasting at least a year and to enter negotiations with the rebels. Government forces were beginning to run short of food and were reduced to making foraging expeditions into rebel territory. The soldiers had not been paid for some time and Ormond feared a mutiny. They still fought well enough, however, and defeated Preston's rebels in open battle, even though outnumbered by the Irish. The battle had no strategic significance, even so, and Ormond led his troops straight back to Dublin.

O'Neill did no better than his rival, Preston, and by mid-summer of 1643 had been driven out of Ulster completely, and was regrouping in Connacht. In Munster things were static, though in Connacht Galway surrendered in August. Although they had never been promised it, the Confederates had thought they would get help from Europe, but it became obvious very soon that this would not arrive. In fact the underlying religious nature of the conflict was reinforced by the fact that the only military supplies of any significance which reached the Confederates came from the Pope. Charles ordered Ormond to talk with the Irish about a truce; this Ormond was able to do because he was popular with his troops while the other, pro-Parliamentary leaders simply were not. The truce, which had no political conditions attached, was signed in September 1643. Charles immediately had a large proportion of the army (2,500 men) transferred to England, where they performed miserably at the Battle of Nantwich and many of them transferred their allegiance to the Parliamentary army. The truce also marked the final breach between the Dublin and London Parliaments.

The Protestants of Ulster rejected the truce. Munro was appointed commander of the joint Parliamentary and Scottish armies and prepared to fight on. He made no attempt to coordinate his strategy with Lord Inchiquin, who, in Munster, was also continuing the fight in the Parliamentary cause. By June 1644, O'Neill had taken refuge in Louth, forced there by 'the invincible power and force of the Scots in the north'. Divisions with the Confederacy meant that he was not reinforced. The Old English were fighting for their Catholic religion; the native Irish were fighting for their land. Where the Old English were hoping for a form of words that would allow them to reassume their old privileges, the Irish were hoping for a change in substance which would allow them to reoccupy their traditional estates. The Pope's Nuncio saw a greater future in the hopes of the Ulstermen, and gave money and support to Owen Roe O'Neill.

It looked as if the Italian's confidence was justified in the early summer of 1646. Munro had decided that he should march south and attack the core of the Confederacy. He and his men were confident after many victories and he chose as his route the road through Armagh, as if challenging O'Neill to do something about it. Reports came to him that O'Neill was approaching with a large army, but he did not allow that to discourage him; the Scots had prevailed against superior numbers in the past. He was not even sure that O'Neill would have the nerve to face him in battle. When he discovered the location of the Ulster forces, he marched straight against them, coming into contact at Benburb, seven miles from Armagh, on 5 June. The pikes of the Ulstermen won them victory; the Scots broke and the slaughter continued into the long summer's evening, till darkness allowed the survivors to escape. Munro got away, but left behind a wig, sword, artillery, stores and half his men. He decided that the Protestants had offended the Deity in some way. The Nuncio, Rinuccini, agreed that God was on the side of the Irish, and had himself elected President of the Confederacy. There was to be no more talk of treating with the enemy. The Confederacy was to go on the offensive, and its first objective was to be the capture of Dublin.

Dublin was not saved by Ormond or by any reinforcements from England or Scotland. It was saved because, once again, the two greatest generals that the Confederates had could not agree to work with one another. O'Neill withdrew his forces in November, while Preston even considered making an alliance with Ormond. This notion passed, however, and Ormond found himself in an increasingly difficult position. Once again, the resolution he chose was based on religion; he preferred to surrender to Protestant enemies than to Catholic ones. He agreed to hand over all the garrisons under his command to Parliamentary command. This done, he travelled through England to France, where he endured exile with the Queen and the Prince of Wales.

He left chaos behind him. The fragile unity of the Confederates fell apart. Preston was defeated leading an attack against Dublin. Inchiquin had Munster at his mercy. The Old English managed to conclude a truce with him in May 1648. Rinuccini excommunicated them all. The Old English dismissed O'Neill from command of the Ulster army. O'Neill advanced south with his men, but had more casualties than he could afford and retreated north again. Rinuccini moved to Galway, and left Ireland altogether in February 1649. There was no more unity among the Protestant forces, as different groups decided where their loyalties lay in the English Civil War. Dublin was all for Parliament, but Inchiquin had declared for Charles in April 1648. Not all of Inchiquin's followers agreed, so there was dissension within Munster. In Ulster, the Scots disliked the Parliamentary General Monck, and began to have second thoughts about their opposition to Charles. Monck neutralised any discontent by seizing all Scottish garrisons.

The Confederates, excluding O'Neill, now entered into alliance with Inchiquin and declared for the Royalist cause. The evergreen Ormond arrived in Cork to lead them. Ormond realised that he needed more allies, and hoped that revulsion at Charles's execution would encourage O'Neill to rejoin. O'Neill would not be cajoled, however, and actually entered an agreement with the Parliamentary commanders of the north, whereby he would be able to get military supplies. Undeterred, if disappointed, Ormond captured Drogheda and Dundalk. When he moved against Dublin itself, his forces were shattered in a surprise attack by Jones at Rathmines on 2 August. The Royalist survivors fell back on Kilkenny. It was all over, because, later that same August, Oliver Cromwell arrived in Dublin with 3,000 Ironsides.

Within a month the newly arrived forces had taken Drogheda. There was a short siege before the town was assaulted and taken on 11 September 1649. The entire garrison, together with as many Catholic clergy as could be found, were put to death. There is some debate as to how many of the town's civilians were killed, but it is certain that no Cromwellian soldier stayed his hand in case of doubt. If an innocent person was killed, then 'the Good Lord would know his own'. In his report to Parliament, Cromwell seems to have felt it necessary to justify the killings, which he did by saying that they were in revenge for the slaughter of settlers by the Irish in 1641. He did not find any irony in the fact that those he killed were in the Royal army and had nothing to do with the earlier massacres.

Drogheda had been on its own, without external support, and it fell easily. O'Neill was quick to learn the lesson, and he proposed an alliance of his troops with the remaining Royalists under Ormond. Whether this new combination would have made a difference was never put to the test, because Owen Roe sickened and died three weeks later. Irish folk tradition has it that he was poisoned, but it is just as likely that the long years of campaigning had weakened a man who was no longer young and that he succumbed to a fever. Whichever story is true, it is fair to say that he was the last of Ireland's truly Gaelic heroes.

Ulster was soon under the control of the Parliamentary forces, with opposition holding out in Charlemont and Enniskillen. Cromwell turned south and took town after town that was held by Royalists. Only Waterford held out, but by the time Cromwell left Ireland in May 1650, the backbone of the resistance was broken. Although the Irish still had 30,000 men in the field, there was no unity of command or purpose. Gradually, individual units surrendered, usually with the condition that the officers could pursue military service abroad and take any recruits that wanted to accompany them. By 1652 the ordinary Irish, once again, were helpless in the hands of the English, abandoned by their natural protectors.

TO HELL OR CONNACHT

Even before this, Parliament in London had appointed four Commissioners to propagate the gospel, suppress popery, provide education, enquire into the state of the judicial system, and to get the tax system operating. When they arrived, in January 1651, they found a country where it was impossible to carry out this programme. The agricultural economy was in ruins, there was famine in many areas and plague was common. The devastation had become so bad that the wolves had become bold enough, or desperate enough, to become a menace to the rural community. The Commissioners decided that their first priority was to set up some form of local government. They chose a military, rather than a civil, form of this. The country was divided into precincts, each with a military governor. Under each governor was a commissioner for revenue and another for the administration of justice. Originally the country had six precincts, but this increased to twelve as more territory came under Parliamentary control. One of the first things done in each precinct was the establishment of preaching ministers.

By the end of 1651 the four Parliamentary Commissioners became responsible for the entire government of Ireland, and not simply civil matters. They had power to interfere, for example, in the surrender terms that Parliamentary generals offered to surrendering garrisons. They were concerned about the possibility of disbanded soldiers becoming brigands, terrorising the country, and encouraged those surrendering to take their soldiers overseas to the service of a foreign monarch. Indeed, they did all they could to make this an easy option. Not all the soldiers went, however, and even after all hostilities had ceased between Parliamentary and Royalist forces, unreconciled Irish soldiers maintained a guerrilla war. They were called tories, a word that was later used as an insult in the English Parliament. They continued to be a nuisance for the next fifty years, and acquired an almost heroic status among the poorer people of Ireland.

In the meantime, Parliament had some claims on it that had to be dealt with. The adventurers, who had put up money to finance the war in 1642, wanted their returns, now that the war was over. In addition, Parliament had a huge standing army, too great for peacetime needs. It wished to reduce this, but could not release its soldiers from service until they had got their arrears in pay. Parliament intended to pay both these groups in land and, on the long-established principle that the loser pays, the land would come from the Irish. In the past, it would have been the leaders who suffered. Now it was determined that any Irishman holding any real estate would be punished.

This was a different exodus from the one which had taken place around forty years previously. Then it had been the nobility and their closest retainers that had been displaced. Now it was families that had been part of the social scaffolding which had held that nobility in place; the families that had provided the men of law, the priests, the church wardens, the stewards were being removed from land they had occupied for many generation. While the Gaelic lords were alive there had always been the fear that they would return to try to claim their own. Now if they were to come back they would find no system of support to maintain the old way of life.

There were different levels of punishment. There was, to begin with, a list of 104 names of leaders who were to suffer loss of life and estate. These ranged from Lord Inchiquin to Sir Phelim O'Neill and so included Catholic and Protestant, Old English and Irish. It also included those bishops who had worked with the Confederate Government. As well as these, all who had taken part in the initial part of the rebellion forfeited life and property, as did any who were guilty of killing civilians and any civilians who had killed English soldiers. This was not all; all Irish were presumed to be guilty who had not worked openly for the victory of the Parliamentary cause. These were to lose a portion of their lands, ranging from one-fifth to two-thirds, depending on the degree of their guilt. Further, they might be required to accept in exchange for their home an acreage in another part of Ireland equivalent to what remained to them. The only exceptions to all this were those who had surrendered under conditions that had been approved by the Parliamentary Commissioners.

All of those who had lost any part of their land were to be moved across the Shannon to Connacht, to which Clare was attached for the purpose of the re-allocation of land. One half of the land forfeited in each of ten counties was to be allocated to the soldiers, the other half to the adventurers. Forfeited land in the other counties was to be available to the Government for use as it pleased. It was announced that all 'transplantable persons' had to be moved by 1 May 1654, and were liable to be put to death if found east of the River Shannon after that date. In practice, it was March 1655 before this was enforced. Families went with their stock and their goods and, quite often, a large portion of their tenants. They found that they were apportioned enough land to support the stock they had brought and no more, as those responsible for the allocation of land found themselves overworked.

One of those who had to make the long journey was Ferdoragh O'Mellan, or Mallen, who lived on the slopes of Slieve Gallion. He is described as a gentleman in the list of pardons of 1652. He may have been a relative of the Friar O'Mealan who kept a daybook of the 1641 Rising. However he had managed it, he had up till now been able to hold on to land around Lissan. There is nothing in his style that indicates that he was a trained poet in the way of the old Irish bards, but leaving his native territory moved him to verse, and he left a poem that portrays the emotional devastation of his enforced move to Connacht better than any other in the canon. It is called 'In the Name of the Father of Victory'. I will quote only three verses here, in the translation by Professor Diarmaid Ó Doibhlin. In the first, he says that St Colmcille will make the journey with them, as well as Colman Mucai, founder of the seventh-century monastery at Ardboe:

> Powerful, gentle Colmcille,
> Colman Mucai, the head of the clergy
> Will be with us on the way
> Let you not be weeping about going westward.

> Do you not appreciate, brothers,
> The way of the world since the beginning of time?
> No matter how great our possessions
> It is little we take with us into the grave.

> Their God and our God are the same
> One God who was and is
> The same God here and in the west
> One God who will live evermore!

One result of the enforced migration of what might be termed the middle classes was that the only representatives of Irish culture and society, the only speakers of the Irish language to remain in east Tyrone were the landless labourers and artisans. It is amazing that Irish speakers persisted right into the twentieth century, and that there were still poets composing in Irish for more than one hundred years after the enforced exodus. It is, perhaps, worth commenting here on the fact that it might not have survived without the help given by some Protestant clergy. The Presbyterian minister Revd Robert Allen, born in Cookstown, was the moving force behind a project to translate the Bible into Irish, to the opposition of the Catholic hierarchy. He spent his last days in Connacht, still working on his mission of bringing the Bible to Irish speakers.

Revd Robert King was a Church of Ireland clergyman in the Sixtowns, near Beaghmore. He wrote a Bible history in Ulster Irish, since he recognised that there were significant differences in dialects among the provinces. An interesting point is that, when Sixtowns Church of Ireland church was dedicated in 1843, the opening hymn was sung in Irish. Perhaps it was not simply the Catholics who used Irish in their everyday conversation, but it was the *lingua franca* of remote, mountainous districts.

The vacuum that was left by the exiled Irish was soon filled by new settlers and by old settlers returning. In 1630, it is estimated that there were about 3,000 settlers in County Tyrone as a whole. The setback of the Rising in 1641 and the ten years of war which followed it were soon forgotten and, by 1666, there were probably as many as 10,000 Planters in the county. This was not the outbreak of peace, however. When the monarchy was restored and King Charles II was returned to the throne, the issue of religion began to spread its poison again. To begin with it was a matter for Protestants; while Cromwell ruled England and Ireland the dominant Protestants were those who did not conform to the Church of England, in simple terms the Nonconformists. With the fall of the Commonwealth, the Church of England, like Charles, had been restored to pre-eminence. In May 1661 Parliament passed a declaration that all persons had to 'conform to the Church by law established'. It was the turn of the Nonconformists – in northern Ireland mostly Presbyterians – to be wary.

In fact it was not the king's intention to make much of religion; he was married to a French Catholic, so too much of a fuss could bring problems in his own nest. Some Presbyterian ministers were evicted because they refused to accept the *Book of Common Prayer*, but it was soon decided to leave the remainder in place as long as they accepted a basic stipend, called the *Regium Donum*, from the king. In effect, by accepting his money they were accepting that they were dependent on him. In fact, there was a general atmosphere of religious toleration. Catholics were allowed to celebrate Mass openly and

Catholic priests and bishops were allowed to carry out their pastoral duties. Not all Protestants were happy with this state of affairs, especially after information became available in 1678 of a Popish Plot in England. There was no Irish involvement in this plot, but there was still enough hysteria for Bishop Henry Jones and Lord Shaftesbury to accuse Archbishop Oliver Plunkett of plotting a French invasion. A Protestant jury in Dundalk threw out the charges, but a renegade Franciscan concocted the evidence that Shaftesbury wanted, and there was no difficulty in finding an English jury to condemn him. He suffered the death of a traitor in Tyburn in 1681. It is remarkable that, in spite of this, the ambience of toleration persisted.

When Ormond became Viceroy in 1662 his main concern was to balance the Irish books. This should not have been too much of a problem, since the huge Parliamentarian army had been reduced to a realistic size immediately after the Restoration. One step that he took was to recruit a regiment of foot guards, 1,200 strong, in England, because he believed that these would be more reliable than the rump of the Irish army that he was left with. The rates of pay of the new regiment were higher than those of other soldiers, and they seem to have been paid. The garrison of Carrickfergus had gone without pay or supplies for so long that they were near to starvation in 1666, when they mutinied. Two companies of the well-paid, and well-fed, regiment of foot guards were sent by sea from Dublin to restore the peace.

Another problem that Ormond faced was that Westminster was jealous of the Irish economy, and passed laws interfering with the trade of cattle from Ireland to England. Other groupings in the English aristocracy felt that Ireland was costing the king too much money and that one of their number would run the country more efficiently. The pressure was kept up till 1669, when Ormond was removed from office and replaced by the ill-tempered and obstinate Lord Robartes. He did not get on well with Charles and was recalled, at his own request, within a year.

In spite of these changes, there was an air of prosperity around the province. Ulster was no longer the poorest province in Ireland; Connacht had taken over that dubious title. In spite of the ban on exporting meat and dairy products to England, new markets were found in France and other foreign destinations. Around the Ballinderry, the earlier export of timber had cleared the forests, and the iron industry was stillborn for lack of wood for fuel, but still salmon fishing was self-sustaining, and salted salmon was exported as far as Venice and Spain. The Plantation was having its difficulties, certainly, but a viable economy was being built up. Although there were few parts of the province exclusively settled by incomers, mingling of settlers and natives seemed to be progressing amiably. In some areas the natives changed their names and their religion in the hope of a better life. In other areas, usually more remote, many Planters married Irishwomen for need of company and, within a fairly short time, their families had become Catholic and might well have been Gaelic-speaking. A peaceful progression was not possible, however, and, as usual, the problems came from outside.

In 1685 King Charles II died. Given his reputation as a womaniser, there is a certain irony in the fact that he had no direct heirs. It was his brother James who came to the throne as King James II. The problem was that he was a Catholic. He also chose a Catholic as his representative in Ireland. This man was one of the Old English, the sixteenth son of a down-at-heels Kildare gentle-man named Talbot. The young Talbot had survived the siege of Dundalk, one of the few Catholics to do so. He was created Earl of Tirconnell in 1685 and arrived in Dublin as Lord Deputy in February 1687 and his reforms soon sent reverberations around the country. Although there seemed no effort to restore confiscated lands to their original owners, local government went through a severe reorganisation. Boroughs, except Belfast, were given new charters which produced Catholic majorities. Protestant officers of the Crown were removed from their posts and replaced by Catholics. There was nothing the settlers could do about it, but hope that it would pass.

William of Orange was James's son-in-law, and a Protestant. He was an unlikely champion of extreme Protestantism, however, since he ensured a high level of religious toleration in his own principality. Nevertheless, he arrived in England with a Dutch army in November 1688, and was declared by Parliament joint monarch of England, Scotland and Wales in February 1689. James, meanwhile, had left the country to take refuge with Louis XIV of France. For the first time, England had a king who did not claim to be an absolute monarch, but one who would work within the constitution, acknowledging the primacy of Parliament.

The exiled James decided that he was prepared to fight for his crown after all, but that he would do his fighting in Ireland. A month after William and Mary had been crowned, James landed in Ireland with a French army. Even before this, trouble had begun. A letter was allegedly found in Comber in December which claimed that the Irish were going to rise on 9 December and kill all the settlers. Copies were made and sent round the province. It was being read to the citizens of Derry when news arrived that Tirconnell was approaching with a regiment of Catholics. This was a delicate moment, since the new king and queen had not yet been crowned, and the Bishop advised the people that it was safer to allow the troops to enter the city. In spite of the Revd Lord's words, thirteen apprentices stole the keys of the city, raised the drawbridge and locked the gates. John Campsie, who had lost his position as mayor because of the recent reforms, declared that they not allow any Papists whatever to live among them, and expelled any remaining Catholics there were in the city.

Before long, Derry became a refuge for Protestants from around Ulster. Soldiers loyal to King James, now known as Jacobites, soon controlled most of the eastern half of the province. Although an assault on Coleraine was thrown back, the defenders removed themselves to the stronger walls of Derry as soon as they felt it was safe to do so. The city received muskets, powder and money which were brought on the aptly named HMS *Deliverance*. The Military Governor of Derry, Colonel Lundy, ordered that all remaining garrisons in the north-west should withdraw to Derry. Many of them did so in a hurry, without bringing their supplies with them, an excellent bonus for the Jacobite troops that were following them closely. Even with the extra reinforcements to defend the city, by April Lundy was pessimistic about his prospects. The trouble was that it was not only fighting men that were arriving in numbers, but Protestant civilians from all over Ulster. Once the city became besieged, these were useless mouths that would have to be fed out of limited supplies. It has been calculated that, as well as 7,000 fighting men, 30,000 Protestant civilians were confined within the walls of the city.

The siege proper did not begin until mid-April, when the approaching joint Irish–French army started driving in the city's outposts. At Lifford the defenders were hacked down, the foot soldiers abandoned by the cavalry, which fled in panic back to the safety of Derry. There had to be a scapegoat for this disaster – the defenders had outnumbered the attackers by five to one. A survivor of the battle, Adam Murray, led a citizens' revolt which ousted Lundy, who had been accused of withholding support at the battle. Lundy slipped over the walls and escaped the fury of the mob. His place was taken by joint governors; a military man, Major Henry Baker, and a clergyman, Church of Ireland Rector George Walker. The defence was reorganised and the supply situation proved not to be quite as bad as previously thought. When King James himself came to the walls to offer terms of surrender, he was greeted by cries of 'No surrender!' and a hail of fire.

The siege was a desultory sort of affair for much of the time. The Jacobites were not equipped for a siege and the fact that Derry was almost an island, with the river on three sides and a bog on the other, meant that it was difficult for the besiegers to get near the walls. Even after a siege train and heavy guns arrived in May, the resulting bombardment killed many of the city's inhabitants without seriously threatening the integrity of the walls. The open area to the south of the walled city was controlled by an outpost in a windmill, and much of the more serious fighting took place here. Apart from the bombardment, the greatest problem for the people crammed within the walls was hunger. When it became obvious that direct assault would not carry the city, the Jacobite commanders decided that they would let hunger take its course. Those within the walls began to die not only of hunger, but of fever. Compassion was a part of General Hamilton's character, and he allowed 10,000 unarmed civilians to leave Derry. This probably cost the Jacobites victory, because it enabled those remaining to hold out for a little longer. The sight of thirty ships in Lough Foyle, visible from the tower of the cathedral, must also have encouraged the besieged; but the sight must also have been tantalising, because for six weeks they did not attempt to pass the Jacobite guns at Culmore Fort. It was not until they received a direct order from Schomberg, King William's commander in Ireland, that they made a direct attempt to approach the city. They seem to have picked a happy day to press forward, because the gunners on shore were, according to a disgruntled Jacobite supporter, drunk on brandy, and their firing was wild. The siege was over.

Schomberg himself arrived soon afterwards. Although there was more than adequate time left before winter set in, neither side offered battle and the winter was spent in a welter of misery in unhappy quarters. It took the arrival of King William himself to force the pace, and the two armies met in battle along the River Boyne. Although the Williamite army undoubtedly prevailed, enough of the Irish and French forces were able to extricate themselves to remain as a real threat. To set against the apparent cowardice of King James, the Irish had their hero: the charismatic Patrick Sarsfield. James had gone, however, and no amount of Irish heroism at Aughrim or Limerick could make any difference to his cause. There might have been some recompense if the original terms of the Treaty of Limerick, which ended the Williamite Wars, had been honoured. Protestants in Ireland had had too much of a fright, however, and they refused to confirm the sensible terms that William had negotiated as being too generous to Irish Catholics. The Irish Parliament passed a series of laws aimed at punishing any divergence from the Established Church. The immediate result was that the percentage of land that was owned by Catholics in the island of Ireland fell to 5 per cent.

☙ 4 ❧

LINEN ON THE GREEN

The first of the Penal Laws were passed in 1695 and prevented Catholics from carrying arms, from educating their children, and from owning any horse worth more than £5. King William tried to limit the application of these laws, but his death in 1702 removed any opposition. After that other provisions were added from time to time, including the expulsion of monks and friars. Westminster found much of this distasteful, but only intervened in the most extreme cases, as in 1719, when the Irish Parliament passed a Bill authorising the castration of unregistered priests. It was not until 1728 that the last of Penal Laws were passed. In total they removed the wealth of Catholics and put great obstacles in the way of their acquiring any wealth in the future.

Catholics were not allowed to buy land. When they died, what land they had was to be divided among their sons, unless one of these turned Protestant, when he would inherit it all. The longest lease a Catholic could hold was thirty-two years. The rent had to be at least two-thirds of the land's yearly value. No Catholic could practise law, join the army, hold any public office, be a member of a parliament or a corporation, or sit in a grand jury. Even such punitive laws as these, however, were unable to stop Catholics investing their money in commercial developments, which often showed a much better return on capital than did farming. Gradually a Catholic middle class developed that grew more vocal as the eighteenth century progressed.

Some of the laws simply did not work. Although 400 priests in religious orders were expelled in 1698, and Armagh had to do without a Catholic archbishop until 1714, there were still fourteen Catholic bishops in Ireland. Bishop Patrick Donnelly of Dromore lived in hiding on the slopes of Slieve Gullion, and became immortalised as the Bard of Armagh. Priests were allowed to remain and were allowed to say Mass as long as they were registered. Since being

registered involved rejecting the authority of the Pope, very few priests both-
ered with this. The result was that Mass was an outlawed thing, which was
celebrated around large boulders around the countryside, still identifiable and
known as Mass rocks. Since not everyone could attend Mass, the practice began
of laymen following the Mass in their minds, as nearly as possible at the times
when an actual Mass was being said. It was the landless peasants, who were not
really the targets of the laws at all, who persisted in the practice of the Catholic
religion. Of 5,500 Catholics who converted to the Established Church between
1703 and 1789, almost all were gentry who wanted to avoid the subdivision of
their land, and who had hopes of a rewarding career for their younger sons.
There were few attempts to convert the lower classes. It was important to
maintain an underclass from which could be recruited the hewers of wood and
drawers of water, as Lord Drogheda put it.

It was not only Catholics that were subject to the Penal Laws. Dissenters
and Presbyterians laboured under them as well. Their ministers were paid the
Regium Donum, except for a short period when there was a Tory Government,
in the last years of Queen Anne. But their members were disbarred from positions of power in civil affairs, even in those areas of Ulster where they formed
a majority of the non-Irish population. Even the marriage and burial services
carried out by Presbyterian ministers were denied validity. Those who served
in Ireland's Parliament were the rump of the old aristocracy, and it is likely
that they felt that a Church should be organised as civil society was, with its
natural leaders, the bishops, conducting its members on the right path. It was
the attitude of the Presbyterians towards the bishops that was at the heart of the
problem; as it was in Scotland, whence most of Ulster's Protestants came. They
did not want the Episcopal system.

What made matters worse for Presbyterians was that there was no pressure on the Irish Parliament to grant them any concessions. Irish Catholics
were still seen as the great threat and the Government calculated that, if the
Catholics were to rise again, the Presbyterians would be forced to side with the
Establishment. By the end of the century, the Government was to be proved
wrong in this rather sanguine approach. In the meantime, in spite of (or because
of) the repressive legislation, Ireland entered, almost uniquely in its modern history, a century of unbroken peace.

This is not to say that it was, at least to begin with, a happy and prosperous
hundred years. The eighteenth century began with a cattle distemper that began
in Monaghan but spread around Ulster, persisting on and off for a good many
years. There were years of poor harvests; in 1718, Bishop Nicholson arrived in
Derry to find that many people had the pinched faces of hunger and want.
He had a gruesome experience a few years later when one of his horses was

accidentally killed. Local people fell on the dead animal with knives and axes, taking dripping lumps home to their families. In 1726 another poor harvest meant that oatmeal was selling at twice the normal price, and whole families had to leave their homes and beg for food, having eaten the seed potatoes that should have been planted the following year. As a result, the next winter produced a full-scale famine. In 1739 it was cold that destroyed the potatoes in their clamps in the fields. Cattle died of cold and hunger. Rivers froze, so that watermills could not work and flour could not be obtained. An idea of just how cold it was can be obtained by the fact that the River Foyle froze over near Derry, where somebody was wealthy enough to roast an ox on the ice.

The combination of weather and want culminated in the great famine of 1741, where people were so hungry that they ate docks and nettles, and where so many died that there were mass burials. The famine was at its worst in Ulster and, when fever broke out in the heat of summer, many were so weakened that they succumbed easily. As big a proportion of the population died as in the famine years of the late 1840s. In Ulster most fatalities were suffered by the poorest of the Catholics. Many of the new settlers cut their losses and were grateful to move on to America. Presbyterians were probably the most ready to emigrate, because they found the tithes that they were required to pay to the Established Church an unbearable burden. Many went in groups along with their minister, although it was probably poverty rather than religion that drove them. Some landlords, and some bishops, were concerned that they would end with none but Irish as tenants.

Linen saved the day. Flax had been grown in Ireland from early times, and made into linen in narrow widths known as bandle linen. From the start of the Plantation some landlords had encouraged their native tenants to grow flax and to spin it into linen in order to give them an extra cash crop that might see them through hard times. Dr Allan Cooke leased Church land near the Ballinderry River in 1619 and, in 1628, obtained a charter to hold a market each week and a fair twice a year in what came to be known as Cookstown. The much-maligned Lord Wentworth became Lord Deputy a few years later and one of the tasks that he set himself was to improve the standard of linen production in Ireland. The method used by the native Irish to spin the yarn was fairly basic and resulted in many breakages. He ordered that no bundle of yarn could be sold that had more than two ends. In Wentworth's time the sale of linen in Cookstown was worth as much as £100 a week, at a time when a cow would only have been worth £1. Much of the yarn was destined for Lancashire.

Some of the tenants, indeed, were weavers, and brown, or unbleached, linen was soon being exported to the English market. The Irish Parliament, seeing this as a way of improving its balance of trade, did everything it could to encourage the linen industry, including paying a Huguenot, Louis Crommelin, to establish a colony of weavers in Lisburn. This support continued well into the century. Lack of funds and contacts meant that Ulster weavers were unable to sell directly to English customers, but English merchants were prepared to come to Dublin several times a year. Here they bought the cloth from factors who acted as middlemen.

The Ulster linen industry was a domestic affair, valuable because it could be carried out by families at times when their labour was not needed for other tasks on the farm. Better, because it was a cash crop it paid the rent. The chosen field had to have plenty of manure dug into it during the winter. The flax was planted in spring, produced its beautiful blue flowers in early summer, and was ready to harvest in August. It had to be pulled rather than cut, which was sore on the hand but produced a longer fibre. The stalks were bundled together into sheaves and these were placed in a flax dam, or lint hole, weighed down by stones so that they would rot in the water. A fortnight later the sheaves were removed from the water and spread out in the fields to dry. It still had to be broken, scotched and hackled before the fibres could be got. The fibres were then separated; the long ones produced fine linen yarn, while the shorter ones could still be used for coarse cloth.

At first, spinning yarn was done in the old Irish way, with a weighted stone, but spinning wheels were distributed by the linen board, free to anybody that had flax to spin. The yarn then went on to a weaver. Although the spinning wheel was operated by women mostly, a loom was a heavy machine, and needed a man's strength to use it. It was not a matter simply of tying on the yarn and letting her go. It could take a week to get a loom ready to operate, and it often took a specialist knowledge and manual dexterity that a farmer might not have. In those cases a man would be paid to come in and get everything prepared. Only when all this was done could the weaver get started. He usually produced a web of linen a yard wide and twenty-five yards long, which had to be cleaned and bleached before it was ready for the tailor. This again was a labour intensive operation, and could take as long as six months. The cloth had to be boiled up to twelve times, and spread out on grass for a week between each boiling. The natural process of sun and rain bleached it. Indeed, this was the first process in the industry to be mechanised.

Farmers were able to commit this time to their flax and linen because a new crop had become popular – the potato. This miracle food did not require a great deal of land, it grew well without requiring too much maintenance and it provided a very nutritious staple diet. All of this, together with the fact that merchants were finding fresh markets for linen and the improved technology of seafaring, helped Ulster to become the most prosperous of Ireland's provinces by the middle of the eighteenth century.

Old factor's house, Lissan.

Cookstown had a long way to go. It had been burned by loyalists from Limavady in 1642 and, even by 1736, little attempt had been made to restore it, other than a few tenements which were built in the Oldtown. The market was still being held, on common land between the townlands of Monrush and Coolreaghs. Part of this was a linen market, because there is a notice in the *Belfast Newsletter* in 1752 giving the date on which a linen market would be held on the south side of the hill in the new town. The new town referred to is the one that was designed in 1750 by William Stewart, who gave the town its layout along a broad, straight street.

By this time, the ethnic background of the people supplying the linen had changed. There were large areas in the surrounding districts that had been inhabited by the native Irish a century before, such as Orritor, which were now densely inhabited by Protestant immigrants from Scotland, nearly all of them Presbyterian. The part of Scotland from which most of them came, probably Ayrshire, already had a tradition of home weaving, and it has been suggested that there was an influx of weavers to the Cookstown and Ballinderry areas because of the encouraging initiatives of Trustees of the Irish Parliament, such as the weavers colony established in Lisburn. Bleach greens had been established since 1711. Beetling, or pounding with a wooden mallet, gave the linen a distinctive finish. This was one of the first processes to be organised on factory lines. Water power could drive a number of mallets to make continuous beetling possible. The technology was not difficult or particularly expensive. There was no need for a constant flow, nor was there any need for a mill dam. The mills worked continuously, from Monday morning to Saturday night.

Merchants who owned these mills needed as much linen as they could get hold of. In addition to buying webs in the traditional way directly from the farmer, they also gave out hanks of yarn to a poorer, landless class of weaver, in order that the supply of cloth was maintained. The Irish Parliament did what it could to encourage enterprise in the linen trade. In 1763 it passed a law making it easier to give leases in perpetuity for bleach greens. Even if a property was entailed, the landowner could lease up to fifteen acres, provided a third of this area had been converted to a bleach green within three years and £10 per acre was spent on improvements aimed at the bleaching business.

The first lease for Wellbrook Beetling Mill was given to Hans Baillie in 1765. The general feeling at the time was that there was a great future in bleach greens, and landowners who had water power available were actively looking for tenants. Not everyone was successful. William Cluff had been one of the builders who had made William Stewart's plan for Cookstown a reality. He leased lands along the Kildress River from the See of Armagh and placed an advertisement in the *Newsletter* extolling its advantages as a site for a bleach green. Unfortunately, the terms of his own lease meant that he did not qualify under the 1763 Act. Without security of tenure, no one was prepared to invest in a bleach green or beetling mill and Mr Cluff had to make do with a much more basic scutch mill, used to break up the stalks of the flax.

There were other provisions in the Act, designed to control the process of selling the linen. A piece of linen that was to be sold on the open market was examined by a seal master to ensure that the web was of the correct size and that any imperfection on the linen could be seen by a potential buyer. He then sealed the web at both ends. When the web was sold, both seller and buyer had to write their names on both ends. Anyone found guilty of counterfeiting a name on a web was liable to seven years transportation. This complicated procedure was meant to cut out middlemen who had made a practice of buying webs from poor weavers before they reached the markets at less than they were worth, then selling them on at a fair price. Dungannon was notorious for the number of people who lived as middlemen. The Act made it illegal for anyone to buy linen and to sell it again on the same day or within a month in the same market or within thirty miles of that market. Drapers, who were anxious to get as much linen as they could, tended to buy from anybody. As a result, this part of the Act was largely ignored for more than a decade. In 1775, however, drapers in east Tyrone put out a joint statement wherein they said that they would no longer buy linen unless all clauses in the Act were followed. This initiative was followed by other drapers throughout Ulster.

There were other laws which provided for quality control of linen. It was forbidden to use lime as a short cut in the bleaching process. Some people used pigeon droppings for this purpose. Anyone who informed on a transgressor was given £10 reward. The guilty party forfeited the linen and had to pay a fine as well. There were different classes of linen web. One of these was the 'Moneymore', which was brown linen, 32in wide, in lengths of either twenty-six yards or fifty-two yards for a double piece. Not all the registered bleachers were satisfied with the integrity of the seal masters and eventually an inspector was appointed, one of whose tasks it was to keep an eye on the seal masters.

If there was short measure in a web, it was no use trying to fine the weaver, who would not have been able to pay up. Instead it was the seal masters who were fined. This was a problem in a big market. On what was called a throng day there could have been as many as 420 attending the linen market in Cookstown; Moneymore might have as many as 1,000. It was impossible for the seal master to check every web in these circumstances, so most of them employed assistants. The seal master at Cookstown, for example, employed a number of assistants and in one year had to pay seventeen fines on their behalf. The fines ranged from 5s for passing a web with a damaged end, through 10s for passing short measure, to 15s for passing a web that had concealed damage. Since the payment for measuring was only 2d per piece, these fines were of a punitive nature. Of the £80 income that might be earned by a seal master in a year, the loss of £8 10s 0d, or over 10 per cent, was a serious matter.

Linen was such an important part of the Irish economy that there was continual pressure to make its production more efficient. Many innovations occurred in the opening decades of the nineteenth century. Spinning wheels were developed that allowed the spinner to use both of her hands on the yarn, which resulted in a better product produced at a faster rate. There was a grant to provide these at the school at Lissan in 1818, where up to 200 girls and as many boys were being educated. The wheels were made locally, and woodturning was an important industry. They seem to have cost about 15s each, although some were as cheap as 10s. There were improvements in looms as well, particularly in the introduction of the flying shuttle, brought to Ireland by a Moravian who settled in Gracehill, near Ballymena. This made the work lighter and increased the output. It also made it easier for women to work at looms. The standard price for a loom at this time was £4 10s 0d.

Wellbrook Bridge.

Not all innovations were successful. James Stewart of Killymoon set up a trial on the Ballinderry of a machine that was designed to retrieve the linen fibre from the flax plant much more quickly and without the loss of colour that the normal process involved. There was great excitement in the district at the prospect and plans were made for local carpenters to copy the design. Unfortunately, after a single trial, the experiment was discontinued, and farmers had to continue with the traditional, time-consuming process.

One problem about the production of linen was the fact that flaxseed could not be harvested in Ireland in the quantities needed, but had to be imported every year. The Linen Board kept strict records of the amounts imported and where they were distributed. Merchants had to report how much seed they had left at the end of the planting season. This was then examined to see if it was still capable of germination; if not it was sold for animal feed or for oil production. There were occasional shortages and, since this threatened income at every level of society, even gentlemen were not loath to get involved in obtaining emergency supplies from England or beyond.

It is important not to let this develop into a picture of a rural paradise, with each man happy at his station. The individual weaver was in a very vulnerable position, whose station was firmly placed at the bottom of the heap. Any change in circumstances threatened his very existence, so he was understandably afraid of change. Even the introduction of the linen laws provoked riots. The increased emphasis on standardisation was an obvious drive towards factory methods. As yet full industrialisation was impossible because no one had developed a weaving machine sensitive enough to deal with the very delicate linen thread. There were other pressures, however. Because there was a small increase in prosperity for tenant farmers, more of their children grew into adulthood and there was a subsequent increase in population. There is an estimate that the population of Tyrone doubled between 1753 and 1791, in line with population trends in the rest of Ireland. Where Church records exist, they give a picture of women marrying early, having more children, and having fewer who died in childhood. In addition to this, the Penal Laws were gradually falling into disuse, and an increasingly confident Catholic population was looking for its share of the pie. There was only so much land available, and it was almost inevitable that secret societies developed who took it on themselves to guard the rights of their co-religionists. Some took quite romantic names, like the Peep o' Day Boys and the Defenders, but the different organisations eventually settled into two; the Orangemen looked after the interests of Protestants, while the Ribbonmen took care of Catholic priorities.

The outside world also had its effects on the Ballinderry Valley. In America, revolution had broken out in 1776. Many of the revolutionaries had family connections with Ulster, but that was no consolation as linen sales fell dramatically and lack of revenue prevented the Irish Government from replacing the troops that the English had removed to America. Things were so bad that it had to suspend all payments, and still required a loan of £50,000 from the Bank of England. Starting in Belfast, a Volunteer movement began to recruit. The fact that its members were reasonably well-to-do is shown by the fact that within a few weeks they were in a position to parade to church in full uniform. To show their annoyance with the Government in Westminster, the uniforms were made completely in Ireland. In spite of this, the Viceroy eventually accepted that the only force available for the defence of Ireland was the Volunteers. In June he distributed 16,000 militia muskets to the organisation. This was a dangerous gamble, because he had no control, legally or morally, over the Volunteers. Whatever the legal position, the gesture encouraged recruitment and within a few weeks membership stood at 40,000, half of them in Ulster. This membership was effectively restricted to landlords, substantial farmers, merchants and professional men, because nobody else could afford to buy all that was required, including £1 15s for a musket. Interestingly, they were organised on democratic principles, and their officers were elected.

These were also the people who had votes in the Irish Parliament. It was almost inevitable that, as they began to feel their strength, they considered the possibility of using that strength to allow Parliament in Dublin to break away from the restrictions imposed on it by the Parliament in Westminster. At a meeting in Dungannon, representatives of all the Volunteer Companies in Ulster passed resolutions demanding the legislative independence of the Irish Parliament. By a fortuitous bit of timing, a new Whig Government took over in London only a few weeks later. Their priority was an end to the American War, and they passed the Irish reforms quickly, in order to have a clear field with the more important item. This was the great achievement of the Volunteers; to establish a Parliament in Dublin that was answerable only to its voters and to the king. This was known as Grattan's Parliament. It was not particularly representative, since in most boroughs the landlord's nominee was elected unopposed. Only in Derry and Carrickfergus did Ulster have free elections. In Belfast there were only thirteen voters; Coleraine had more, with thirty-six.

Having felt their power, the Volunteers tried to press forward with a programme of reform. There was even some pressure for alleviation of the Penal Laws. This was opposed by most Protestant clergymen. John Wesley wrote to the *Freeman's Journal* that, 'I would not have Roman Catholics persecuted at all. I would only have them hindered from doing hurt; I would not put it in their power to cut the throats of their quiet neighbours.' By now, however, the Volunteers had lost their potency. The war in America was over and the regular

Clock tower, Lissan.

army and militia were back in Ireland. Future petitions for reform were ignored by Parliament. The Belfast Volunteers remained in existence; they were of a very different nature from most other Volunteer companies. They were nearly all Presbyterian for a start, and most of those who had gone to university had been educated in Scotland and were radical in temperament. They were delighted at the idea of the French Revolution and had a banner made showing the Storming of the Bastille in 1789. They even sent a declaration of support to the National Assembly in Nantes. It was these radicals whom Theobald Wolfe Tone visited in 1791 in order to get their support for the plight of Irish Catholics. This led to the formation of the United Irishmen, the aim of which was neatly summed up in its title.

Very few landowners joined this new, ultra-radical organisation. Its membership was composed mainly of middle-class businessmen and professionals, and they showed the limits of their radical vision in 1792 when they turned out to suppress demonstrations by Antrim weavers who had the cheek to claim better wages. They did, however, see themselves as Irish patriots, and one of their great achievements was to revive interest in Irish culture and music. They organised a great festival of harpers in Belfast's Assembly Rooms. This link between Presbyterian radicalism and a resurgent Catholicism was alarming to the English Government, since the United Kingdom was now at war with France and the war was not going particularly well. Pitt and the Privy Council put pressure on the Irish Parliament to grant the vote to those few wealthy Catholics who could meet the stringent property qualifications. They had already won the right to enter the lucrative legal profession, so some of them might be in a better position to accrue voting qualifications.

The trouble was that all of this controversy filtered down through the levels of society till it reached society's poorest members. Sectarian warfare developed in County Armagh, which was already the most densely populated rural area in Ireland, in the 1780s. The Protestant Peep o' Day Boys went beyond mere faction fighting. Better armed than their Catholic neighbours, they broke into Catholic houses and, as Lord Gosford reported, 'treat many of them with Cruelty'. Some of the local Volunteers actively sided with the Protestants and on at least two occasions fired on Catholic groups with fatal results. There were reports that some Protestant gentlemen were so upset about this that they loaned guns to Catholics for their defence. As usually happens in this sort of strife, Catholics began to fight back and there were soon parts of the county where Protestants did not feel safe.

Matters were not helped when, after the beginning of the French War, the Government set about recruiting a militia. Since this involved taking a breadwinner away from his family, since the militiaman was not allowed to serve in

LINEN ON THE GREEN

his own county, it was considered an imposition. In theory, recruits were to be chosen by ballot, but in practice the local sheriffs tended to pick Catholics first. In one way this suited Protestants, since they were able to stay at home and look after their families. There was a dangerous side to it. Many of those recruited were already members of the increasingly well-organised Defenders, and they were now getting military training at government expense. Many of its members were part of a Catholic proto-middle class, somewhere between merchants and weavers. They were literate and idealistic, and set it as their task to reverse some of the land settlements of the previous hundred years. To cement their sense of identity, they bound themselves with oaths and symbols. It was after a clash between Peep o' Day Boys and the Defenders at the Diamond, in which the Defenders were defeated, that the Orange Order was set up. In the first flush of victory, the Protestants turned on local Catholics, placarding their houses with the advice to go to Hell or Connacht, and by attacking homes, destroying looms and webs. In two months, 7,000 Catholics fled from County Armagh. Local magistrates did little to uphold law and order. As a result of the outrage that this enforced exodus caused all over the country, many Defenders applied to join the United Irishmen, who by this stage had also gone underground and become an oath-bound secret society. Recruiting for the Defenders even increased, as Catholics all over the country heard for the first time the tribulations of their brethren in the Black North.

In any organisation that grows as quickly as this it is impossible to keep a high level of security, and soon Defenders were being brought before the courts. After the autumn assizes in 1795, dozens were executed and hundreds were transported. The Catholic Archbishop of Dublin weighed in on the side of the Establishment by excommunicating everyone who belonged to the society, but even that was not enough to quash their sense of indignation. The leaders of the United Irishmen saw this determination and saw in the Defenders a way of putting numbers in the field of battle that they could never do themselves. By this stage their organisation was limited to two groups: bourgeois radicals in Belfast, Lisburn and Dublin; and Presbyterian farmers in Antrim and Down. New recruits were urgently needed, because news was reaching Ulster that the French were prepared to put a force on the seas to support them. They were also encouraged by the latest successes of the French armies in continental Europe.

Lord Camden, who was Lord Lieutenant at this time, was not a man to do anything by half measures. He forced a Bill through the Dublin Parliament which indemnified magistrates if they exceeded their powers during the current emergency. An Insurrection Bill allowed martial law to be imposed and suspects to be sent to serve in the navy; it also allowed the courts to apply the death penalty to anyone administering illegal oaths. Finally, he replaced the militia, who had been infiltrated by the Defenders, with a yeomanry which was almost completely Protestant and which allowed its members to serve in their home counties. In mid-Ulster, Orangemen were among the first to join. In spite of all this, the United Irishmen seemed to be getting stronger. At this critical moment, a French force of 14,450 men sailed to Ireland, reaching Bantry Bay on 22 December 1796. However, through a mixture of mismanagement and stormy weather, no landing was made, and the ships withdrew.

The French attempt aroused the revolutionary zeal of more Irishmen, and even more joined the United Irishmen. The Government was faced with a large body of armed men whose intention it was to sever the links with England. At this stage the revolutionaries were at the height of their powers, and a rising at this time might even have succeeded. The leaders, however, lacked confidence, and preferred to wait for another French invasion, which they believed was imminent. This gave the Government time to get its forces in order. It knew that it was dealing with an organisation that showed great solidarity among its members. When leaders of the United Irishmen had been arrested in the autumn, there was a mass turnout of people who harvested the prisoners' crops. General Lake was sent to Belfast. His intention was to use terror to keep them in order, since he believed that Belfast was at the centre of sedition in Ireland. Military searches began at once and were soon extended to the neighbouring towns. As is usual in Irish history, the United Irishmen had been penetrated by informers, and Lake was able to round up most of the leaders, together with over 5,000 firearms. The most dangerous prisoners were taken to Dublin, while the remainder were put on a hulk anchored at the Pool of Garmoyle, in Belfast Lough.

That was not the end of the terror. The Monaghan Militia demolished the presses of the *Northern Star*, silencing it forever. Elsewhere, the yeomanry were turned loose, striking terror. They demolished houses and lashed anyone they suspected of sedition. One man in Broughshane had 250 lashes on the back and another 250 on the buttocks, and there are reports that this was not unusual. The yeomanry had Lake's full support. When a captain in the Dublin Militia complained about the burning of Kilkeel, he was court-martialled. When the Monaghan Militia, in spite of the destruction of the *Northern Star*, were discovered to have seventy men in their ranks who were also sworn members of the United Irishmen, four privates who refused to inform on their comrades were shot in Lisburn. When the jury trying William Orr, a farmer from near Antrim, found the evidence against him unsatisfactory and recommended mercy, he was executed anyway. Lake made no attempt to disarm the Orangemen; General John Knox claimed that if he did, the whole country would have been in flames. This General Knox was the younger brother of Thomas Knox, whom we will now meet.

Tyrone could not avoid this social convulsion, and one of the first yeomanry forces in Ireland was raised by Thomas Knox of Dungannon; indeed, it was later claimed that this was the first. The first yeomanry lists were published in 1797, and Tyrone was shown to have the highest membership of any county – 2,889. Together with William Richardson, Knox had worked out a plan, known as the Dungannon Association, by which a yeomanry corps could be levied throughout Ireland. The resolutions and plans of this association were signed by the county's magistrates. Landlords were to organise meetings of their tenants and the tenants would be asked to support these resolutions. When that was done, selected men were invited to offer their services. The list would be submitted to the Government. If the list was approved, officers were given commissions, while arms and uniform were distributed to the rank and file.

The troubles that had accompanied the expulsion of Catholics from Armagh had reached the linen producing areas of east Tyrone and south Derry. The *Northern Star* had commented, when the idea of the Dungannon Association was first mooted, that the real disturbers of the peace were Orangemen and that anyone genuinely interested in law and order should deal with them first. To counter this, there were resolutions disavowing all lawbreaking at an Orange parade at Gosford Castle. Landlords also got involved with the Order, ostensibly to direct it away from lawlessness. Under these circumstances, it was easy to accept Orangemen into the yeomanry and, by 1798, there were some who spoke of the Orange Yeomanry.

It is possible to have some sympathy for the Government's position. Because of the war with France, most regular soldiers had, once again, been removed from Ireland. Their place had been taken by the militia, who were mostly Catholic and who had been infiltrated to an unknown extent by United Irishmen and Defenders. The English Government had transferred units of Fencibles, regiments which were the equivalent of the Home Guard in a later war, to reinforce the militia. The problem was that these did not represent a rapid reaction force, and magistrates in more remote parts of the country, such as Tyrone, felt that they did not offer a reliable response. The magistrates were concerned about the possibility of the United Irishmen/Defenders organising militarily and paralysing law and order locally. Knox was advised that there was no possibility of the Dungannon system working without the approval of Dublin. It was not until September 1796 that final approval was given.

Knox was concerned that the two strands that would together form the yeomanry should be kept distinct. The possible reason is that he did not want some of the other magistrates, in particular James Stewart of Killymoon, to know about the Orange connection. Stewart had been a Volunteer and was no friend of Orangemen. It was important that people like Stewart did not realise the real nature of the proletariat volunteers until the whole enterprise had been sanctioned by the Government. Indeed, as far as the officers were concerned, about one in three of the Tyrone Militia had served as Volunteers, thus showing a fairly radical background. They are unlikely to have volunteered to officer an organisation whose rank and file were as anti-Catholic as they turned out to be.

Meanwhile, numbers of United Irishmen in Tyrone had risen to 14,000 by May 1797. There was no possibility that the Tyrone Yeomanry could counter this force on its own. The combination of the Insurrection Act should have helped them, but the United Irishmen seemed to grow in strength no matter how many of them were sent to gaol by the yeomen. There was a sense of danger around the countryside and some magistrates who lived in the countryside were moving to the safer surroundings of towns. James Stewart complained that he would soon be the only magistrate operating in the Ballinderry Valley. The United Irishmen felt strong enough to burn out some of Stewart's tenants near Stewartstown, while within that town people who resisted the invitation to join the United Irishmen and joined the yeomanry instead were themselves being cut and maimed. Stories began to circulate that United Irishmen were infiltrating the yeomanry; even that some were joining the Orange Order. There was also the realisation that the yeomanry was forcing government supporters to show their hands. It was no wonder that many loyalists were not coming forward to volunteer, even though some of the original recruiting had been straight from Orange lodges.

To show whose side he was on, Knox ordered his yeomanry to ignore any unregistered arms that they found in the possession of Orangemen. Next he organised a review of yeomanry in his father's park in Dungannon. At this he urged his soldiers to wear their Orange ribbons. To ensure that he had enough men, he encouraged Orangemen who did not want to enlist to attach themselves to existing units as unpaid supplementaries. Finally, he began to organise his men into brigades, so that they could be used as conventional troops if needed. This initiative was copied throughout the organisation.

As it became apparent that 1798 would see the crisis in the radical movement, the yeomanry was called to full-time duty. Forward piquets were established and fall-back positions identified which were to be defended at all costs. The intention was that the full-time yeomen would concentrate against outbreaks of violence, while the supplementaries would continue to guard their home districts. The system was so well organised in Tyrone that no outbreak took place, and Knox was even able to release a large contingent to reinforce Antrim. Even the landing of the French in Mayo in the autumn of that year caused scarcely a ripple along the Ballinderry.

The continuing Napoleonic Wars were a time of relative prosperity for Ulster. There were many government contracts to be won, and there was money circulating in the province. Some of the money came from the lubrication used by the English Prime Minister, Pitt, to encourage members of the Irish Parliament to vote themselves out of existence. Since the Pope had recognised the legitimacy of George III's rule, there was no justification for repressive laws against Catholics; they were threatening no one. Yet the Protestants of Ireland were reluctant to grant full emancipation to Catholics, since that would put Catholics in an effective majority in the country. Emancipation could only be offered in the context of a single United Kingdom, with its built-in Protestant majority. After a great deal of wheeling and dealing, the United Kingdom of Great Britain and Ireland came to be ruled by a single Parliament in 1801.

After the war the economy became depressed, not only in Ireland, but throughout the United Kingdom. Lancashire in particular suffered, and there was a great deal of civil unrest. At about this time the Drapers' Company sent a delegation to investigate the condition of their estates in Loughinsholin, in the northern half of the lower Ballinderry Valley. The picture they drew gives us a fascinating insight into conditions in mid-Ulster at the beginning of the nineteenth century and how the countryside looked at that time.

The land around Moneymore had been leased to Sir William Rowley. The lease had ended and the Drapers decided to become direct landlords. In 1817 they sent a deputation to their portion. This stretched from Moneymore along the eastern slope of Slieve Gallion and on round to what is now known as Draperstown, but was then the Cross at Ballinascreen. Moneymore itself was built very close to the edge of their portion, so close in fact that some of the houses were limited to very small gardens and curbed any improvements that might be intended. It was a town of roughly one hundred houses and it had one grist mill. There were only two houses that 'would answer to the name', as far as the delegation was concerned; the Manor House and the house belonging to the curate of Desertlyn Parish. Near the town were two other residences with claims to gentility: Springhill House, belonging to the Knox-Conynghams, and Lissan House, home of the Ponsonby-Staples family. Beyond that, most of the homes were no more than cabins. People with a little more wealth, or perhaps a greater pressure of family size, sometimes rented more than one of these. There were sixty-eight different holdings. The town had a monthly fair for cattle and linen. Although there was permission for a market, this had fallen into disuse. Around Moneymore the company owned some 5,000 acres of cultivated land and another 1,200 acres of turf bog and rough pasture. There were a few wealthy tenants who had strong farmhouses but even these did not limit their activities to farming. The uncertainties of the agricultural economy encouraged them to earn money in as many ways as possible.

On the eastern slopes of Slieve Gallion the company owned another section of land, Brackaghslievegallion, about six miles long by three miles wide. Because of the depth of soil, cultivation was possible nearly to the top of the mountain. People here lived in separated dwellings; there was no town or even a group of houses. It was much more densely populated than Moneymore and, whereas most of the inhabitants of the town and its surroundings were of Scottish extraction, those who lived on Slieve Gallion were almost exclusively descended from the native Irish.

The general techniques of farming and ways of life were similar in both these sections, and in Ballinascreen, where most of the inhabitants were Catholics, both native Irish and Scots who had settled in the district before the Reformation. Two of the strongest farmers had tanning businesses as well. This was probably necessary, as individual holdings of land were very small to begin with and some had been subdivided. Each holding or sub-holding had one or two cabins on it. The cabins were made of mud, thatched with straw or else with reeds or turves. They were rarely watertight. Floors were of bare earth. If there was a chimney at all it consisted of a simple hole in the roof. More often, the door was left open when the fire was lit. Horses, cattle, goats and pigs lived in the same house, their quarters separated from their human masters' by a simple partition. In all three sections furniture and clothing were poor, but in Brackaslievegallion they were 'miserable in the extreme'. The delegates were intrigued to notice that clothes in this section were not simply coarse material worn through, but seemed to be made up of cast-offs. It turned out that there was a strong trade in used clothes between Scotland and the poorer districts of Ireland.

Husbandry was of a limited kind. Most families grew only oats, potatoes and flax. There was no attempt at any sort of crop rotation; the same piece of ground might be used to grow oats for two or more years. The family subsisted on the oats and potatoes. The flax was spun into yarn, and was often sold as such. In most houses, however, it was woven into cloth before being sold. The sale of the cloth, supplemented by the sale of fat pigs, brought in enough cash to pay the rent and to buy next year's flax seed. Even the best farmers made little effort to improve what they had. Few of them put up barns or other buildings that would have helped them care for their cattle. Their fields lacked hedges or fences. The only fences that they used were march fences, marking the boundaries of their properties. As a result, much time was spent trying to keep the livestock out of the crops. It is important, in the light of modern prejudices, to emphasise that that the delegates were unable to differentiate between Planters and natives when it came to farm management.

The reason for the lack of fencing was the total deforestation that had taken place in the early decades of the Plantation. There were few trees in the section, so people and animals lacked the shelter that these would have provided normally. In addition, lack of tree cover on an exposed hillside would have led to a great deal of erosion and allowed precious nutrients to be washed away.

The town of Moneymore was made up of more substantial cabins, built of rough stone and whitewashed. Its neat appearance was marred somewhat by the fact that there were dung-heaps in front of many of the houses. This aspect of country life was prevalent in towns for most of the century, but was modified in later years by moving the dung-heap to the back door. The town boasted three public houses – the same number as exist today, almost 200 years later. It had no inn, however, which was a problem for visiting merchants and dealers on fair days. The numbers were substantial; taking linen alone, 1,000 weavers, each month, sold their webs to one hundred drapers or their agents. This did not include those who had come to buy and sell cattle. The linen market was held on the open street, whatever the weather, and by the end of the day the dealers were glad to crowd into private houses for whatever shelter their money could buy. Their horses found shelter with the poorer residents.

The Lower Ballinderry.

As mentioned previously, most of those living in the Moneymore section were Scottish in origin and Presbyterian in religion. In fact, the brewery that had existed in the town from the first had recently failed, due to the attitude of the majority to intoxicating drink. The next largest grouping was the Catholics, 'principally of the lower class', as the report delicately puts it. It is equally delicate when it describes the Established Church – it actually calls it the Church of England *and* Ireland – as having a 'respectable congregation', although not numerous. Finally, there were about fifty Methodists. This last group had an English minister, a stocking weaver from Leicester, who provided a Sunday School for the community, together with the curate from Desertlyn Parish. In Brackaghslievegallion, Catholics were more populous than Presbyterians, while in Ballinascreen there were very few Protestants of any denomination.

The rector of Desertlyn was over ninety, and inactive, but he continued drawing his annual £700. His curate, who was diligent in carrying out his duties, had private means and was content in his role. The Presbyterian minister got £100 a year from his congregation, and another £70 from the *Regium Donum*. He also farmed some land. His meeting house was small and in need of repair. There was a small Catholic chapel on the hill just outside the town. The only schools were a Sunday School in Moneymore, mentioned above, and another one in Desertmartin. In spite of these, many people demonstrated their literacy by writing petitions to the delegation (at least, the petitions were written in 'many different hands').

There was no medical provision for the poor nearer than the City and County Infirmary in Derry. Most made do with a clinic in Cookstown, though the care and facilities there were described as rudimentary.

The estate was not operating at anywhere near optimum levels, that was clear. The delegation put aside the temptation to improve the tenants by getting rid of the old ones. That would be too much like buying a pig in a poke; who was to say that the replacements would be any better? Rather, they decided, the occupiers should be made to desire improvement. As a beginning, they felt that creating more freeholders would be an incentive to treating the land more carefully and, in particular, encouraging the use of crop rotation. In order to lessen the number of mouths that required feeding directly from a farm, they decided that more tradesmen were needed, so they started apprenticeship schemes. Some of the delegates had been mortified by the immodesty of some of the garments worn by young women, so they were to be provided with clothing that preserved their decency. Houses were to be built in the towns so that newly qualified tradesmen were not required to live in a subdivision of a father's holding. Trees had to be planted, some to grow to maturity as timber for building, while others were coppiced to provide wood for fuel. Strong fences and walls were built to protect the young trees from marauding browsers.

Farm building, Lissan.

The education of children was to be taken in hand. Schools were built in Moneymore, at Lecumpher and at Moyheelan. To protect religious sensibilities, these were to be non-denominational, and religious instruction could not be given to a pupil without his parents' consent. In order to alleviate the hardship of those poor who were ill, the Drapers' Company would build a dispensary and a house for a doctor in Moneymore. The company contributed £10 towards setting up a soup shop. A Market House, inn and public stables would also be needed, to be built on the site occupied by the library and old courthouse.

They then turned their attention to the spiritual needs of the people. At £700 per annum, the incumbent of Desertlyn Parish was well looked after. Things were tighter for the dissenting congregations. The company decided to pay each Presbyterian minister either ten or twenty guineas a year to supplement his income. Catholics were more problematic. In spite of Catholic Relief Acts, the Master of the Drapers' Company thought that it was part of his duty to uphold the position of the Reformed Church over 'the Romish religion'. To get around this problem, it was decided to give the Catholic priest, Fr Mackle, a personal donation of £10 each year in recognition of his good character and moral conduct; this would mean that the money was being given to the person rather than to the priest. It was also agreed that this form of words could be used in the future. The Jesuits would have been proud!

To give the local economy a kick-start, since it was almost moribund after a dreadful harvest in 1816, the company bought flaxseed which was distributed on credit to farmers. It also provided seed potatoes. Finally, it forwarded £493 to the various clergymen to be offered as loans to farmers whose stock had died from starvation and needed to be replaced.

When it came to building the new premises in Moneymore, the company felt that there would not exist in Moneymore tradesmen of the skills necessary to complete the work to the high scale envisaged. To maintain standards, the members decided to have all doors, windows and joinery made in London by a London joiner, who would then send a competent individual to Moneymore to see that everything was correctly fitted. The resulting buildings, they felt, would be a model that locals would wish to imitate. Those members who were in Moneymore now departed and left the supervision of the construction to a clerk of works.

Another deputation came from London to see how things were progressing. The Drapers' Company was anxious that all its tenants (especially the Catholics) should benefit from any improvements. The fact that they formed the poorest section of the community did not arise from their religion, but from the fact that they had lost everything in the many upheavals they had endured and by the fact that they still found it difficult to buy property. Several women were brought in from Scotland to promote the two-handed method of spinning, and spinning wheels were distributed free or part-price to those who could not afford to buy one. Ground was donated for a new Presbyterian meeting house, and a row of cabins that had been used as brothels was demolished in the process. The Catholic chapel was extensively repaired. Trees were planted in several locations around the estate. All this work brought money into the town and a general air of prosperity began to be built up.

In 1820, new rents were set and new conditions were put in place for tenants. This was not the end of the involvement of the Drapers' Company in the development of Moneymore. Unlike most absentee landlords, they did not hold the Agent to account simply on the matter of rents received, but were also concerned about the welfare of their tenants. They built new roads to make it easier to bring home the turf or to attend the market. When it became obvious that the old market hall was too small, they built a new market yard complete with corn stores. In all of this they provided a model as landlords that should have been copied more. Even before the Land Reform of the late nineteenth century, they encouraged their tenants to buy the freehold of their land when they could.

One of the facts discovered by the delegates from the Drapers' Company on their various trips was that the nature of the estate had changed in the years since the original Plantation. Tenants had reclaimed land from mountain and from bog, so that their holdings were bigger than they had been originally, yet they were still paying the same rent. In a sense this echoed the situation in the early 1600s, when nobody had any real idea how big the portions of land that were being distributed were. It may have been this that was the instigation of the Ordnance Survey of Ireland. This came in two parts. The obvious task was to survey and map the island of Ireland, and this was carried out with commendable accuracy. To add to that, however, someone came up with the ambitious scheme of getting local gentlemen to provide memoirs of each parish in the kingdom, so that flesh might be added to the topographical bones, as it were. The project was begun in the 1830s but unfortunately never completed. The parishes of County Londonderry were covered in detail, however, and there is quite a bit of information about those parishes which are situated in the County Tyrone side of the Ballinderry River. In some parishes the information is rather perfunctory, but in others there is great detail. For anyone interested in the local history of the north-west of Ireland, they are as valuable as *The Domesday Book* is to the English.

In 1834 Lieutenant Charles Bailey of the Royal Engineers completed his report on the parish of Ballinderry. The parish was divided into six townlands and comprised 1,947 acres, of which about 500 acres was bog and unreclaimed ground. The river at that time varied from 80ft to 100ft broad, and was about 5ft deep at Ballinderry Bridge itself. It was useless for navigation for there was, and still is, a bar of sand and gravel where it opens into the lough. The river was full of trout and, in the autumn, dollaghan (or bull-trout as he called them) were common up to 15lbs in weight. They were sold at 3*d* per pound in the local towns. He comments that they are soft and bad eating, so they seem to have been caught after spawning, late in the year. There were also some salmon in the river, but these were caught more rarely. There was a corn mill and a kiln at Derrychrin, near Ballinderry Bridge. Another mill in the townland of Lanaghy (he probably means Lanaglug, further upriver) had failed because of lack of reliable water, since it had been built on a side stream. From the bridge two gravel roads cross the parish, one to Coagh and the other to Ardboe. The ground about was extremely flat, and the great expanses of bog were interrupted only by small hills of gravel. There were few trees or hedges, while the cottages, he considered, were poor and dirty. He summed up Ballinderry as 'a poor and uninteresting tract of country'.

Most of the inhabitants were Catholics. Although the Penal Laws had long been repealed, there was still no chapel, and Mass was heard in the open at Derrychrin. They lived in cottages that were built of stone or mud, with small windows and thatched roofs. Inside they were divided into two rooms or, more rarely, three. There was little comfort, and the people lived mainly on potatoes, washed down with milk, or on oatmeal made into porridge or oatcakes. They did have ready access to turf from the bogs round about. They seem to have had two main holidays in the year. St Patrick's Day was celebrated in the 'usual way', presumably by drinking and dancing. Easter Monday was spent in 'more innocent amusements', like cock-fighting!

There was very little flax grown in the parish. Agents of cotton and linen mills in Belfast went round most of the cottages and distributed either linen or cotton yarn, which was then made into a web. When the web was collected, the cottier was paid for his labour. Cotton was the more usual fabric, since it was more robust and easier to work than linen. Most of the work was done by children and was paid a very cheap rate. For those few who did produce cloth or yarn on their own account, or who wanted to sell farm produce, the only option was to walk to one of the local markets at Coagh, Moneymore, Magherafelt or Cookstown.

The biggest farms in the parish were about ten acres, with many as small as three. The fields were small and irregular, surrounded by earthen banks. Farmyard manure was the main fertiliser, with a little lime if the farmer could afford it. Where labourers were employed, their wage was 1*s* per day in summer, reduced to 10*d* in the shorter days of winter. What carts there were in the district were small, and great use was made of wheel-less slide cars or slipes. Anything bigger would not have suited the narrow lanes and soft soils of the district. Timber was such a rarity that any logs that were found in the bogs were used for building, while the stumps were cut up and used for fuel.

It is interesting to compare the observations of the local rector, Thomas Paul, written a few years earlier, in 1825. Many of his comments echo those of Lt Bailey, but he is prepared to be a little more florid in his language. He describes the beautiful serpentine winding of the river towards the lough. His house and one other, at Ballyronan, were the only gentlemen's residences in the parish. Unlike the lieutenant, he mentions the County Derry part of the parish, noting the castle at Saltersland, the only remnant of a failed settlement on the lough shore.

He found the peasantry sharp and intelligent, well mannered and well spoken in English. They supplemented their diet of potatoes with eels and pollen. Because of the low-lying nature of the countryside there was occasional fever. He was taken by the fact that there were very few marriages, but many christenings. The number of christenings was matched by the number of wakes and funerals. There were three schools in the parish, with books provided by a number of charitable agencies. Children were often kept away from school to prepare yarn for the loom, to gather potatoes or to draw home turf. Farmers did not practise crop rotation. The livestock consisted of horses together with black cattle of wretched quality. Few farmers kept sheep. The agents who collected the webs of linen and cotton transported them to Belfast by water from the harbour at Ballyronan.

An interesting contrast is the parish of Kildress, about eight miles upstream from Cookstown, which Lt Bailey surveyed in 1833. This locality he describes as mountainous, with the northern half in particular having a very bleak and wild appearance. There was little cultivation in much of the district, with huge boulders protruding from heather for more than half of its area. There were no towns or villages, the largest group of houses being at Orritor, a few miles from Cookstown. The only good arable ground was in the south-east, where some wheat was grown. In more mountainous areas people scratched a living with 'indifferent crops of oats and potatoes'. Although the smallest farms were about the same size as those in Ballinderry (indicating that three acres was the minimum required to feed a family), some of the larger farms were up to twenty acres. These larger farms were usually in the higher areas and generally had a portion of unreclaimed land. With newly let land, rent was deferred for three years to allow for the expense of bringing this land into cultivation and of building a stone house; a lease of twenty-one years began from this time. Most of the cottages in the parish were stone and lime. In the lower ground they were clean and surrounded by shelter belts of trees, though this was impractical on the windswept higher slopes.

Most of those living in the mountain areas were Catholics, who still spoke Irish. There were two Catholic chapels, one at Dunamore and the other at Killeenan, as well as the Established parish church and a Presbyterian meeting house. Killeenan chapel was said to be the oldest, built over 150 years previously. It was in a poor state of repair, but services were still held in it. Dunamore chapel had been built only a few years previously, in 1828, at a cost of £60. It could hold 260 people and was usually full when Mass was being said. Before this chapel was built, Mass had been said in a ruined chapel in Roisbrack. The Church of Ireland parish church was also relatively new. It had been built in 1818 at a cost of £1,600. The average attendance on a Sunday was 350, but there was room for about 50 more. The Presbyterian meeting house had been built in the same year as Dunamore chapel, but at greater expense, costing something under £500. It could hold 240 worshippers. The parish was not thickly populated.

There were only two schools in the parish. At Killeenan a school had been operating since 1828. The Catholic master taught, in 1833, four Protestants and sixty-two Catholics. At the other school, in Tamlaght, another Catholic master taught nineteen Protestants and thirty-one Catholics. The sole support that the masters received was 1d per pupil per week.

Most farmers grew oats, potatoes and flax, although in the few areas of good land wheat was also grown. Flax was only grown in small quantities. All holdings had bog attached, and the tradition was for farmers to take their excess turf to market in Cookstown, where they would exchange it for lime to fertilise their land. Most agricultural produce was sold at Cookstown Market, but there were also fairs in Gortin twice a year and a monthly one in Tullynacross, where livestock could be sold. Most farmers got their main income from spinning and weaving, with the linen being sold in Cookstown or Moneymore. One other source of income here was the quarry industry. There were several limestone quarries, though some of these were already worked out. There were also quarries where freestone was obtained for building. There were suggestions that a new road should be made, connecting Cookstown with Omagh. The most obvious natural feature of the district was the Ballinderry River, which ran through the middle of it. This stretch of river often overflowed its banks in winter, bringing natural fertiliser to the water meadows. In the townland of Corkhill – where Wellbrook Beetling Mill is located – there were four water-powered mills.

One feature of the parish was the number of small lakes. The biggest of these was Camlough, the source of the Ballinderry River, at fourteen acres. Almost as big was Loughbracken, but many of the lakes were not much more than pools. They were of little use to farmers because they were in the middle of bogs and their edges were nearly always marshy, so cattle had difficulty drinking from them. They could not even be used for soaking flax, since they were too deep.

The Ballinderry at Wellbrook.

The picture that is painted by these Ordnance Survey memoirs, and by the earlier report of the Drapers' Company, is of a countryside of small farms whose inhabitants are poor and living near the margins, but whose security of tenure means that they are in a position to work themselves out of poverty. There are dangers. For one thing, their main source of income, producing webs of linen, is under threat from increasing industrial production of fabrics. For another, it is only the success of the potato crop (a source of food which, at the time, allowed a large amount of food to be produced in a small area of well-manured ground) that allowed the farmer the time to work at his loom. If circumstances changed either of these factors not only their livelihoods would be threatened, but their lives.

❧ 5 ❧

HUNGER AND AFTER

James Mullin was born in 1846, the only son of a Cookstown man and his wife. His father died when he was still a baby and his mother reared him on her own. She was a good mother to him, with a stout heart and strong hands; a woman prepared to face up to the realities of life. In the summer she worked for local farmers, and was highly regarded by them because of her strength and her ability to take charge of a gang. In winter she switched to spinning linen thread for the local weaving factory. By this time looms had mostly disappeared from cottages. Her pay for a long summer's day was between 6*d* and 8*d*, little more than half what a man had been earning thirty years before. Her work in winter would have earned less than that.

They lived in a house that had been rebuilt on the site of a tumbledown cabin and the rent was 50*s* a year. During his father's lifetime the rent had neither been asked for nor paid, but a new landowner discovered this and threatened his mother with eviction if she did not pay her arrears. She did this by half-yearly instalments. In this she was helped by the fact that hers was a two-room house. She and James were able to occupy one room and to sublet the other to a family. In the garden was a pigsty, which she sublet to yet another family. This accommodation was less than salubrious, because it lacked window and chimney, so they made a hole in the roof for the smoke and left the door open for the light. Whenever possible, this family cooked and ate outside. The rest of the garden was used by James's mother to grow enough potatoes to see them through the winter.

As a very young child, he had no direct memory of the famine. What he did remember was the day-to-day hunger that continued even when the worst was over. He remembered his mother spreading his porridge as thinly as possible over his plate to make him think that he had more food than he was actually getting. When he complained, he was told to say a prayer over his food and it would then satisfy him. It didn't work. Even after the famine, the staple food was potatoes. People ate them at every meal, with buttermilk and a little salt to add flavour. The potatoes were boiled in their jackets in a black pot over the fire. When they were cooked they were turned out into a basket. Round this the diners sat on three-legged stools. Each would lift a potato from the pile, peel it with his nails, and then eat it like a hot apple, washing down each bite with a mouthful of buttermilk. There were few variations on this fare. Nettles were gathered in the spring and made into broth with a little barley, some lard or dripping if it could be got and, very rarely, an oatmeal dumpling. On very rare occasions there would be enough money to buy a sheep's head at the Saturday market and this, too, would be added to the mixture.

By listening to his mother as he grew older, he realised that his part of Tyrone had missed the worst of the famine, and that his family and neighbours had not suffered as those in the south and west had done. Nevertheless, as early as September 1845, there were signs of blight in fields of potatoes as near as Donaghmore. In one night the tops had rotted, and there were signs of rot in the tubers as well. Tyrone got off lightly that year, as did Fermanagh and Derry. These three counties had the lowest incidence of blight in the entire island. Even where blight had struck, it was possible to find some healthy tubers. Matters were helped by the fact that there was an excellent oat harvest that year, which offered more porridge and oatcake where there were fewer potatoes.

The next summer was crueller. Luxuriant growth in July promised a good crop, but the tops turned black and withered in August, and there were even fewer sound tubers than the previous year. The Prime Minister, Peel, was so alarmed that he repealed the Corn Laws, which had protected the income of the landed gentry for decades. It was a futile gesture. There was no flow of cheap grain into Ireland, and Peel was rapidly deposed as Prime Minister. Meanwhile, back in Ireland, the country entered the coldest, longest winter in living memory. The new Government had decreed that the poor and destitute would only be fed if they worked for it. A series of public work schemes were put in place. In Tyrone overall, 11,500 were employed on these schemes. A return of snow in February meant that 'the weaker and worse clad ... were not able to endure it' and when the snow reached 3ft deep around Omagh, the relief work had to be suspended. Even when it was possible for work to be done, the rates of pay were scandalously low. This was because the Government insisted that those working on relief schemes should be paid 2d per day less than the usual local rate. Men were paid for digging drains at 4d per perch, which was roughly 5m. Given the nature of the ground and the fact that large stones had to be removed continually from the line of the drain, it was almost impossible to earn enough to feed a family. As they weakened with hunger, the men were able to earn less and less. If bad weather stopped work, they were put on half pay breaking stones. Even so, in most areas there were more applicants than there were positions.

As well as providing employment, local relief committees were expected to provide food for sale. They were expected to fund this from locally raised subscriptions. There were detailed instructions as to how this was to be managed and, if these instructions were followed, a government grant was added to the funds. They could only sell the food in small quantities, and only to those who had no other way of obtaining food. The food had to be sold at the local market price, though there was a concession that allowed the committee to discount food or to provide money to those who could not pay – but only if the local workhouse was full. Most local committees did distribute food and funds without reference to the population of the workhouse. Some committees found that it would be cheaper to give away food than to embark on some of the relief schemes proposed. Anyway, a literal adherence to the instructions was impractical in the circumstances of east Tyrone. If meal was sold at cost price, then the fund would have the same amount at the end of the year as it had at the beginning. This was not what the subscribers wanted.

At this stage the workhouses in the area could cope with those who were absolutely destitute. The people who needed help were those with large families who might be working part-time but could not afford to buy food at the inflated prices that now prevailed. Farm labourers often worked for only a few days at a time, while weavers had little to do during the ongoing depression in the linen industry. They might only earn half a crown per week, which would hardly be enough to provide a single meal per day for a family. Most committees wanted to supply meal at slightly over 1d per pound. In order to prevent someone buying more than needed and reselling the excess, each family was limited to 2½lb a week for each member. They would only sell to those who had not cows, corn or any other means of support.

Tyrone had one of the lowest rates of destitution in Ireland. Cookstown Union, that first full year of famine, provided food, not always free, to 16 per cent of its population. To support the work, Famine Relief Committees were set up at Desertcreat, Ballyclog and Ardboe. In Cookstown, on 2 November 1846, magistrates and local gentry met in what was known as an extraordinary presentment session. The good folk met in the courthouse. Outside, in spite of atrocious weather, a huge crowd had gathered. Possibly in a desire for shelter, the crowd pushed open the doors and invaded the meeting. Col. Stewart of Killymoon calmed the situation, saying that the meeting was being held for the benefit of these people and that he would try to ensure that there would be work they could do close to home. The crowd began to get bored as the magistrates went into discussion mode and the arguments began to get long-winded. They demanded that they should have a spokesman and be able to contribute to the debate. All thought of debate disappeared when a taxpayer from Drumanny said that there was not much destitution in his part of the county. Col. Stewart was forced to close the meeting and ask the crowd to disperse. The latter blocked the door and announced that no one would be allowed to leave until something was done to alleviate the conditions of the poor and hungry. Some of the magistrates made their way out and home without any trouble, but one gentleman was pushed back on the stairs. Indignant at this violation of his person, he called loudly for the police to arrest someone. In an instant there was a fight caused, a newspaper reported, by those labouring classes that the meeting was trying to help, and carried out for the sheer 'love of licentious riot'.

By St Stephen's Day that year Cookstown and Dungannon Workhouses were full. Sleeping galleries were built around the large common rooms, while in Dungannon wooden sheds were built and houses rented in the town. In spite of these efforts, Cookstown Workhouse was declared dangerously overcrowded a month later, when only seven paupers out of eighty-nine applicants were accepted. Realising that the rejected paupers had nowhere else to go, the Cookstown guardians asked permission to give a little food to anyone they had to turn away. The Poor Law Commissioners thought that this was far too generous and vetoed the proposal. By this time, Cookstown was only able to collect two-thirds of its rate.

There is one way in which the relief works around Cookstown and Dungannon differed from those undertaken in other parts of the county. In most areas roads were the main theme; amenities which were for the general good. In north-east Tyrone all of the work decided on took the form of drainage schemes. Landlords here believed that if they had to pay for work to be done, then the work should bring them some benefit. The workers seem to have been grateful for anything. The Board of Works Inspecting Officer for Tyrone found that the work was going on well, the country was quiet and the people were orderly and well behaved. This was in spite of the fact that there was a great deal more destitution in the county than the gentleman from Drumanny was prepared to admit.

At least some of the credit for this might be attributed to the work of the relief committees, one would think. Not all relief committees seem to have been equally dedicated to their charitable labours. In October 1846, when it was obvious that the crop had failed, each county lieutenant was asked to divide his county into relief districts and to nominate local committees. In Tyrone, the first committee that Lord Charlemont appointed was that of Cookstown, and he went on to appoint many more, based on petty sessions districts. Although

Cookstown was the first to be appointed, there is no record of any correspondence between Cookstown Relief Committee and the Relief Commission in Dublin. On the other hand, we know that committees in Stewartstown and Ardboe were operational by December, followed by one in Pomeroy early in the new year. The rector of Desertcreat complained that the Cookstown Committee limited itself to picking names for the Public Works Schemes. Other evidence indicates that the Cookstown Committee did not even attempt to raise a relief fund, in spite of a direct instruction from the Government to do so. Any funds raised seem to have been collected privately, and the rector complained that they were spent to the benefit of, and within, individual estates. This hotchpotch mixture of official and local relief committees created such an administrative nightmare that, as the long winter of 1846/47 continued, the Government lost faith in the system. There was a new Temporary Relief Act, passed in February 1847, which was designed to allow the Poor Laws to cater for famine as well as the usual destitution. In effect this meant that the Government was prepared to allow help to be given outside the workhouses, to be known as outdoor relief. The public work schemes were run down.

Just about the time that the Temporary Relief Act was becoming law, there were signs that things were rapidly deteriorating in Tyrone. In Coalisland the fund could not hold out as distress was increasing daily, with families now starving who would never have been expected to reach such dire extremes. In Ardboe the relief committee was supporting 190 families, but there were 300 more who were in as bad a position, but who had a few acres and thus did not qualify for relief. Around Pomeroy 'much distress is now prevailing'. The poor in this area no longer had any money for food, be the price ever so cheap.

The new system was soon in operation. In most areas outdoor relief took the form of soup kitchens, though that was perhaps a misnomer. People formed into orderly queues, each with some sort of container, but what they got was a stirabout made from Indian corn, with some rice to thicken it if any was available. By July over three million people were being fed every day. This prevented many thousands from dying of hunger, but there were other threats to existence. Where not enough care was taken in the preparation of the food, people contracted dysentery. Even where care was taken, the diet provided lacked Vitamin C, and many people developed scurvy. The unhygienic conditions in which they lived, combined with their weakened condition, made them particularly vulnerable to typhus, which they called famine fever. Because people tried to move from areas where there was nothing to areas where the famine was not so bad, they succeeded in spreading typhus throughout Ulster. The disease was passed on by lice, so people who gave the refugees shelter made themselves vulnerable. James Mullin remembered the fear of fever in Cookstown.

A hoverfly on a dog rose.

After the terrible winter, the summer of 1847 was a fine one, and the grain harvest was a bumper one. The same sun that ripened the grain kept the blight at bay; the problem was that hunger had driven most people to eat their seed potatoes, so there was a very small acreage planted that year. The poor still had nothing to eat, but the Government now closed the soup kitchens in almost every district. According to them, the famine was officially over. The burden of relief was passed back to the Poor Law Guardians and to the landlords who financed them. Many of these landlords had already spent a fortune in supplementing government initiatives, and some of them were bankrupt. Others simply defaulted on their payments. The standard of care in some workhouses, already low, fell even further as they became even more overcrowded. In one Fermanagh establishment, 432 inmates died in one year, 20 per cent of the admissions. In Ballyshannon the sewers were overwhelmed. In Cavan the workhouse was bankrupt, because the estate of the principal landlord was in chancery and there were no resident gentry. Granted these were in the harder hit west of the province, but even in the land around Lough Neagh a significant number of people were suffering hardship. Although manufacturers in England were sending yarn to places like Castledawson to be spun into cloth, many weavers had been forced to sell their looms in order to buy food, and were unable to take advantage.

An important clause in the 1847 Act was that relief could not be given to anyone who rented or owned more than a quarter of an acre. Some families died because the father was determined not to give up his holding. In tens of thousands of cases the man bowed to the inevitable, and gave up his land. Often, this meant giving up his home as well. That winter was bitterly cold; it was not a time to be without shelter. Heavy snow fell in February 1848, the month that the Irish saw as the first month of spring. From somewhere the belief spread that the hard frost would kill the blight in the ground. Cottiers and small farmers felt confident enough to go to any lengths to get seed potatoes. Since there was a limited supply of these, some walked twenty miles for a few stones of seed and paid as much as 10d per stone when they could get them. In the meantime the hunger of spring, that cruellest of seasons, when the stores of winter are gone and the first fruits have not yet arrived, drove even more people into the workhouses. Crowded together in unhygienic conditions, the poor died in droves. As the Poor Law income diminished, there was no money for medical provisions, and too little to buy adequate food. During the year the regulation that said that able-bodied individuals could not be fed unless they were signed into the workhouse – where they would soon cease to be able bodied – was eased a little. No extra funds were provided; it still had to be paid for by the rates. It made little difference, however, and there was no large-scale change to outdoor relief. Where it was provided, it was often funded by private charities. This is not to say that all landlords gave generously. Many begrudged the cess they had to pay, while in some areas bye-laws were passed to forbid people from giving handouts to all vagrants. There was a general outcry when it was announced that there was to be a levy on all Irish Unions to help out the poorest districts in the south and west of the country.

The workhouses staggered on. They had more than a quarter of a million inmates in June of 1850 and again in June 1851. By this time one million Irish had died of hunger and disease, and that does not include those who died after they had emigrated. Another million had fled the island, going to Great Britain or to the New World. A haemorrhage had started that would last for one hundred years. Worse, the begrudging attitude of the Government towards providing relief had coloured Irish perceptions of England and the English in a way that has persisted even longer than that. Some modern Irish nationalists see the actions of the British Government as giving substance to the comments of Thomas Carlyle. He said, 'Ireland is like a half-starved rat that crosses the path of an elephant. What must the elephant do? Squelch it – by heavens – squelch it.'

In fact, the Government provided less than half of the expenditure on famine relief. Much of this consisted in cancelling workhouse debts in 1853, when it was all over. They laid out about £7 million altogether, over a period of seven years. This sum pales significantly when compared to the United Kingdom's tax revenues over the same period, which was about £370 million. The Government had no difficulty in finding £69 million to fight the totally unnecessary Crimean War. It was a salutary reminder that the United Kingdom was not ruled by representatives of the people but by representatives of the landed classes. It is important also to remember that, even during the worst of the famine, Irish landowners, many of whom lived permanently in England, were able to collect about 75 per cent of their rents.

The tragedy of the Great Famine was bad enough, but even as its worst effects started to ease it was replaced by another plague, the plague of sectarianism. The killings at Dolly's Brae in County Down had taken place while famine fever was still rampant. Although Presbyterians had suffered with Catholics under the penal laws, they had a frank distrust of any system that depended on the power of individual bishops. In the early years of the nineteenth century, there had been a shift in attitudes among those people who were members of the Established Church, the Church of Ireland. They grew more evangelical in nature, and closer to the world view of Presbyterians. From about 1820 on, there developed a simple two-way split in the population of Ulster: Protestant and Catholic. There had been bigotry before that, as illustrated by the Orange Order and the Ribbonmen. It had expressed itself in the hunger for land, as if the soil of Ulster had been consecrated to one faith or another. Now Protestants became wary not only of individual Catholics who might have designs on their land, but of an increasingly powerful Church organisation which seemed to be keen on demonstrating its new freedoms. Less than one hundred years after Oliver Plunkett, Catholic Archbishop of Armagh, had suffered an appalling death simply for being archbishop, an Archbishop of Armagh was living openly in Drogheda, where a Catholic business class had developed that was wealthy enough to sustain him and to build schools and churches. The Catholic archdiocese stretched from Toome in the north all the way south to Drogheda and the Boyne. The Catholic population was concentrated in two major areas: Louth and South Armagh on one hand and Tyrone and South Derry on the other.

We have already seen that in the first half of the nineteenth century the Catholics of the Ballinderry Valley were for the most part too poor to build chapels that were in any way triumphalist; at Derrychrin they were still saying Mass at a Mass rock. This was also true in Ardboe. Even where chapels had been built, it was at moderate cost. In Stewartstown a chapel had been built in 1797, but it had no seating. The original building had been so poorly built that it had to be repaired in 1807. It was rebuilt completely in the 1840s as part of a church-building programme. Work had to be stopped through the famine years, but was started again as soon as things got back to normal.

Glacial Erratic near Churchtown.

Most parishes in Tyrone were large enough to need a curate as well as a parish priest, and by 1836 Cookstown had two curates. With grants from the Government, Maynooth College had been expanded in the 1840s and was now producing many more priests. At the same time there was a great increase in the number of nuns and Christian Brothers. Ironically, while provision for Catholics was being improved, the number of Catholics in Tyrone, and in Armagh Archdiocese altogether, went into serious decline. It has been calculated that the Catholic population in the archdiocese dropped by 70,000 in the second half of the century. The largest proportion of this was in Tyrone.

Another factor was the actual attendance at Church services. A commission had been established in 1834 to try to establish statistically the demography of Ireland. It found that only 40 per cent of the Catholics in Cookstown Parish attended Sunday Mass. This might seem an alarming figure, but there were reasons for it. There is a long list of reasons that excused people the obligation to attend Mass on Sundays. Apart from age and health, there was the distance from the church and whether a person had proper clothing. To overcome this problem, a parish would have held a Mass, known as a station Mass, in each townland in turn. There would usually be one a week, and people would attend the stations in each of the neighbouring townlands. One indication that Catholics were anxious to practise their faith is the number of children who were presented each year for Confirmation. In Cookstown, these are completely out of kilter with the 40 per cent attendance rate on Sundays.

If even in the reasonably unified Catholic Church we can find what appear to be anomalies, think how many more questions there will be to answer when we look at Protestantism during the same period. Just because most Protestants might be seen as a unity in political terms – although that is true no more and may never have been true – there is within the Protestant community a multiplicity of approaches towards spirituality and worship. Given the input of determined elders or members of select vestries, this is almost bound to be so, even in the dominant Presbyterian and Established (Church of Ireland) Church. In the middle of the nineteenth century Protestants accounted for 44 per cent of the population of Tyrone. Almost half of these worshipped at the Church of Ireland, slightly fewer were Presbyterian. Less than 2 per cent of the population were Methodists, while Independents, Baptists, Brethren, Quakers and Moravians when added together totalled only 1 in 200 of the population. An individual's membership of any congregation was neither unconditional nor necessarily permanent. It could be determined by the power of a landlord, the popularity of a preacher or simply the fact of getting married. Lord Castlestewart subsidised Orritor Presbyterian congregation and granted them land on which to build a church and this sort of support helped several of the smaller denominations to establish themselves.

The position of the Church of Ireland was different from all the other denominations. Since it was the Established Church, the state in prayer, it had a number of civic responsibilities as well as catering for the spiritual and pastoral needs of its parishioners. It was traditionally the Church of Ireland which was responsible for levying local rates for many of the functions nowadays carried out by local authorities, as well as looking after Church expenditure. The vestry was responsible for maintaining the roads in the parish, for example. The care of the destitute was its main concern, however. It had to licence local beggars, who were nominated by two respectable parishioners. It provided coffins for paupers. Theoretically it was also supposed to care for foundlings. Desertcreat Parish tried to get out of this expense by declaring in 1750 that the owner of a house was responsible for rearing any child born in the house or found on the doorstep. Nearly all parishes simply paid a local couple to care for abandoned children, or sent them to the foundling hospital in Dublin.

This social care was not limited to members of the Church of Ireland. Cappagh Parish donated money towards the building of a Catholic chapel in 1801, and Orritor Parish made a £50 contribution towards the building of a Presbyterian meeting house. In spite of this, the payment of tithes was soundly resented by those who were not part of the Church of Ireland community. Presbyterians and Catholics both disliked the idea that they were paying towards the upkeep of another denomination's clergyman. When, however, the Government was minded to disestablish the Church of Ireland, Presbyterians closed ranks with their Episcopalian brethren against what they saw as a Catholic attack on Protestant privilege.

Most Presbyterian ministers were the sons of ministers, or of the small merchant class, or of farmers. They lacked the social elevation of most Church of Ireland clergy, but they were all educated to university standard. The fact that they were of the same social level as most of their congregation meant that the concerns of that congregation, no matter how local, were an important priority in the meeting house. Although they received the *Regium Donum* they were mainly dependent on the stipend that they collected from their congregation. This was supposed to have been agreed before the minister's installation but there were often problems in raising the stipend; its payment was a nice way of letting the minister know what his people thought of him. Since many of the Presbyterian congregation were tenants of small farms, the minister's income could also be curtailed during times of agricultural depression. During the famine, whole areas were excused stipends. After that crisis, the average stipend in Tyrone was about £55 a year.

One remarkable factor was the attachment between a Presbyterian minister and his flock. They stuck together through thick and thin, and many ministers served forty or even fifty years in the one meeting house. When a Cookstown Presbyterian church celebrated its centenary in 1935, there had only been two ministers in its history. This sense of continuity was reinforced by the fact that sons or sons-in-law might take over from a retiring minister.

This intimate, democratic relationship, and the notion that the session was the employer of the minister, meant that a Presbyterian clergyman was always under scrutiny and if he failed to set an appropriate model of moral and religious behaviour he was considered to be in breach of contract. One minister was sacked for immoral behaviour, while another had to answer complaints that he had a number of sermons which he preached in the same order year after year, simply going back to the first when the last was finished. On the other hand, five members of the Moneymore congregation complained that their minister's preaching was far too intellectual, and that he neglected his pastoral duties. Sometimes a congregation might be split, as again happened in Moneymore. Half of the congregation complained that their minister was a ranter, attacking other denominations rather than encouraging Christian behaviour in his own. The disgruntled members seceded, setting up a second Moneymore Presbyterian church. This was a two-way system, however, and Presbyterian ministers took seriously their task of supervising the morality of their flocks. One rebuked a member of the congregation for selling bad butter at Carland in 1876.

Methodist ministers were regularly moved at their annual conference. Although this meant that they were seeing new congregations at fairly short intervals, the fact that they usually boarded with those on the circuit wealthy enough to look after them helped them too to a state of intimacy that resembled that of the Presbyterians. Since not all circuits had wealthy members, the minister often, in bad weather, had to sleep in damp beds or remain in wet clothes. Although the Methodist minister might have to travel great distances – one near Aughnacloy was estimated to have to ride twenty-five miles every Sunday – even opponents recognised that the system gave them easy access to the hearts of their flock. In fact, there were complaints that the relationship between some Methodist ministers and their female followers was friendlier than it should be.

It is obvious from all this that there were great differences among Protestants in the middle of the nineteenth century. There was one difference more fundamental than all the others: the difference between the rulers and the ruled. Although more men, both Protestant and Catholic, were entitled to vote, property qualifications ensured that these voters were still in a minority. Politics was for the Big House, and the tradition that the landlord's nominee was duly elected persisted long after the famine. In 1868, Tyrone was represented by members of two aristocratic families. T. Lowry Corry was an uncle of the Earl of Belmore; Lord Claud Hamilton was a brother of the Duke of Abercorn. Both had served a long time and, in the general election of that year, they were returned unopposed. Things seemed as they always were, and continued so until 1873, when Lowry Corry died and it was necessary to have a byeelection. Since the famine, the Orange Order had been growing in terms of membership and of popular support. In the countryside, the Order represented the interests of the class of people that would be called yeomen in England. Since it was not at all obvious that the interests of the landlord class coincided with those of tenant farmers, it seems reasonable that the Grand Orange Lodge of Tyrone, meeting in Killyman, should decide to nominate Ellison Macartney, a barrister who lived near Clogher, as a candidate in the election. The alarm sounded in the houses of the great landlords.

The great men chose the brother of the dead MP, H.W. Lowry Corry, as their candidate. He did well in the matter of flattering tenant sensibilities, but there was little that was solid in what he had to offer. Macartney, on the other hand, promised to pursue specific changes in the 1870 Land Act that would benefit tenant farmers; he was not above adjusting his speech to suit his audience. It was obviously going to be a straight contest between landlord gentry and tenant farmers. Even those landlords who were also members of the Orange Order were alarmed and they repudiated the upstart candidate. There began a campaign of vilification that was directed not simply at Macartney but at the Order itself. Macartney was described as the candidate of the 'Fenian Orange party'. More realistically, some landlords believed that the Orangemen were throwing stones in a pond without knowing what monster slept in the depths. It could be that the disturbance would be enough to waken a Home Rule candidate.

In the event, Macartney lost by thirty-six votes. It was obvious to the gentry that they were losing their power. Nomination by an earl or a duke no longer guaranteed election. It would be necessary to trim to the wind so that they did not lose their influence altogether. They had very little time to get their act together because there would be a general election within a year. In Tyrone, it was almost certain that Macartney would be elected, leaving only one seat for the landlords. It seemed obvious that one of the sitting MPs should retire rather than suffer a humiliating defeat. Even the Prime Minister, Disraeli, got involved. He suggested that Lowry Corry should stand down, since he was the junior in terms of political experience. Lowry Corry would have none of it. He had already laid out a large amount of money; he calculated that he had spent at least £100 a day for twenty-three days. It also seems that he distrusted Claud Hamilton.

This time all three candidates spoke about the land issue, but Macartney was by far the best politician and he was able to collect Catholic votes as well as Orange ones. He came a clear 1,500 votes ahead of Lowry Corry, with Hamilton a further 400 votes behind. Claud Hamilton's anger at this, which simmered for years, had the effect of splitting the Abercorn–Belmore monolith which had controlled Tyrone politics for decades. It happened because these were hard times, with bad harvests. Even though some landlords gave help unstintingly, once again there was unemployment, lack of fuel, and, especially in the upland areas, only twenty years after the famine, there was real hunger.

By 1880 the landlords had decided that the policies followed by Macartney were conservative enough to be supported by them. As a result, they chose only one candidate for the general election of that year; they returned to the tried and tested Claud Hamilton. After all, having a duke as a sponsor took precedence over being sponsored by a mere earl. Lowry Corry took early retirement from politics. A new element came into the equation when the Liberals, for the first time in decades, put up a candidate for Tyrone, E.C. Litton. Litton aligned himself with those seeking land reform. He made it clear that he believed that farmers should own the land they worked. In a constituency of small farmers, he could be sure of a good showing. Sure enough, he was elected, and the losing candidate was once more Claud Hamilton, who seemed destined to be always the bridesmaid.

At that time members of Parliament were paid neither salary nor expenses, and a sitting member needed a substantial private income in order to be able to carry out the job. The offer of well-paid employment was often enough to tempt a less well-off individual away from the rigours of Westminster. This was so in

Litton's case; he was appointed as a Land Court Commissioner and resigned his seat. The bye-election was contested by a Conservative – not Lord Claud – and a Liberal. A third contestant was a Unitarian minister who was a supporter of the Land League. Although the reverend gentleman came a very distant third, and the Liberal was elected with the help of Catholic votes, his presence was a forerunner of a very different type of politics in Ulster which continued for the next hundred years. In spite of the fact that priests had encouraged Catholics to vote for the Liberal candidate, Dickson, almost half of Catholic votes went to the Land League candidate, Revd Harold Rylett.

At the heart of the change was land. Most of Ireland laboured under a grossly unfair system of land ownership. A tenant had no rights. He could be evicted or the rent could be raised at the whim of the landlord. The majority of landlords lived in England and rarely if ever visited their property, which was managed by an agent. By the second half of the nineteenth century, even Parliamentarians at Westminster recognised that there was a need for reform. In 1879 a National Land League was formed, demanding protection for tenant farmers. This would normally have been grist to the mill of Presbyterian farmers who, radical by tradition, distrusted landlords. Two things stopped them from joining in the fight. One was a practical matter. Tenant farmers in Ulster already had better conditions than their southern equivalents. Their lease was subject to a thing called Ulster Custom. This allowed the tenant security in his home as long as he paid his rent. He also had the right to transfer the remainder of his lease to any other tenant, although the landlord had the right to veto an individual of whom he did not approve. The original tenant also had the right to demand payment from the newcomer for any improvements that he had made to the farm. In all this, the landlord remained passive. This Ulster Custom had been given legal status by the Land Act of 1870. In a sense, then, the Ulster farmer already had the rights being sought by the Land League.

The second reason, although less practical, was no less important. The president of the Land League was Charles Stewart Parnell, and he had linked land reform with the much more contentious issue of Home Rule. While Protestant farmers at this stage had little animosity towards their Catholic neighbours – a farming community cannot thrive without mutual help – they did not trust Catholic priests and many actively feared the Pope in Rome. Some of this was a residue of folk memories of Irish rebellions in the past, but it was leavened by an interpretation of the Apocalypse of St John which equated the Pope and Rome with the Beast and with Babylon. The only thing that protected the Protestants of Ireland from domination by the Pope was the Union of Great Britain and Ireland, which guaranteed a Protestant majority in any legislative body. That protection would be removed if the electorate was limited to

Ireland, where any Parliament would be overwhelmingly Catholic. Given what they saw as the assertive nature of the Catholic priests, it seemed inevitable that Home Rule would become Rome Rule.

It was the Orange Order that led the attack against the Land League. Lodges that supported land reform were expelled from the organisation. The landlords also attempted to regroup. Through the Conservatives they formed the Tyrone Protestant Constitutional Association, whose aim it was to ensure that every Conservative supporter was on the electoral register. Matters went beyond this in the border counties of Monaghan and Fermanagh when, in 1883, a feared invasion of Ulster by Parnell's ideas was met with a series of violent incidents. There was trouble in Tyrone as well. James Mullin had an uncle by marriage who was a butcher in Dungannon. There was in the neighbourhood of Cookstown a group of Protestants who called themselves the Killymoon Wreckers, from their self-imposed task of wrecking, in the middle of the night, houses belonging to Catholics. On one occasion they decided to visit Dungannon and, accordingly marched round that town to demonstrate their strength. When they came to Shambles Street they were met by a row of butchers, all Catholic, and all carrying their cleavers. The Wreckers halted, nonplussed for a moment, but one of their number decided that the butchers were bluffing. As soon as the unfortunate man entered the street James's uncle stepped forward and split open his skull with his cleaver. Though he was found guilty of manslaughter and served two years in jail, he was treated with great circumspection by Protestant and Catholic for the rest of his life.

The most famous of the organisations that were committed to revolutionary violence in the second half of the nineteenth century was the group known as the Fenians. As James Mullin reports, it proved a magnet for many young men who carried a romantic ideal of an Ireland independent of English control. They had more enthusiasm than military sense, and never questioned their ability, more or less unarmed, to face the might of the British army. In the meantime, they drilled in the evenings and spent occasional Sundays conducting field days in the Sperrins. The Fenians were opposed by the local Catholic clergy, who were claiming pre-eminence in the Catholic community. Since the would-be rebels felt the need to attend Mass before going off for their day in the hills, they were an easy target for a diatribe from the priest, who often concentrated on their future dwelling-place in hell. The Fenians replied by calling the priests 'English beefeaters', since most of them had been sustained in their student days at Maynooth by an English scholarship.

As far as mid-Ulster was concerned, the whole thing was a storm in a teacup. The volunteers were told to stand by for action within two weeks, but nothing happened. A couple of members were arrested, to be detained without charge.

James himself was mortified that he was not important enough to be taken by the police. It could be said that the whole movement fizzled out, but for one thing. The Land League was its offspring.

The Land League brought a new element to Catholic voters in Tyrone. Before this, with the encouragement of their priests, Catholics had tended to vote alongside most Presbyterians in support of the Liberal candidate. Now Parnell's Irish National League began to organise in Tyrone, with one of the first branches being established in Pomeroy in 1883. The vocal and physical opposition which had already taken place in Monaghan and Fermanagh was now repeated in Tyrone. Meetings of the National League were met by counter-demonstrations by the Orange Order. These counter-demonstrations were often led by Protestant gentry and clergymen, with the result that they were sometimes supported by the forces of the crown. In Dungannon a combination of Orangemen and soldiers kept National League members from entering the Market Square. In Dromore, at the other end of the county, police took the other side, and dispersed an Orange counter-demonstration with a bayonet charge. A boy of eighteen was killed in the Dromore incident, but it was the example of official support for Orangemen that Catholics noted and by 1885 the Catholic voters were solidly behind the Land League.

Branches were set up around the county and volunteers took great pains in ensuring the registration of all voters who would support the Home Rule Party. They were given extra help by Catholics who had once been Liberal activists. This was so successfully done that a nationalist won the East Tyrone seat in 1885. In fact, at this election Parnell's party won a majority of the thirty-three seats in the nine counties of Ulster. By the following year Protestants had got their act together, and unionists won North and South Tyrone, while the Home Rule Party won East and Mid-Tyrone. There was no attempt by either side to try to persuade the other; every effort was made to ensure that one's own supporters came out. Home Rule branches tended to be organised by Catholic parish and normally had the support of the clergy.

It is important to remember that not everybody had land, and there were those for whom the idea of being able to buy the land you rented was irrelevant. James Mullin was one of these. As he grew up it was simply accepted that he would be a farm labourer. Since he was obviously a bright lad, his neighbours had his future planned out for him. He would work for a large landowner, impress his employer with his intelligence, get transferred to the household staff and work his way up to become a butler. It did not work out quite this way. He had to report for work at six in the morning. Since there was not a clock in the house, James got into the habit of staying awake 'after his first sleep', as he puts it, and waiting for the horn of the linen factory to call out to its workers at five. While he was waiting he would read by the light of a paraffin lamp. At six he began his work in the fields, usually looking after the cattle. There was a break for breakfast and another in the middle of the day, but by the time James got home he was usually so tired that he went straight to bed. After two and a half years of working seven days a week, without holidays, he was moved to the farmyard, with the easier job of looking after the poultry. This state of affairs was not to last, unfortunately. On his very first day in this new job he found a quiet space where he could stretch out on the straw to read his book for a while. The farmer was too smart for him; having expected some such trick from his young labourer, he had hidden all day long in the stable so that he could keep an eye on James. The neighbours grieved that the prospect of being a butler had been lost to him forever.

When the Parnell scandal of 1890 split the Home Rule party, both sitting Tyrone nationalist MPs turned against the Chief, in line with clerical and most lay opinion. That they had chosen the popular option was shown in 1892, when a Parnellite candidate took only 123 votes in Mid-Tyrone.

Landlords were solidly behind the unionist cause. In East Tyrone the dominating personalities were J.B. Gunning Moore, the Constituency Association's president, and Lt Col. R.T.G. Lowry, its treasurer. This meant that the Parliamentary candidate was open to Presbyterian accusations that he was a landlords' pawn. The local unionist Association was small, with limited resources. Its main income came from local landowning families. The largest donor was Gunning Moore, who gave £15 in 1899. Donations of £5 or £10 were more common. The Association's straitened financial circumstances were not helped when, in 1907, the entire subscription was lost. The unionist Joint Committee had been forced to make grants of £50 to £100 each year, but the Association was still near to bankruptcy.

These difficulties seemed to have been overcome when, in 1909, A.D. Saunderson was chosen as unionist candidate. He sent a cheque for £100 as an earnest of his good will, and enthusiasm for the new candidate encouraged others to bring their contributions up to date. Saunderson met the unionist voters of Cookstown in January 1910 and was given a great welcome. During his campaign, he made frequent reference to the fact that he came from a staunch unionist family. His opponent was the sitting MP, Tom Kettle, who won by the largest majority since 1895. He had attempted to avoid the sectarian slanging match that passed for politics in most of Ireland, but had not been able to persuade any unionists to vote for him.

This may have been the reason that local landowners refused to bail out the Association, although they claimed it was because of the financial mismanagement that had caused the original problem. There was another election in 1910, when Kettle resigned and Willie Redmond took his place, which cleaned out the Cookstown coffers altogether. It was lucky that there was not another election to fight until after the Great War.

When voting in local government elections became more democratic in 1898, nationalists set about ensuring their voices were heard in local council chambers. They did gain control of Omagh urban council in 1899, but were unable to gain control of Tyrone County Council, even though nationalists formed a majority in the county. This was an important piece of propaganda during the Home Rule crisis of 1912, since Tyrone was a key county in the balance of power. It was not until 1920 that nationalists gained control of County Tyrone under what proved to be a short-lived experiment in proportional representation.

The Home Rule Party was reunited under the leadership of John Redmond in February 1900. The new party's official party organisation, the United Irish League, set up a branch in East Tyrone the following year. This did not become a popular organisation in nationalist Tyrone for a couple of reasons: there would be a very satisfactory Land Purchase Act in 1903, thus removing the UIL's reason for existence, and the local priests simply did not like it. Catholics turned more readily to the Ancient Order of Hibernians (AOH), and by 1911 it had surpassed the UIL as the main political organisation for the Catholics of East Tyrone. The AOH had as its focus the development of Catholic loyalty to the Irish Parliamentary Party (IPP). It allowed no factionism, and was powerful enough to prevent the Irish Republican Brotherhood (IRB) from developing in the county. Arthur Griffith and Sinn Féin had no more success when they tried to organise in Tyrone in 1908.

Cardinal Logue hated the AOH, resenting the way that it called itself Catholic while remaining under secular control. He claimed that people were brutalised or coerced into joining the organisation. There was no stopping the AOH, however, and even respectable MPs, like East Tyrone's Tom Kettle, joined up.

One of the most significant developments of the period before the Great War was the passing of the Parliament Act of 1911. This meant that the House of Lords would no longer have a permanent veto if the House of Commons granted Irish Home Rule. In the euphoria that a seemingly golden future cast over Irish nationalists, most failed to notice the preparations being made by their unionist neighbours. The latter first formed political clubs, but these quickly developed into the Ulster Volunteer Force, or UVF. It was only as 1913 progressed, and the UVF demonstrated itself to be a credible force, that some local nationalists began to realise that unionists in Tyrone would not allow themselves to go gently into a Home Rule Ireland. At the same time nationalists could not believe that Tyrone, with 55 per cent of its population Catholic and nationalist, could be forced to join a political entity separated from the rest of Ireland.

When the Irish Volunteers were formed late in 1913 they found little support in Tyrone. This was largely because local nationalists thought that such an organisation was simply playing the unionist game their way. In that first year the only branches of the Volunteers formed in the county were in Carrickmore and Clogher. That changed when news arrived of the UVF gunrunning to Larne. Both the AOH and the UIL played a large part in setting up new branches of the Volunteers. Many Catholic clergy sanctioned the movement, and it was obviously going to spread further. So many active young men joined the Volunteers that the Gaelic Athletic Association (GAA) suffered a crisis of membership. Tyrone was at the heart of failed talks held in Buckingham Palace to try to get out of the impasse. In the end, Asquith decided that he would allow partition of Ireland for the time being, with Tyrone to be part of the bloc excluded from Home Rule. His motto was, 'Wait and see!'

Then war was declared.

✤ 6 ✤

WAR AND PARTITION

The Great War was like a plague of Egypt, destroying husbands and sons and fathers. Women helping with the hay, women who might never have gone further than Portrush, saw clergymen walk towards them across the fields and knew that their men had died far away, near towns and rivers and on fields whose names the women might never be able to pronounce. It was easier for those whose men were officers because they were informed directly by the War Office. For wives and mothers of the rest, there was no such personal, private intimation. They had to look at the long lists of casualties published in newspapers and pasted on windows by sympathetic shopkeepers. Those women who lived in the country could not visit the town or even the shop every day and for them the unexpected visit was always a threat, always a dread. For those who could read the list as it went up it was worse, since they had to be braced to receive the worst of news while surrounded by neighbours.

Right from the start of the war local men died. Men who had served with the colours and who had remained in the army reserve had been called up straight away. Robert Falls had enlisted in 1903, when he was eighteen, and had served in the Mediterranean and in China. He always enjoyed running and had won cross-country events in Peking and a marathon in Malta. When his term of enlistment was complete, he worked for a while in Scotland, before returning to Cookstown and a job in the farmyard at Loughrey, in what was then the Ulster Dairy School. He was called back to his old regiment, the Inniskilling Fusiliers, and went to France with the British Expeditionary Force. William Nixon, one year older, was a lifelong friend of Robert's and was called up to the same battalion at the same time. They both died on the same day. At the Battle of le Cateau, on 26 August 1914, the 2nd Battalion, Inniskilling Fusiliers, had been driven back by a German attack. The unit regrouped and launched a counter-attack which regained the lost ground. It was during this counter-attack that the friends died. They were the first of many Cookstown inhabitants to die in the war.

William and Robert were both members of the Church of Ireland, but it was not only Protestants who fought or who lost their lives. John McCaffrey had the military in his blood. Three great-uncles had fought in the army. Two had died at the Battle of the Alma, in the Crimean War; another had survived the Indian Mutiny. Although he was a Catholic and a nationalist – he was a section leader in the Irish Volunteers – John enlisted in the Inniskillings very early in the war. He was transferred to a regular battalion, 2nd Royal Irish Fusiliers, in September, and sent to France. His unit was involved in the fighting around Ypres, where he was wounded. He died of his wounds on 16 November, aged only nineteen.

Other than those who, like John, were transferred to regular army battalions, most of those who volunteered in Ireland during August 1914 were assigned to the 10th (Irish) Division, one of the first 100,000 who answered Kitchener's call to arms. An infantry division in the British Army is meant to be a self-contained fighting unit. It is made up of a number of brigades, and each brigade is made up of a number of battalions. At fighting strength a battalion has about 1,000 men. In addition, a division has its own cavalry and artillery, its own pioneers to do construction work and its own transport to make sure everything is got to the right place on time. At its full wartime strength a division could number 20,000 men. Not all the soldiers of the 10th Division were Irish, and the division was never given the opportunity to fight as an entity, since different brigades were sent to different parts of their battlefield in Gallipoli, but those who volunteered for it were those who were impatient with the politics of Ireland's rival leaders, Edward Carson and John Redmond. Rather than wait to gain political advantage, they volunteered because they were distressed at what Germany was doing to neutral Belgium. The division was sent to land at Suvla Bay to try to open up the Turkish defences in order to take the pressure off the original landings. By this time Gallipoli was gaining a worse reputation for slaughter than the Western Front. In a few days 10th Division became almost a spent force, sent to attack against impregnable defensive positions, forced to defend in countryside that allowed snipers to get within a few feet without being seen. Altogether, the British lost 21,000 men and the Allies a staggering total of well over 40,000 before the campaign was brought to a close.

Most of those who enlisted from this region joined one of two divisions. Protestants and unionists tended to join the 36th (Ulster) Division as members of 9th Battalion Royal Inniskilling Fusiliers. Catholics and nationalists preferred to join 16th Division, which was almost completely Irish, but which wasn't officially permitted to use the title till much later in the war. It is probably true to say that most Northern Catholics joined the Connaught Rangers. Both divisions were sent to the Western Front in late 1915. At first they were attached to other units in order to learn the skills necessary for survival in such a hostile environment. These were supposed to be quiet sectors, but even in the quietest sector there was danger, and news was soon coming home of death and injury. The Cookstown and district members of these two divisions were lucky in that there were no fatalities in the winter of 1915/16, but there was a steady stream of bad news reaching homes in the area, concerning men in the regular battalions and others in the 10th (Irish) Division, which was now serving in Salonika.

Pressure on all fronts got worse in early 1916. Although Henderson Moore had been born in Bellaghy, he had a job in Moneymore. He had joined Moneymore Company of the Ulster Volunteers and, when war broke out, it was with them that he enlisted in 10th Inniskillings. In March his battalion was based in Thiepval Wood, a place which was to become notorious within a few months. Henderson was one of a number of men posted in saps in front of the British line. On the afternoon of 10 March the Germans, aware of movement in and around the woods, launched an artillery barrage. After a pause, they fired again, hoping to catch men out of their trenches as they helped the wounded from the first barrage. The firing went on well after dark, and did not stop till the early hours of the following morning. When it was possible to check on casualties it was found that ten men from the battalion had died, including Henderson Moore, who had been killed by shrapnel. He was buried the same morning.

The following month, it was the turn of the 16th Division to suffer casualties. John O'Neill had been born in Ardboe, one of a family of fourteen children. He found work on a farm at Ballysudden, just outside Cookstown, where he stayed during the week. On a Saturday night, after his week's work was done, he normally cycled home to spend Sunday with his family. One Saturday night early in 1915 he failed to arrive home. His mother was worried and on the Monday John's father went to the farm to make enquiries. The farmer knew nothing, and the two men went into Cookstown to see if they could discover what had happened. It turned out that the army had been recruiting in Cookstown that weekend and that John was one of a number of young men who had enlisted. He had just turned eighteen. Army life suited him. He served with 7th Inniskilling Fusiliers, which was part of 16th Division. After training he moved with his battalion to France, arriving there in February 1916.

He would have been well used to life in the trenches by the end of April of that year. On 26 April, his battalion was holding the line at Hulluch, which was part of the Loos salient. Intelligence reported that there were indications that Germans were going to launch a gas attack. One of the signs was that rats were escaping from the German trenches, trying to avoid gas that was leaking from the storage tanks. The attack began early in the morning with rifle and machine-gun fire, followed by shelling from German artillery. At about 04:45, while it was still dark, the Germans released the gas. As it was carried towards the British lines, soldiers worried whether their gas masks would work; they hadn't been tried out in action before this. The German assault followed close behind the gas and was determined enough to reach some of the Inniskilling trenches. They were driven back, but were able to take some prisoners with them. There was another attack soon after dawn, and the fighting continued for some days. By the time the fighting had died down, seventy-one of all ranks of 7th Inniskillings had been killed. One of these was John O'Neill. Another was William Wilson. He had been born in Ballyronan, and his parents lived in Church Street, Cookstown. As a member of the Church of Ireland, he helps to disprove the idea that 16th Division was exclusively Catholic nationalist. He was thirty-one when he died.

As spring turned into summer it became obvious that 1916 would see the first great battles of Kitchener's New Armies. The Germans had launched an attack on the French fortress complex of Verdun and it began to look as if the manhood of France would be sucked to destruction within the cauldron of fire. The French High Command sent a desperate call to Field Marshall Haig, commanding general of the British Forces, asking him to launch an attack that would take some of the pressure off the French Army at Verdun. Haig agreed, and gave orders that his staff should initiate planning for what was to become known as the Battle of the Somme.

It has to be said that, before the Battle of the Somme, the highest echelons of the general staff were not completely confident that they could rely on the citizen soldiers of the New Armies. The generals were particularly worried about the ability of units to keep in formation as they attacked. Then someone had a bright idea. Since the attack was going to be preceded by the most intense artillery barrage yet undertaken by either side, there was no need for the assault troops to hurry forward. Those fortunate few Germans who had survived the shellfire would be too stunned to defend themselves against advancing infantry. Why not let the troops advance at a brisk walk, as if they were heading out for a stroll in the country? In that way the generals could be confident that their men would arrive at the right place at the right time and in proper formation. Nothing could be simpler!

The day chosen for the attack was 1 July. Some among the soldiery remembered that this had been the date of the Battle of the Boyne in the old calendar. Those who took this as a good omen were sadly disappointed. The 36th (Ulster) Division was to be in the first assault. Luckily for the Ulstermen, in a way, their general did not altogether trust the claims of the artillery that German survivors

Tributary waterfall.

would be in no position to defend themselves. He ordered his troops to climb out of their trenches a few moments before the whistles went, so they had a few minutes' advantage over the troops on either side. Equally, no canny Ulsterman was going to stroll across open country while an enemy was trying to shoot him; they got to the enemy trenches at best speed. As a result the Ulster Division got further forward than almost any other troops in the original assault. They had casualties almost straight away. Leslie Bell from Moneymore was shot soon after he moved off. Unable to move, he had to lie there until rescued by stretcher-bearers. Those who reached the German lines were in a worse pickle. The troops on either side had been unable to advance at all, so the Germans were able to concentrate on these forward troops and to fire on them from three sides. At times they were completely surrounded. By the time they were relieved, on the second day of the battle, the division had suffered horrific casualties, and over 2,000 of its soldiers were dead.

Families all along the Ballinderry were bereaved. In Kildress and Pomeroy, in Sandholes and Newmills; in Lissan and Moneymore and Coagh; along the river at Ballinderry Bridge, near the lough at Ardboe and Ballylifford and Ballyronan; on the farmlands of Mowillian and in the outskirts of Cookstown; most of all in Cookstown itself, parents and children mourned. On the first day of the Somme battle thirty-four men were killed who had connections with the district; nine of them came from Cookstown. It was as universal a loss as is possible in life. Everyone old enough to remember those times knew one or more of the dead. The only equivalent that was as shocking to the entire community was the loss of the *Princess Victoria* in 1953, when the whole of Northern Ireland seemed to be talking of those who were lost. The difference in 1916 was that the information arrived in bits and pieces; there was no organised system for releasing the information promptly. While it is understandable that the authorities had difficulties arising from the sheer scale of the disaster, it was surely very distressing when, as often happened, the first news that a family got was a letter from one of the dead man's comrades.

Although that July was the worst month of the war for the people of Northern Ireland, it was not the end of bad news for those at home. In September it was the turn of 16th Division to fight in the long drawn-out battle, when they took two German-held towns. Once again men from the area died. Among the best known was Lt Col. John Staples Molesworth Lenox-Conyngham from Springhill House outside Moneymore. He was a professional soldier who had retired from the army in 1912. At the beginning of the war he had returned to his old regiment, the Connaught Rangers, and was Commanding Officer of the regiment's 6th Battalion. He was a popular commander, even though the majority of the men in his battalion were Belfast nationalists. His death came when he was leading his men in Guillemont, revolver in one hand, walking stick in the other, encouraging the others by his disregard for danger. The wooden cross erected on the site of his death by his own soldiers is now in the Church of Ireland Cathedral in Armagh.

Both divisions had suffered so badly that it was not until 1917 that they were able to participate in another full-scale battle. This was the Battle of Messines, the first unambiguous victory won by the British since the start of the war. The Ulster Division and the Irish Division attacked together on the first day of the battle and easily reached their objectives. Unfortunately the well-earned success of this battle was squandered in the subsequent Third Battle of Ypres and in the slimy mud of Passchendaele. Thomas Gibson from Coagh was resting with his comrades of 9th Battalion, Royal Inniskillings, at Vlamertinghe in the early days of August. Though the ground was wet and muddy, like soldiers everywhere they made the best of it. In the late afternoon of 15 August, the battalion was ordered forward to support the front line, spending that night in Capricorn Trench. The following afternoon they were ordered to move forward once again. As soon as they left their trenches they came under fire from German artillery. Although they took very few casualties at this stage, progress was very slow, since the ground was pitted with shell holes and was slippery with mud. The Germans now brought machine guns to bear on the advancing Irishmen and forced them to take cover. They were now almost like sitting ducks and the German shells started to fall among them. The mud was so soft that it threatened to drown the wounded, who had to lie without aid while the explosions ripped the ground around them all of that night and most of the following day. Thomas died at some time during this bombardment. The survivors never found his remains. His name is one of nearly 35,000 names inscribed on a memorial wall at the back of Tyne Cot war cemetery. This is the largest of Britain's war cemeteries, holding 12,000 graves. There are so many that it is impossible to take them in at one glance; there are always graves beyond your peripheral vision. In spite of the size of the place, the memorial wall has to curve back and forth on itself in order to contain all its names. It is a place of wonder at the suffering that man can inflict on his own species.

The long dying continued till the end of the year, till the men were too exhausted to move and even the politicians were appalled at the scale of the sacrifice. By this time so many Irishmen had died, North and South, Protestant and Catholic, nationalist and unionist, that it was impossible to maintain 16th Division and 36th (Ulster) Division as purely voluntary units. In order to allow them to remain as Irish and Ulster in character, regular battalions were now being assigned to them. War on the Western Front was not a matter simply of set-piece battles. The daily routine of being in the trenches, or even in support just behind the lines, was a dangerous one. There was the 'daily hate', with the artillery of each side shelled the other, and the ever-present danger of snipers. Even on the quietest day, the British needed 2,000 replacements just to keep their numbers steady.

The long winter of 1917/18 may have seemed the most nightmare-ridden of the war. So much effort had gone into two years of major attacks, yet the Germans seemed as steady as ever. It was alright for politicians and members of the general staff to know that the Americans were coming, with all that implied in terms of men and logistics, but for the man sitting with his muckers in a smelly, damp dugout, waiting for the call of stand-to before dawn, there seemed to be no end in sight. Equally, for women who were trying to run farms on their own, or old men who still had to do the milking with arthritic hands because their sons were at the front, the long winter nights passed slowly. And the greatest disaster was yet to fall.

The Germans also anticipated the coming of the Americans, but with fear. The blockade of their shores by the Royal Navy meant that they were being denied essential supplies from overseas. This was made worse by a series of bad harvests. The people were hungry enough to be desperate, and that desperation was to show itself in revolution before the end of the year. The Kaiser and his staff decided on one risky throw of the dice, planning an all-out attack on the Allies which would throw them back to the English Channel and force a ceasefire before the Americans could land enough men to make a difference. To do this, they introduced a different form of fighting. The attack would be led by storm troopers whose job it was to pierce the Allied lines but to keep moving forward. The troops that followed would deal with any remaining pockets of resistance. In this way it was believed that the defenders would be kept off balance and would be unable to offer an organised resistance. The German attack came to be known as the Kaiser's Battle.

The 16th and 36th Divisions were together again, on the front line, facing the brunt of the German assault. The Tyrone Volunteers, 9th Royal Inniskilling Fusiliers, was one of the battalions that took part in the fighting retreat which followed and within a week had lost seventy-two dead. One of these was James Mitchell, from Tamlaght, just outside Coagh. He had survived many battles but he was killed in hand-to-hand fighting as the Inniskillings tried to extricate themselves from a hopeless position. Even when the German attack had stalled, the danger was not over. John Neill had left Cookstown, where he had been a member of the Ulster Volunteers in the town before leaving to work in the shipyards of Clydebank. Although he was in a reserved occupation and could have sat out the war in relative safety, he volunteered for the Royal Field Artillery, and had been in France since July 1916. While he and his mates were having tea on 17 April 1918, the Germans launched what was called counter-battery fire. John was killed at once.

By the end of the German offensive, the two Irish divisions had suffered the heaviest casualties of any in the army. Some relatives at home later got the reassuring news that their menfolk had been captured and were safe in German prisoner-of-war camps. These cannot have been too comfortable, all the same, because the German army came under greater pressure as more and more American troops arrived in Europe. Prisoners were a low priority when it came to food, clothing or medical supplies. Although there are no stories of German brutality to prisoners – quite the contrary, in fact – prisoners could expect no more than was available for the German soldier, and that was little enough. The British High Command decided to disband 16th Division, but to maintain 36th (Ulster) Division. Since 10th (Irish) Division had been converted into an Indian division by this time, this meant that the Ulster Division was the only one left to take a share in the triumphs of 1918. The decision was one which caused great resentment in Ireland, particularly among the Catholic population of Ulster, and the bad taste it left in nationalist mouths was one of the reasons that remembrance of the Great War was left as a unionist activity.

For all that so many had died and so many more had been maimed, there was much to be grateful for when the men returned. The vast majority had survived, after all, and for many of the survivors the sense of camaraderie which they had shared was a valued memory for the rest of their lives. There was also a sense of achievement at a personal level; those who had been to the front had managed to survive in one of the deadliest environments on the planet. As a team they had set out to avenge the rape of Belgium and, although it had taken longer and cost more than they could ever have imagined, they had succeeded. After the first euphoria had worn off, however, they came down to a very cold reality. All of them had left friends behind, and there was the question of why death, or luck, had chosen some and spared others. To compound the matter, veterans came back to a world of fewer jobs, where positions had been taken by those who had avoided the war. Poverty and want were new lodgers in many homes.

For those who had enlisted for political reasons, whether unionist or nationalist, there was a new reality to be faced. A new armed force, based on a breakaway section of the Irish Volunteers, had started what was to become the Hiberno-English War of Independence. On top of that, political supporters of this force had taken on the name of an Irish cultural organisation and, as Sinn Féin, had won a landslide victory in the general election. It looked as if the civil war had not been averted by the start of the Great War, but simply postponed.

Taken as a whole, County Tyrone had been good hunting ground for Sinn Féin clubs. By the end of 1917, 2,135 members belonged to thirty-six clubs within the county. They were not evenly spread, however. In East Tyrone, which was part of Armagh Archdiocese, Cardinal Logue was a tireless opponent of

Sinn Féin. He was helped by the fact that the AOH was very strong in this area. Many Sinn Féin supporters were young men who had transferred their allegiance from the Irish Volunteers or the Gaelic League. Dr James Gillespie from Cookstown was also prominent but he, like many other members, was reluctant to embrace out-and-out republicanism. There had been a bye-election in Cookstown in April 1918 and the Redmondite candidate, T.J.S. Harbison, had defeated his Sinn Féin opponent by almost 600 votes out of a total of 3,000 cast. The contest was fought on the straight issue of Home Rule versus a republic. One factor may have been that it was Sinn Féin policy to boycott the British Parliament. At this time most Ulster Catholics believed this to be a dangerous policy; what would the Ulster unionists get up to if there was no one to keep an eye on them?

The Government chose this time to drive a few more voters into Sinn Féin ranks by threatening to extend conscription to Ireland. Although there was a general consensus among Irish people that such a move should be resisted, it was Sinn Féin who took the lead, advising young men to use violence to resist conscription. Knowing that it would be the police who had to enforce conscription if it did become law, they also advised the population to avoid associating with the police. The message gained an added edge because many of the people who were speaking for Sinn Féin were lawyers and younger members of the clergy. By arresting some Sinn Féin organisers in Strabane in July of 1918, the police began to weaken the influence of the Irish Parliamentary Party compared to their revolutionary opponents.

New Parliamentary boundaries were established before the general election, which was to be held in December 1918. Tyrone was now divided into three constituencies: North-east, North-west and South. There were Catholic majorities in both North-east and North-west Tyrone, but there was a danger of splitting the Catholic vote and allowing the election of Carsonite MPs unless Sinn Féin and the Redmondites could come to an arrangement. Bishop McHugh of Derry and Dean Byrne of Dungannon worked hard to arrange a compact but with no apparent success. It was not until Cardinal Logue became involved that there was an agreement that Harbison would stand for North-east Tyrone, while a Sinn Féin candidate would be given free rein in the North-west. The Sinn Féin candidate was Arthur Griffith, who was in prison at the time, but both candidates of what was called the Green Pact were duly elected. The fact that 30,142 votes had been cast for nationalist candidates within the county, as opposed to 24,993 for unionist candidates, did not prevent the unionists from claiming Tyrone as part of the Northern Ireland that was to be excluded from the terms of the Home Rule Act. Nationalist opposition to this sleight of hand lacked unity. Sinn Féin as a whole set up an independent body,

Dáil Éireann, and ignored Westminster. Harbison, together with the few IPP members who had managed to hold on to their seats, took the fight to London and opposed the Government of Ireland Bill of 1920, which divided Ireland into two unequal portions.

Through the trauma of the War of Independence, Tyrone nationalists managed to maintain enough unity to gain control of the County Council in June 1920, in an election held under proportional representation. Nationalists in the county – and in Fermanagh, where they had also gained control of the council – thought that this would take the wind out of partitionist sails and at least ensure that the two counties would have to be included with the southern portion of the country. When it became obvious that this was not going to be the case, Harbison, a solicitor and a constitutionalist, stated in the House of Commons that the nationalist population of Tyrone would be justified in any form of resistance that they took to prevent themselves being coerced into a Northern Ireland to which they felt no sense of loyalty.

In spite of this level of opposition to partition, there was very little effort made in the county to conform to the policies of Dáil Éireann. Although one or two revolutionary courts were set up, mainly in the west of the county, they got little support from the local population and soon fell into disuse. A contributing factor to this was that the revolutionary police were somewhat headstrong in enforcing their decisions. A local man was shot dead during a raid on a poitín still. The AOH was content to follow the Sinn Féin leadership as long as they concentrated on keeping control of the county council.

One positive thing which Tyrone nationalists got involved with was the Belfast Boycott. In Belfast, especially in the heavy engineering industries and in the shipyards, Catholics had been forced from their work by Protestant mobs. In retaliation, nationalist areas of the north, and all of southern Ireland, chose to boycott Belfast products. Even bread carts that came from Belfast were attacked. The organisation of these and other actions allowed Sinn Féin to extend their control over the nationalist population and began to institutionalise the sectarian divide that started to develop all over Northern Ireland, bringing an internal partition before partition had been established as a political solution in the island as a whole.

Some violence by the IRA also took place within Tyrone. In spite of this, the republican leadership in Dublin was disappointed at the level of activity in the county, as in the north as a whole. What fighting there was tended to be in the west of the county. When the IRA started ambushing police patrols, they were opposed by the Ulster Special Constabulary, newly formed in October 1920. Since this force was drawn from the local unionist population, and many of them had seen service in the Great War, their local knowledge and military training made them a formidable enemy. Dublin tried to counter this by reorganising their northern insurgents and by sending a new commander, Eoin O'Duffy. His orders were to cut off the unionist heartland of eastern Ulster from the western hinterland. He intended to carry this out by concentrating on attacking police and military patrols. The first fatality among the security forces in east Tyrone was in May, when a police sergeant was killed near Greencastle. Once again, most activity took place in the west of the county, with two special constables being killed near Drumquin. The fighting gathered no momentum of its own and, when the Kerryman Charlie Daly came north to command a division, he complained of the 'slave-mind and lack of enthusiasm' that he found.

The Government of Ireland Act, passed in December 1920, gave a new urgency to nationalist cooperation. The first election to the new Parliament of Northern Ireland was held in May 1921. This, like the local elections, was to use proportional representation. The two debatable counties of Tyrone and Fermanagh were amalgamated into a single constituency with eight seats. George Murnaghan, an Omagh businessman who had been an IPP MP, wrote to his successor, Arthur Griffith, warning of the urgency of the situation and the need to unite nationalist opposition to partition. The result was another pact between the two nationalist parties, and three Sinn Féin candidates were elected; Harbison was the sole survivor of the old IPP. In spite of the fact that nationalists had obtained 57 per cent of the vote, the seats were evenly divided between nationalists and unionists, four each. It would be easy to justify putting these two counties into either of the proposed new jurisdictions.

The insurgents in Ireland agreed to a ceasefire with the Crown forces in July 1921. Even when they met delegations of nationalists from Tyrone, Sinn Féin offered sympathy but no guarantees as to where any future border would run. There is evidence that Sinn Féin had not even begun to formulate its policy on the north before negotiations began at the London Conference in October. The Irish plenipotentiaries were innocents compared to Lloyd George, and were no match for him in diplomacy. Although Griffith and Michael Collins had argued for the essential unity of the island of Ireland, they were forced to accept dominion status – little more than was offered under the original Home Rule Act – for twenty-six counties, with exclusion for the other six. As a sop to their sensibilities, a boundary commission was offered which would determine the final line of the border. The resulting agreement, signed in December, gave unionists all that they might have wished.

In Cookstown, even before the final documents had been drafted, there was an attempt by the Special Constabulary to destroy any nationalist opposition to the new Northern Ireland state. This had taken responsibility for internal security in November. Tyrone County Council passed a motion repudiating the Belfast legislature and pledging their allegiance to Dáil Éireann. The new Government reacted by introducing a Bill which would enable it to dissolve any councils that did not accept its authority. Even before the Bill had been passed, the Specials had occupied the council offices. At the same time they were flexing their muscles with the people of Cookstown, as Dr Gillespie wrote to de Valera.

When the Anglo-Irish Treaty was published, it posed a number of questions for the nationalists of Northern Ireland, the answers to which depended on where you happened to be living. For Catholics in Belfast there was no hope of being included in the new Free State, so it was important for them to oppose the Treaty in its entirety. For Catholics in the disputed counties of Tyrone and Fermanagh, on the other hand, the battle against partition was already lost. Their hope was based on Article 12 of the Treaty, which seemed to offer the possibility of the border being adjusted to meet the aspirations of local people. Tyrone County Council actually changed its alliance to the Northern Ireland Parliament, on the assumption that this would only be a temporary expedient. The Council wanted to be in existence so that it could present a united front to the upcoming Boundary Commission. Cookstown Rural Council refused to go as far as this, and was dissolved, along with Strabane, for rejecting unionist rule.

Michael Collins, probably the most charismatic of the southern leaders, had enough influence to ensure that the vast majority of Tyrone Catholics, and particularly the clergy, endorsed the terms of the Treaty. Collins's own attitude to the emerging Northern Ireland was, at the very least, ambivalent. On the one hand, he had signed an agreement which endorsed its existence. On the other hand, he was encouraging northern Catholics not to recognise the institutions of the Northern Ireland Government. A number of Catholic teachers refused to accept their salaries from the new Ministry of Education. For a period of ten months they were actually paid by the Irish Provisional Government. These secret payments ended in November 1922, a few months after Collins had been killed in the Irish Civil War. Collins was also playing a double game in military terms. He wanted to keep the Northern IRA on his side in the Civil War which seemed inevitable, so he kept them happy by providing them with arms even after the Treaty had been accepted by Dáil Éireann.

Because of this, the IRA in Tyrone kept up a level of activity at the beginning of 1922. In this they were doing a disservice to the Catholics of the county, since these civilians were left open to retaliation by the Special Constabulary. In Gortin, the parish priest was forced to work at filling in a trench that had been dug across a road by the IRA. When the final split between pro- and anti-Treaty sections of the IRA occurred in March, republican morale in the county was at its lowest ebb. Most of the pro-Treaty group went to the Curragh, where they were trained for the Free State Army. Those who rejected the Treaty made their way across what was now a national border to Donegal, where they found like-minded units still in existence.

While the military option was fading, political opposition to partition ensured much closer cooperation among constitutional nationalists than there had been in the past. In the British general election of November 1922, nationalists were elected to the Westminster Parliament in both Tyrone and Fermanagh by significant majorities. Although this underlined the fact that there were nationalist majorities in both counties, there was general frustration with the fact that the Boundary Commission had not yet been set up. What was worse was that the Northern Ireland Government had already passed a Bill abolishing proportional representation for local elections. With a little attention to ward boundaries, it was an easy matter for Tyrone and Fermanagh to be 'painted with a deep Orange tint', as Michael Collins put it. After the changes 5,381 unionist voters in Tyrone appointed twenty-one unionist councillors; 8,459 nationalist voters only managed to elect eighteen. That was not the end of nationalist woes. In another Westminster general election in 1924, the intervention of two de Valera candidates split the nationalist vote and allowed two unionists to take the seats. Tyrone and Fermanagh now had a deep Orange tint indeed.

Whether it would have made any difference to the Boundary Commission that was finally appointed is debatable. To have met the aspirations of Tyrone nationalists, almost the entire county would need to be transferred to the Free State. The Chairman of the Commission, South African Richard Feetham, saw it as the Commission's task to offer only minor alterations. Though the Commission operated for a couple of years, it was a case of the mountain labouring and bringing forth a mouse. The status quo prevailed. For almost fifty years, Cookstown and Tyrone remained unionist strongholds.

❧ 7 ❧

WHERE THE
FISHERMAN STRAYS

It is intriguing to think that mankind has been exploiting the riches of Lough Neagh since they first arrived in Ireland, so many thousand years ago, at the beginning of our story. Nowadays the commercial fishermen concentrate on the eels for which the lough is famous, but pollan and trout are also taken, depending on the time of year. Where in the past dugout canoes were used, nowadays motorboats with powerful inboard engines provide a faster and safer – if much noisier – way of getting to the fishing grounds. Although a chart of the lough does exist, this is based on a survey that is more than one hundred years old, and has been updated simply by calculating the difference made to depths at the various times where the level of the lough was lowered. Those who use the lough for work rather than for pleasure, such as the fisherman or the skipper of a sand dredge, must carry an internal chart of the lough's underwater topography.

Many of the families who now fish the lough did not move there until the upheavals of the Ulster Plantation drove them from their own land, or the pangs of the Great Hunger led them in search of food. In the days before flood control and drainage, the area around the lough shore was not a great place to live. Regular winter floods meant that houses had to be built on raised ground and that families could be isolated for much of the year. Less regular summer floods meant that crops (and to a lesser extent livestock) were only safe on the limited higher ground. Lives lived in such isolation meant that the fishing community for many years was very difficult to get to know. This has changed a lot in modern times, because improved drainage means that homes are rarely isolated as in the past, while the children all go inland to large secondary schools and so get to know and become friendly with other children from well beyond their immediate community.

The Battery – pleasure boats and fishing boats mingle in the harbour.

It is well known that Lough Neagh is the largest lake in the British Isles. What is less well known is that it is the fifth largest lake in the whole of Europe. Six good-sized rivers flow into it, while only one, the Lower Bann, takes its water to the sea. For its entire shoreline Lough Neagh is surrounded by Lough Neagh clays in the southern two-thirds or by basalt to the north, but the inflowing rivers pass over a much wider range of rock types. These rivers supply a rich source of nutrients – often too rich – and also provide good spawning grounds for the various fish species that need flowing water in which to spawn, such as trout and salmon. In this, the Ballinderry is a perfectly typical river.

Because of the nature of the surrounding shore, from Ballyronan round to Sandy Bay in County Antrim, much of the southern lake has been filled with sediments and is much shallower than the area that is defined by basalt rock. An interesting feature that shows up in the chart is an underwater ledge that goes all the way round the lough, varying in width from half a mile to less than a quarter of a mile. The depth of this shelf is fairly constant, between 7 and 10ft. The margin of this shelf is an important mark for fishermen. In the days before GPS and echo sounders, each fisherman would have identified landmarks on the shore that would have told him where it was.

Beyond the ledge, which the men used to refer to as the gut or the hard, most of the bed of the lough is made of mud; in fact mud makes up about 75 per cent of the total bed. It is generally flat, with an average depth of about 30ft, though there are variations. One of the most striking of these is opposite the Ballinderry mouth, where there is a deep trench, again with a muddy bottom, which is about eight miles long and three-quarters of a mile wide. This, and other, smaller, holes are rich in fish. The mud contains the invertebrates that are necessary for trout and eels and it is in areas like this that fishermen set their lines. In the past these were good holding areas for pollan, and fishermen used draft nets to catch this species during the winter. In very hot weather, when oxygen levels in the water are low, many eels retire to these deep muds and enter a state of semi-hibernation, so they have great economic importance.

One of the alarming features of the lough as far as visiting boatmen are concerned is the way in which what appears to be open water can suddenly be interrupted by flats that rise out of the mud. While most of them are still quite a distance below the surface, some of them reduce the depth to a few inches. The author had a nasty experience once when he realised that he was sailing towards a cormorant that was standing on a submerged rock. It looked for all the world as if it was walking on the water. Freshwater lakes, particularly those which are rich in nutrients, can have very murky water, with light only penetrating a few feet deep. These raised areas have increased sunshine and therefore can sustain more aquatic vegetation at the bottom of a food chain that leads up to fish.

The lough is very open to any wind blowing, and a steady wind over a few days will set up surface currents. There is a counter to these in the opposite direction moving under the lough, and all of these are influenced by the movement of water through Lough Neagh to leave it at Toome. These underwater currents have produced a series of bars on the lake bottom. It is these, in turn, which contribute to the sandy shores of Traad Point and Ballyronan Bay, as well as a number of other bays around the lough shore.

Mud gives way to sand and gravel for about 15 per cent of the floor of the lough. This is another important environment for fishermen, especially a band that stretches along the lough opposite the mouth of the Ballinderry River. Eels prefer a hard bottom at the beginning and end of the fishing season, but some eels can be found here all through the year. It is in this area that fishermen begin their season, usually using long lines containing hundreds of hooks.

The low-lying ground around Moortown was subject to regular flooding, and fen bogs as well as peat bogs have formed over the millennia. The area would have been wooded until the great pressure of population which followed the

Plantation and the Famine. There are five townlands in the parish of Ardboe which have the prefix 'Kil' or 'Killy', indicating woods, in their name. The woods near the shore would have been scrubby in nature, with alder and birch in the wetter areas, while ash and probably hazel would have grown in slightly drier areas. Much of the shore has been cleared of this sort of wet woodland but there is a good example of wet woodland at Ballyronan, where Cookstown District Council maintains Ballyronan Wood as a local nature reserve. Like much of the surviving woodland, it is growing on land that was exposed by the lowering of Lough Neagh.

The lough was first lowered in 1847, and most recently in 1959. Just how much the water level has fallen can be seen by the old jetty at Ballyronan, which now rises high but uselessly above the surface. Flooding was also controlled by a series of sluice gates, with the most important one at Toome, where the Lower Bann leaves Lough Neagh. Although a great deal of land has been gained by the various schemes, little of it is of much value to agriculture, since the water table remains high and the soil is very water retentive. Fishermen, many of whom owned small farms, may have been self-sufficient in the past. Now there are very few who could survive without another job.

Different methods of fishing have been used over the years and boat design has evolved to meet the needs and lifestyle of the fisherman. At the turn of the twenty-first century there were about 220 boats used for fishing the lough. A dozen or slightly more were made of wood, but the vast majority were made of fibreglass, which is much easier to maintain than wood. When boats were made of wood, the traditional hull was made of Russian spruce; the wood used for the gunwales was Oregon pine or Douglas fir; while oak was used for the ribs and the stem and stern. They resembled boats that are to be found in many of Ireland's sea loughs, such as the Lough Foyle punt. The boats were clinker built and could be sailed using a calico sail when there was a suitable wind. Otherwise they were rowed.

When internal combustion engines became more readily available in the 1940s, it proved possible to put a small petrol engine in these boats without too much difficulty. In practice, most boat owners used petrol till the engine had heated properly before switching over to paraffin, which was much cheaper. The problem was that a paraffin-driven engine had little torque and could only drive a small propeller. This limited the speed that a boat could achieve, a handicap when the size of the lough is considered.

In the 1950s men began to experiment with diesel engines. These have much greater torque and can drive a bigger propeller, so they could move a much bigger boat much faster. A design based around this engine developed which I think is unique to Lough Neagh. Fine in the bows and broad in the stern, with a bottom that is almost flat, these boats can rise like speedboats on the plane and cover great distances in a short time. At the same time, their broad beam makes them steady work platforms, stiff and hard to upset, as well as being capable of holding as much equipment as is needed. There is even room in most of them for a small shelter in the bough, giving a level of comfort that the old fishermen wouldn't have believed possible.

This local hardware store is typical of country stores before the motor car.

Over the years different nets have evolved to suit the different methods of fishing and the different fish being sought. The most important of these, and the one most often used for eel, pollan, trout, perch and even salmon, is the draft net. The net is about 100ft long, with a line of floats holding one side up and a weighted line making the net hang vertically in the water. It is set in a large semi-circle and then drawn into the boat by two men standing at the stern. The fish are caught in a bag at the end of the net, called the bung.

The trammel net has the same design of one line with floats while the other is weighted. It is about half the length of a draft net and is over 6ft deep. It is anchored in the water, either just below the surface, when fishing for trout, or at the bottom, when fishing for perch. Fish are caught when they try to force their way through the net; presumably they think that they have just encountered a line of weeds. Their gills get tangled and they cannot escape. This type of net has become more effective since the introduction of nylon, which is more difficult for the fish to see.

Other methods have been tried, but have subsequently been banned. Fyke-netting was too deadly, while trawling did too much damage to the fragile floor of the lough. The final type of fishing for eels that is used on Lough Neagh is line fishing. The line used can be well over a mile in length, made of strong nylon. Shorter side-lines are attached to knots on the main line every 13 or 14ft and attached to these are the hooks. There are usually about 400 hooks on a line. The bait used is live worms or small fish, such as young perch or pollan. The lines are set in the evening so that they are in position overnight, when the eels are most active. The fisherman goes out in the morning to lift his catch. He keeps the eels alive in a barrel on his boat until he reaches the shore, where they are transferred to a holding cage to keep them alive until they are collected for the market. The condition of the eels deteriorates while they are in the holding cage, so it is important that they are collected regularly. To stop overfishing, each fisherman has a daily quota, which depends on market conditions. The live eels are taken to the Fishermen's Cooperative at Toome, where they are graded by size before being flown to the Continent. The larger eels go to Germany, where they are made into jellied eels. Smaller ones go to the Netherlands, where they prefer their eels smoked.

Fishermen's families also eat the eels, of course, but their recipe is more straightforward. The eels are skinned, cut into short lengths and then fried slowly. The pan needs no oil, since the oil from the eel itself is enough. In fact, the cook has to keep pouring off the excess oil. This is kept carefully, always in a glass container, and will be used during the winter to treat cuts and scratches and the general aches and pains that come from a hard life in the open air in all weathers. The fishermen claim that the oil is so fine that it gradually leaks out of any container, even glass. The use of eel oil has a long tradition in the area. Local people say that the monks at Ardboe used the oil for their lamps as far back as the sixth century.

The number of people actively fishing the lough has declined in recent years. As roads and communications have got better, more and more of the young folk have looked for steadier, more reliable employment elsewhere. Although this is particularly true of the south and eastern shores of the lough, where the jobs of Craigavon or Belfast are no great distance away, there has also been a drop in fishing on the western shore. In some cases this is because the young men prefer other employment, but there is also the fact that the lough is less productive than it once was, and is unable to support the same number of fishing families that it once did. In 1980 there were 500 fishermen active. Of these, the vast majority lived in Ardboe Parish, particularly in Moortown, which has only six miles of shoreline. This is still the most isolated shoreline, which may explain the persistence of old ways.

It takes at least two people to fish a boat, and a few still have three in the crew, the number needed in the past, when someone had to man the oars. The crew often consists of a father and son, or two brothers, reflecting the close family ties that still exist in the area. This can be seen when an examination is made of where people live. Often there are three or four fishing families with the same name living within a quarter of a mile of each other. In the past that would have produced a clachan, since there were limited areas that were dry enough for building a house. With modern drainage and the lowering of the lough this is no longer a problem, however, and houses and bungalows can be built along the road, with easy access to shops and schools, or in small housing estates, which can be some distance from the shore. This is not the disadvantage it once was. In the past, most of the routine maintenance of lines and nets was done near the boat. With modern cars and vans, it is no disadvantage to do the work away from the shore and transport it there. In fact, I have seen a line being baited as far away as Moneymore. When a married son moves away, the uniting bond that holds family groups together can be the family cove, or moorings. Fishermen tend to be very loyal to their coves, even if marriage means that they live closer to another one. Where a son inherits the family home, he usually has it renovated to be brought up to modern standards. For this reason, there are very few of the traditional thatched cottages left. A rare example is Coyle's Cottage, in Kinturk, which is preserved by the local community group.

The lough shore is not an area in which to disparage someone to anyone else. The kinship lines in the area mean that your listener is probably related to the person you are insulting at least once!

Commercial fishing in Lough Neagh has not always been a peaceful affair. Other than the timber from the woods of Killetra and Glenconkeyne, the most valuable asset that the English found in mid-Ulster was the fishing. At the end of the Nine-Years' War, which saw the destruction of the Gaelic way of life in the area, the fisheries of Lough Neagh and the Lower Bann were invested in the Crown. There was some wheeling and dealing for about sixty years, and some very nefarious actions, before the lease was granted by Charles II to Sir Arthur Chichester. From that time the rights were owned by the Donegall family and by the Shaftesbury Estate. The matter was theoretical as far as the lough itself was concerned. The value lay in the catching of salmon, and this was done mainly in the rivers.

In the latter half of the nineteenth century, however, the eel fishing in the lough began to take on a commercial significance. With a view to making as much money as possible, the Shaftesbury Estate went to court to enforce their claim to the fishing rights. The case went to the House of Lords on appeal and the local fishermen won the right to fish the entire lough except Toome Bay, where they could not employ draft nets. The decision was made because it was decided that Charles II did not own the fishing rights and therefore the grant to Sir Arthur had been illegal. A second case was brought to the House of Lords in 1911 and, by a single vote and against the legal advice of the Lord Chancellor, it was decided that Charles had acted legally after all.

In 1925 the fishing rights of the Lower Bann, above its tidal reaches, and of the lough itself, were leased to the Toome Eel Fishing Company. This company sold on the rights in 1959 to a Dutch consortium. In 1962 this new company had the injunction of 1911 extended to the entire lough, threatening to destroy a way of life that had existed at least for several centuries. The fishermen organised themselves into the Lough Neagh Fishermen's Association and challenged the injunction in court. The case lasted nine weeks, the longest civil case in Northern Ireland's history. In the end the fishermen lost; ill feeling was so bad that there was talk of violence, and unconfirmed rumours of guns in boats.

The fishing war ended in a different way, however. Within three years the Fishermen's Association had raised enough money to buy a 20 per cent stake in the Dutch company. By late 1971 it had bought the remaining shares. It was a great victory for the common people over the propertied class. The ownership was taken over by the Lough Neagh Fishermen's Cooperative, and this organisation has managed fishing on the lough ever since.

Big changes had come to Lough Neagh and its shores long before this. The Second World War did not have the immediate impact on the people of mid-Ulster that the Great War had. For most of the people on the lough shore it was life as usual, although there were the usual petty restrictions that accompany national emergencies. Those who farmed had a better market and better prices, and they even began to get subsidies by 1940. Cash was a welcome guest in many houses, and made many a house more comfortable, many a household more reconciled to bureaucracy. In 1941, however, news came of a project that was to have devastating consequences for thirty-five local families. It had been decided to build a military airfield in the townland of Kinrush, effectively cutting Ardboe in two. The division has become so settled that people from Moortown and those from Ardboe hardly think of themselves as neighbours any more. The people who had to move got what was considered a good price for the land; £50 per acre. In addition, they got a disturbance allowance and moving expenses. Further ready cash was got by selling the livestock at auction. All the same, there is a great hunger in Irish people for land and it was hard to give up what had been so long fought for. It wasn't just farms that went; two shops, two shoemakers' and two forges had to be cleared. Although some families were lucky enough to get settled locally, others had to go as far away as Stewartstown and Newmills to live. Perhaps the ones that had to go furthest were the lucky ones after all, because those who stayed locally had to witness the land that had been enriched and fertilised by their hard work become encased in metal and concrete. It was little comfort to be told that, if the Air Ministry ever decided to resell the land, previous owners would be given the option to buy it back.

Work started on the airfield in December 1941, only two days after the attack on Pearl Harbour had brought the United States into the war. The contract had been awarded to an English company. Although the supervisory staff arrived quickly enough, it was some time before the necessary machinery could be assembled. There were few jobs for the locals at this stage. The men needed special training before they could operate the great earth-moving and levelling machines. Hedges, houses, ditches and trees had all to be levelled before work on the runways themselves could begin. Because the work was being carried out by outsiders, there was no allowance made for local sensitivities. Trees that had been used as marks by fishermen for generations simply disappeared. Even sites held sacred because they had witnessed Mass during penal times were obliterated.

Whether most people were concerned about this is unsure, because now there was plenty of work available. The airport, which became known as Cluntoe, was only part of a network of airfields being built around Lough Neagh. Ordinary tradesmen and labourers were needed for the army camps that were growing up in the area to support them. The labour shortage was so great that many handymen who were not formally qualified as tradesmen simply signed on and got on with it. There was even money for wives, since workers who came from beyond the area were prepared to pay good money for lodgings. Men from the cities were particularly delighted to be living in an area where food rationing was simply a theory.

The men worked in gangs, each run by a ganger whose main qualification was that he could he could read plans and ensure that the work was following them. Some of these were from England and brought with them a store of bad language that was a revelation to the locals. Each gang had a young boy, called the Nipper, attached to it. The Nipper's job was to organise the tea. He collected tea, sugar and milk from each worker and made a huge can of sweet, milky tea for the ten o'clock break and for dinner time, in the middle of the day. There was a widespread belief that the Nipper collected all the leftovers and sold them on the black market. Some claimed that he probably made more money than anybody except the ganger.

There was also a great deal of work available in supporting industries. Local quarries were working at full stretch, and the trade of quarryman was a reserved occupation; they were not allowed to join the armed services even if they wanted to. Those lucky farmers who had a tractor and trailer got as much work as they could handle. Anyone with a lorry was also in demand. At that time there was no local cement being produced. It was brought by train to Moneymore and Cookstown stations, and brought on from there by road. So many heavy loads were brought by road that the roads themselves began to collapse, and pedestrians began to complain that they were not safe to walk along.

It was not only pedestrians who felt that they had something to complain about. War-time regulations set wages on a county-by-county basis. The further from Belfast, the lower was the rate of pay. Workers in County Derry were paid $1d$ an hour less than those in County Antrim, while workers in Tyrone were paid $1d$ less than that. There was a strike for parity of pay, since men working at Langford Lodge or Aldergrove, on the other side of the lough, were earning $8s$ a week extra for doing the same work. Quite a few workers were fined before things got settled.

The first phase of the work was finished in eight months. By the late summer three runways had been completed, together with a three-mile long taxi-way and hardstands for thirty heavy bombers. As well as the buildings that were concerned with the running of the airfield, there were those concerned more with the welfare of personnel, such as a hospital, cinema, church and living accommodation. Some installations were reminders of the more serious purpose of the base; bomb dumps held incendiaries and high explosives, and two petrol dumps each held 72,000 gallons of high octane fuel. Local residents were told that this fuel was unsuitable for ordinary engines, but there are reports that, after the war, local fishermen were never troubled by petrol rationing, since they had an alternative source to call upon! Many of the old buildings are still standing, incongruous now, since there is nothing visible around them to explain their position. Others still fulfil a function, having been converted into houses.

Many of those who had been attracted to the regular work and wages had come from Donegal. Now that this first phase was completed they found themselves in a sort of limbo. Since it was late summer, many found work with the flax harvest or bringing home turf. Northern Ireland was a closed society at that time, in the sense that only people who were citizens were allowed to work there without a permit. Most of the Donegal men had to return home, although some married local girls and settled down.

The first service personnel to arrive were from the RAF. Soon after, the first aeroplane arrived, to the delight of the children from the local primary school. It was not long, however, until Americans started to arrive. Cluntoe was one of the airfields used for the huge build-up of resources before the invasion of Normandy. The Americans were like people from another planet. They were tall and healthy looking, dressed in uniforms which were well cut and made of the best materials. Many local people got work on the base, even youngsters, and got to know the Americans very well. One of the perks of this was that you got to see the film shows.

The increasing number of aeroplanes coming and going was a source of rich entertainment and often, on a Sunday, there would be a gaggle of visitors from as far away as Cookstown, watching mechanics perform maintenance on the planes, which were parked on the hard stands around the perimeter. At that time there was no mains electricity in the district, so the few radios that were owned locally were powered by battery. These were not the compact batteries of modern design, but were large glass contraptions, filled with dilute acid, called wet batteries. Most families had two of these, with one in operation while the other was taken away – usually in the bread van – to be recharged. A battery had to last a week, so listening time was rationed. People were anxious to hear news about the war that was brought so close by the sight of planes across the perimeter fence.

Ardboe was no longer a quiet place. Part of the function of the base was to get battle-ready for fighting in the skies over Europe. Glass domes were built to simulate the gun turrets of bombers, and the noise of machine guns blended with the roar of planes overhead as young men fired hundreds of rounds in the specially built shooting range. Out on the lough, boats would tow targets for planes to bomb, or set adrift floating targets that the gunners would try to hit. Night-flying exercises were particularly exciting, with the lights of the runway contrasting with the blacked-out countryside for miles about.

Many of the Americans seemed to miss their families and seemed to appreciate the friendship of the local children. Besides giving out gum or sweets to children they met, the Americans also had a Christmas party for children from the district. For many it was their first fairy-lit Christmas tree, and their first present from

Santa Claus. The Americans, particularly those from rural districts, were also keen to see aspects of local life, and even to help out with it. They bought fresh eggs and eels, bringing even more money into the local economy. Local women were employed in the laundry, while young men got jobs as orderlies for the officers, many of whom where there for rest and relaxation between tours of duty. Other jobs were less salubrious, such as maintaining the latrines.

From about 1943, the build-up of Americans intensified, as the date for D-Day approached. One of the most famous American paratrooper units, 82nd Airborne Division arrived. Its headquarters was in Killymoon Castle, but different regiments were spread around a large portion of Northern Ireland. Unlike many Americans that had been here for a while, these were battle-hardened veterans who had already fought in North Africa and in Italy. They remained for only a short time before going on to earn more credit for their role in the invasion attack on the Cherbourg Peninsula in Normandy.

After that invasion, things began to wind down, and men were transferred to England or to Europe. By the end of the year an official from the Air Ministry was offering farmers the opportunity to buy their land back. The lough was quiet again, but the old way of life was gone.

By the 1960s it was recognised that the nutrient level of Lough Neagh had become highly eutrophic. Since then, in fact, it has become over-fertilised and is classified as hypertrophic. According to research published by the Government a few years ago, the waters of Lough Neagh are among the most highly polluted in Europe. Farmers were blamed as being the main source of the pollution.

Two main substances were involved. Nitrates and phosphates seep into the water system and make their way into the lough. Their origin is in fertilisers and animal waste. Their main effect is to encourage the growth of a scum-like algal bloom. This reduces the amount of oxygen available to fish and to those invertebrates that constitute a large portion of fish food. Since Lough Neagh has problems maintaining its oxygen levels at the best of times, this forms a great threat to the welfare of the ecosystem. The original problem was from phosphates, mostly coming from pig slurry finding its way into the water system. Attempts were made to control this and other effluents. The phosphates still seem to be making their way into the system. It may be that this is a result of much building development in the countryside. Most of these houses are away from main sewer pipes and need septic tanks. These require care and maintenance that they do not always get. In order to ensure that they do not have a detrimental effect on the environment it is important that no more septic tanks drain into a stream or ditch than that stream can cope with. Perhaps the introduction of reed-bed sewage treatment would be a step forward.

A particularly worrying development that the report highlights is an increase of nitrate pollution of over 70 per cent in the last thirty years. The scientists say that 80 per cent of these nitrates are coming from fertilisers that farmers are applying to their land in order to increase their yield. Although representatives of the farming community claim that nitrates do not cause a problem, Lough Neagh is the biggest source of drinking water in Northern Ireland and nitrate in water is a danger to health. If nitrates get into the human system and turn to nitrogen, then a substance is produced that reduces the ability of a person's blood to carry oxygen. The person then shows the same symptoms as what used to be called blue babies. The levels in Lough Neagh have not reached that sort of concentration yet, but the need for monitoring the water is obvious.

Eels are by far the most important catch in Lough Neagh. For many children their introduction to eels is to see one on a hook that that was meant for something more like a fish in looks. The sight of the squirming creature, exuding slime as it attempts to force itself off the hook by the sheer strength of its long body, is enough to put a child off eel suppers for life. When, horrified, the child tries to kill the unfortunate captive by dashing it against a rock, to no avail, the prejudice against this seemingly invulnerable creature is confirmed. Yet, if given time, the eel will get itself off the hook and will move, almost like a snake, as it goes back into the water. The sight gives some idea of the mystery of these creatures.

Each one was born far away, across the Atlantic Ocean, in the Sargasso Sea. This area of the ocean, near the Caribbean, is at the centre of a long, slow eddy the size of the North Atlantic. It is to this strange area that the adult eels swim from all around the Atlantic shores of America and Europe, following paths in the sea that have been hard-wired into their central nervous system for millions of years. Our eels leave on moonless nights in late October, around the time the first frosts chill the evening air. Their journey is winter-long; they never return, though their offspring do.

It is possible that only the pregnant females reach the Sargasso Sea. Here they lay their eggs in the spring, and die. The eggs hatch into larvae that do not resemble an eel in any way; their shape is more like a willow leaf, but completely transparent. As the larvae get caught in the ocean currents they start to drift north. As it drifts, its body shape changes until it resembles a tiny, transparent eel, known as a glass eel. During this drift it starts to gain some colour and is now relatively easier to see. It has become an elver. When they come near to the shore, near the mouth of their river, the elvers split into two groups. The males remain in salt or brackish water, never growing longer than 1ft or 19in. The females are more intrepid, and now begin yet another stage of their epic journey. Although up till now they had been more or less drifting, they now develop an instinct to swim against the current. Not even weirs or waterfalls will stop them. When the elvers are running they form what are almost like ropes around the sides of obstacles, climbing over one another until they reach the top and can swim on. Some, as they reach the end of their journey, will even make their way across wet grassland in order to reach a pool. By this time they have become a yellowish-green in colour. It is called, not surprisingly, a yellow eel.

The females remain in fresh water for somewhere between seven and ten years. They feed voraciously and grow until they are about 3 or 4ft long. It is only then that they go through their last bodily change and become fully adult, a silver eel. The following autumn the epic life cycle begins again. In the dark autumn evenings they swim past Toome and down the Bann and out into the mysteries of the sea, where their life began. Occasionally a female does not make this change to sexual maturity. When this happens, the eel continues to grow as it feeds and becomes a giant of its species. It is from these that stories arise of huge eels 'as thick as a man's thigh'. It is not known how long such eels can live.

If the story of the eel is the story of an epic voyage, then that of the pollan is the story of a fish that is going nowhere. In fact the species is trapped in Ireland and occurs on only three lakes; as well as in Lough Neagh they are found in Lough Ree and Lough Derg, both on the Shannon River, and on Lower Lough Erne. When the ice melted some 10,000 years ago, they were among the first species to colonise the new, freshwater systems in Ireland. As the ice continued to melt, the land rose. The water around Ireland became saltier than the pollan could cope with, and they were trapped. The healthiest population is that of Lough Neagh, where they feed on a type of freshwater shrimp, as well as other aquatic invertebrates. To look at they resemble herring, with a streamlined silver body. On their back, however, near the tail, is a small fatty fin which is known as the adipose fin. This is a characteristic of members of the salmon family. The most common size is about 170gm, but some have been recorded as big as 1.2kg.

Pollan do not live in any other European country. There is another landlocked population in Lake Baikal, in eastern Asia, and another population around Alaska, which lives in the sea but breeds in fresh water. In spite of being the subject of a European Conservation, the species is not thriving in any of its Irish homes. Half a century ago pollan was an important part of the mid-Ulster diet, especially in the meat-free weeks of Lent. Pollan were even exported as food or fish bait. Now the sale of pollan is restricted to a few shops near the fishing centres and only a few fishermen still use juvenile pollan as bait. The population seems to have gone into a serious decline. There are various theories to account for this. At one time it was thought to be the result of Lough Neagh becoming over-enriched with nutrients, the process known as eutrophication. A more commonly held theory now is that the introduction of roach to the Bann system has set up a competition for food that the pollan is losing. It would not be the first fish species to become extinct in the lough. There was once a healthy population of arctic char, trapped like the pollan at the end of the ice age. This population was lost in the nineteenth century.

Of course the lough and its shores have many visitors over the course of a year. Even before the eels have begun their long autumn journey, new arrivals begin to gather from the north. Duck which have bred in the arctic tundra fly down the west coast of Scotland, hopping from island to island until they reach the north coast of Ireland. Here the groups split up along routes that have been followed for thousands of years. Large groups of duck and swans (and sometimes geese) follow the line of the Lower Bann until they reach the twin lakes of Lough Beg and Lough Neagh. Once again there is a split, as dabbling ducks like teal and shovelers stop among the shallows and flooded fields of Lough Beg, while diving duck, like pochard and goldeneye, who prefer deeper water, fly on to Lough Neagh.

Slightly later in the year the whooper swans arrive from Iceland. These magnificent birds are best known around Toome, where travellers between Belfast and Derry can see large flocks of them grazing in the fields to the north of the main road. Small parties fly further south, and a group can be seen most winters around the old airfield at Ardboe. They feed on the wet grassland, although in the past their favoured habitat was aquatic vegetation along the coast and in marshes. For some reason, during the 1940s they began to move to agricultural land, where they now seem perfectly at home. For a time a good number were killed each year as a result of flying into electricity lines. The electricity service has now taken measures to make their lines more visible to the swans and fatal impacts occur less often. The swans do not stay in one place all winter, but move about between Lough Neagh, Lough Foyle and Lough Swilly, apparently as the notion takes them. It is these lines of swans, flying east and west, that the old people used to call wild geese, mistaking the white of the swans for the white of their own domestic geese. In March or April the swans leave for Iceland. At that time of year there is often a steady easterly wind which helps them slightly and certainly doesn't impede them. They are expert at using the wind and will fly low over the waves or as high as five miles, whichever suits. With a favourable wind they can make the 500-mile flight to Iceland in as little as thirteen hours. In unfavourable conditions, it can take almost five days, and the birds are lucky that they can rest on the sea if necessary.

Many wading birds also make the autumn journey south to the welcoming shores of Lough Neagh and Lough Beg. Among the most obvious are curlew and lapwing. Both these species, as well as redshank, were once common breeding birds along the Ballinderry Valley but changes in agricultural practice and drainage of wetlands has left them with fewer suitable sites for their nests, and birdwatchers now look out for those rare nests that do occur. The agricultural authorities have recognised the harm that was done by some of their policies in the past and are now trying to redress the balance, encouraging farmers to leave damp corners in their fields. With all three species it is important not to search for nests, but to look for signs that birds are nesting. The male bird can usually be seen in display flights above its territory. A marauding fox will often follow a human trail, knowing that it often leads to food. If you leave a trail leading to a nest on the ground you are simply providing the fox with a bonus meal.

Each bird has specific needs. Redshanks breed early, often arriving at their chosen site in February and beginning their nesting in April. They need short grass to conceal their nests, a high water table providing damp or muddy areas for the adults to feed, and longer vegetation where the young birds can hide and find suitable invertebrates on which to feed. The young birds have usually fledged by the end of June.

The curlews that spend their winters around Lough Neagh are not the same birds that breed here. The breeding birds have spent their winter further south and return in early spring. They look for damp, rushy pastures, and will hide their nests in long, grassy vegetation. They usually lay four eggs, which will hatch in twenty-eight days. The young birds are fledged in another five weeks.

Lapwings are usually seen in flocks during late summer and winter and their group aerobatics are wonderful to watch. Those who stay to breed need short vegetation, or even bare ground, near open water, which can be anything from a drain to a lake. They breed from mid-March onwards. If there is enough suitable ground, they will nest in loose colonies, since this gives them better protection against predators. In spring the male's display flight is easily spotted as he tumbles from the sky. When the birds are sitting, however, or the young have hatched, it is necessary to keep an eye on an arc of ground up to 200 yards in front of you. If you get any closer to the nest you will see signs of agitation.

The main threat to all three species comes from the management of the wet grassland on which they depend. Increased livestock numbers are at the heart of the problem. Cattle can trample the nests. Over-grazing can remove the tussocks that redshanks are dependent on. Spreading fertiliser or rolling grass to increase the productivity of a field can crush nests. Paradoxically, lack of grazing can also produce problems, since wet grassland can then be taken over by rank grasses and shrubs, destroying the habitat altogether. Another threat to the birds derives from the reduction in suitable habitat. Predators have fewer areas to concentrate their attentions on and are more likely to come across a nest. Equally, because the patches of suitable ground are often unable to sustain more than one nest, birds are less successful at driving away predators such as hooded crows and magpies.

Another little breeding bird that is just about holding its own along the

Cam Lough, the source of the Ballinderry.

western shore of Lough Neagh is the tree sparrow. This bird is often passed over because of its superficial resemblance to its cousin, the rowdy house sparrow. It is quite easy to tell the two species apart, as long as you get close enough or have binoculars. Both sexes in the tree sparrow look the same and resemble the male house sparrow. The distinctive feature is a black cheek-patch on the side of the tree sparrow's head. Once you see this, you know you have the rarer species.

The tree sparrow nests in holes; these can be in trees or in walls. It will also nest in the burrows of sand martins and in nest boxes. Like most small birds, they will have as many broods in the year as they can manage. During the summer both adults and young feed on invertebrates. During the winter their diet changes to grain and to weed seeds and they move to cereal fields, where they sometimes form mixed flocks with yellowhammers, chaffinches and, con-fusingly, house sparrows. Tree sparrows had been extinct in Ireland for some time and only began to re-establish themselves in the 1950s.

They chose a bad time to come back, because changes in farming practice have been putting pressure on their food sources ever since. Many fields are ploughed in the autumn, so there are fewer fields of winter stubble for them to forage in. Grassland has become a monoculture of rye, and multi-cutting of silage means less grass gets to set seed. Their summer diet is also under threat. There are fewer weeds in the countryside and that means that there are fewer insects and small invertebrates available as food. This is made worse when ponds and open ditches are filled in, wetlands drained and the margins and corners of fields, which used to be left alone as being too much bother, are brought into cultivation because of new machinery. Even nest sites are under pressure. Many hedgerows are no longer tended, becoming so spindly that they do not give adequate shelter to young birds. The old trees and ruined walls that provided the holes for nest sites are being removed for the sake of tidiness. In an effort to minimise the problems this causes to the birds, a project is placing suitable nest boxes at sites along the shore. Some of these nest boxes are also being placed along the banks of the river to encourage the birds to extend their ranges.

Many different species of duck breed around Lough Neagh. Mallards are the most common of these, and seem prepared to breed almost anywhere. It is not uncommon for a mallard duck to lead her newly hatched family, following in a line, through a lough-side village on the way to water. Although mallard seem very tame in certain situations, where they are leading their ducklings to water, or where they are used to being fed by people, at other times they are the wildest of wild birds. The very duck which will accept bread from your hand on the beach at Ballyronan will rise from the water quacking its alarm call if you encounter it further along the lough shore. The drakes, in spite of their clean-cut looks, are not gentle partners. A group of drakes around a duck will sometimes get so excited that they will drown her.

Another very handsome species which breeds along the lough shore is the shelduck. They look out for rabbit burrows in which to lay their eggs, and the incubation period is spent safely underground. The young birds leave the nest as soon as they are hatched and follow the parents. They are much more of a pair than are mallard, and both parents look after the young. The drake is very aggressive and very territorial and will drive away any other shelduck that he considers to be trespassing. The intruder invariably retreats, but the drake will try to grab hold of the other's tail so the fleeing bird will have to tow an irate territory owner after it as it tries to take off. The drake does not limit his aggression to other shelduck, but will attack any species that comes too close, and will even kill the young of the mallard and of other duck. Although this may seem brutal, the lough is a brutal place. Young birds face an array of enemies, from lesser black-backed gulls and herons on the water to foxes and rats on land and pike under the water. The fact of the matter is that very few ducklings grow to maturity. Seen in this perspective, the aggression of the shelduck may be praiseworthy after all.

Lough Neagh used to hold large numbers of breeding tufted duck, but their numbers have plummeted over a number of years, from something like 30,000 in the 1980s to about 6,000 at present. This decline has been seen in all the diving duck species, although scaup have started to show signs of reversing the trend. Interestingly, populations of dabbling duck species have held steady, although the coot has also shown a significant decline. In spite of study, any explanation would only be speculative.

A more positive success story is that of the great crested grebe. The very existence of this species was threatened one hundred years ago when its attractive feathers became fashionable accessories for women's clothing. They are no longer under threat and are thriving on Lough Neagh, which, together with Lough Beg, holds nearly a quarter of the population of the British Isles. In national terms, Lough Neagh is a reservoir for this species from which it can expand its range into suitable habitat. The pair gets together in the early spring and establishes pair bonds by performing a sort of dance with their heads and necks, crests flared, providing a very attractive sight for the onlooker. The birds are so well designed for swimming that they find it almost impossible to move on land. For this reason they build a floating nest. When the young birds hatch they have very distinctive black heads. Like most water birds, they leave the nest as soon as the entire clutch has hatched. They are not without shelter, however, since they travel around on the backs of their parents.

✤ 8 ✤

THE BANKS OF THE BALLINDERRY

We will now consider the Ballinderry River. It is one of the problems of a river that it continues to look well even when, under the surface, it is anything but healthy. We human beings continue to abuse it, assuming that it can cope with anything we (literally) throw at it. For hundreds of years this has worked, but in the twentieth century, rivers and the environment generally began to reach a critical point. Possibly the first indication that something might be going wrong occurred back in the 1960s, when salmon and large trout began to appear in the rivers, covered with a disfiguring white fungus. The disease was known as UDN, or Ulcerative Dermal Necrosis. It was probably caused by a virus, although none was actually identified, and the first sign was the appearance of small bleached areas on the head, back and tail, which were then covered in a slimy, bluish-grey growth. The affected area then became ulcerated and infected by the fungus, which was the most visible sign. Along the Ballinderry and its tributaries, the disease affected both salmon and dollaghan.

Although the salmon disease, as it was generally known, was not a direct result of pollution, its effect on fish populations made people realise the fragile nature of the river environment and to consider more carefully the stresses that were being put on it. This was at a time when ecology was starting to look at the damage pollution was doing to the world generally and there was concern about mercury in tuna, soap suds in industrialised rivers and DDT in everything. Television documentaries opened up a debate about a situation where whole sections of America's Great Lakes had become dead zones. There was a real fear that something similar could happen here, especially given the fragility of the Lough Neagh ecosystem.

At first, of course, farmers were blamed. They were accused of applying the relatively new artificial fertilisers at too high a rate, and of being too ready to use pesticides. The excess of both of these was washing down into the rivers with deadly results. Apart from the obvious and indiscriminate dangers of pesticides, fertiliser in the water was over-enriching it, encouraging blooms of algae. These blooms diminished the amount of dissolved oxygen that was available for other creatures causing distress and even death. The first fish kills were seen, and distressed fish rose to the surface in an attempt to get oxygen straight from the air. Lack of oxygen had a greater effect on trout and salmon than on coarse fish, and more salmonids died. Farmers were also blamed when silage effluent got into the water and poisoned fish, and this was a time when more and more farmers were turning from the traditional cutting of hay to the more reliable gathering of silage.

But farmers were not the only problem. In England much of the pollution in rivers was caused by industries that had extracted water from the river and returned the impure water straight back. There is little of that type of industry along the Ballinderry. The greatest danger is from the extraction of sand. Almost the entire valley is bedded with sand as a result of the ice ages. Some impression of the depth of this sandy deposit can be seen when travelling along the Cookstown to Omagh Road near Dunamore. There are several sand quarries along this stretch, some of them with walls well over 100ft high. Sand has to be washed and sorted, however, and there is the danger of a very fine silt, a by-product of this washing, getting into the water. It can be held in suspension for a long time and if it settles on the eggs of trout or salmon it can kill them.

Trout eggs.

Even publicly owned institutions were getting in on the act. This was extremely difficult to deal with, because of the principle of crown immunity. Originally, this meant that the King or Queen could not be sued as a result of damage he or she had caused. This was extended to cover the state; this in turn meant that a government department could not be sued even if it was manifestly in the wrong. In the rest of the United Kingdom this had been changed by a law of 1947 which removed crown immunity from everything but the sovereign himself. This law did not apply to Northern Ireland. Indeed, the Water Service claimed crown immunity until as recently as 2006. The result of this anomaly was that government-run establishments could pollute with impunity. For many years the sewage works in Cookstown was not physically capable of dealing with the town's sewage; the town had outstripped its facilities. As a result nitrates and phosphates were being introduced to the river just as it slowed down into a meandering stream.

Another problem occurred on the Lissan Water, one of the Ballinderry's tributaries. There had been a creamery owned by the Milk Marketing Board on the banks of the Lissan Water for a long time, in fact it is now the largest milk processing establishment in Northern Ireland. When a cheese factory opened on the same site, there were cases of milk being released, presumably by accident, into the river. This killed the fish for some distance below the factory.

Some aspects of the situation were almost farcical. Alan Keys, a local farmer, had always had a great interest in the state of the local rivers. He had been visiting the site of a fish kill on the Lissan Water and he decided to walk further upstream, to check the condition of some salmon redds (nests) that he had noted earlier in the winter. As he arrived, he was horrified to find a JCB tractor driver extending his bucket out over the river, directly over the gravel ford where the salmon redds were located. He was able to stop the driver before any damage was done, and he asked the man, who was employed by the Department of Agriculture's Drainage Division, who had ordered this work to be done. It turned out that the man was doing it on his own initiative; he had finished another job earlier and had noticed what he considered an obstruction blocking the flow of the river. As far as he was concerned, it was his job to remove any obstructions from the river in case they contributed to flooding at times of high water. At this same time, the development of angling was in the hands of the Fisheries Branch of the same Department of Agriculture. There seemed to have been no communication between Fisheries and Drainage branches, although they were both dealing with waterways.

In the end, a number of individuals, some representing clubs or other organisations, came together to see if anything could be done. They formed an organisation called the Ballinderry River Enhancement Association, most commonly called by its initials, BREA. At first it met in hotel rooms and people's houses, but its work was professional from the start. It helped that every fishing club along the Ballinderry and its tributaries was represented, which gave it the clout to face up to government departments and the credibility to be taken seriously by everybody. To begin with it decided to consolidate what it could. Since the Plantation of Ulster, the legal rights to the fishing in County Derry rivers was held by the Honourable the Irish Society, usually just known as the Irish Society. They were prepared to grant these rights on a long-term lease to BREA, through a number of trustees.

One of the more difficult issues to begin with was the problem of pollution by individual farmers. The membership all came from the local area and many of them were farmers. They were neighbours of the farmers they were going to have to confront if they were to succeed in their aims. No one was looking forward to such unpleasantness. One of the first major fish kills to occur after BREA was set up involved fish above and below Ballinderry Bridge itself. It was possible to trace the dead fish upstream to where a small ditch entered the river. Silage which had escaped from a farm had got into the river this way. The farmer concerned happened to be a brother of one of the BREA committee members, but that did not prevent the association from bringing his wrongdoing to his attention. Other farmers began to take BREA seriously.

It was necessary to obtain an inventory of what conditions were like for fish within the system. Some of the information could be got from research being done by local universities. For example, one survey showed that, after a drainage exercise carried out by the Department of Agriculture for Northern Ireland, in a whole mile of the Ballymully River below Moneymore there was only one item of food suitable for trout. In order to find out exactly what they needed, some members of BREA taught themselves the skills necessary to carry out environmental surveys on their own. Given the fact that most of them were anglers, it is not surprising that their first concern was for stocks of game fish: trout, dollaghan and salmon. Given the fact that dollaghan was the species endemic to Lough Neagh and its rivers, they took this as their point of departure.

As mentioned elsewhere, dollaghan resemble sea trout in that they breed in the rivers, but spend most of their lives in Lough Neagh. They were common until after the Second World War, but after that they declined in numbers as well as in size. Using electro-fishing and counting the nests (or redds) of breeding dollaghan, BREA established that there was only one healthy population of dollaghan in the Ballinderry system, and that was in the Ballymully River. They decided that they had to use this as the basis from which to restock the entire system. There already existed a hatchery on one of the smaller tributary streams, near the hamlet of Orritor on the Gortin Water. They acquired this and set about learning how to operate it. In the first instance this involved cleaning it out.

A young trout.

The first couple of years were disappointing, since in the first year their stock fish was stolen and in the second the fish eggs they had obtained all died because they had been covered in silt. Many of the volunteers had a farming background and were used to make do and mend. They solved the silt problem with the help of the wife of one of the directors, who donated a nylon stocking which was fitted to the inlet pipe. This turned out to be a great success. In fact, when the volunteers returned to work after a weekend where there had been a heavy flood, they discovered what appeared to be the leg of a woman, about 10ft long and with a neatly turned ankle, stretched over the fish tank. Not a drop of silt had got through.

It would be tedious to follow every step in their progress, but some aspects need to be mentioned. They established working relationships with both of Northern Ireland's universities and with what was then the Department of Agriculture. These relations were – and are – not always easy, as the priorities of each were not always identical. At the moment, for example, orthodoxy among government scientists is that hatcheries are a threat to nature, in that they risk diluting the purity of the DNA of fish in a river system. To this BREA reply that DNA is always being diluted. Among migratory fish, up to 10 per cent return to a river other than the one in which they were born, while the eggs of non-migratory fish are frequently transferred between rivers on the feet of waterfowl and waders. This makes sense, because otherwise a population of fish may become too inbred and lack the capacity to resist a disease or other threats. In the same ways, zoos around the world are always searching for fresh blood in order to maintain the welfare of their stock.

As the expertise of BREA increased, it began to gain respect beyond Northern Ireland. One of the insights that the members had from an early stage was that it was the ecosystem of the river that was important, not simply the trout. If the river could not sustain breeding trout then it didn't matter how many fingerlings you put in the water; they would live an abbreviated life and leave no successors to take their place. To help them decide on water quality without having to resort to expensive chemical testing, they identified a number of invertebrate species that could only survive in pure water, another group that could survive in water of intermediate quality, while a third group was chosen because they were the only ones who could survive in polluted water. In order to be able to get as wide a feedback as possible, a small, durable chart was produced which showed these species and the chart was distributed free to fishing clubs and schools, and to interested individuals. This was possible because of another skill that BREA had acquired: the ability to get funds from a variety of sources, in this case WWF. The idea was so good that it was copied almost directly by the Environment and Heritage Service of Northern Ireland.

Mark Horton, Co-ordinator of RIPPLE.

In all this work, they began to build up a picture of the natural history of the river and its banks, and to see other species that were important, some of which also needed help. One of the most beautiful is the otter. This delightful animal is present along the full length of the river, and can be surprisingly tame at times. This does not apply if you are walking with a dog, since dogs consider it their prerogative to chase any animal that they can smell, anywhere, anytime. In these circumstances all you are likely to see is a glimpse of something moving fast and a splash. If you are lucky, you will see the otter swimming past you underwater. A more satisfying way to see them is when you are moving quietly along the river. Most of the ones that I have seen appeared while I was fishing. Sometimes the otter seemed to be following me downstream, as if it knew that my clumsy feet would be disturbing fish from their hiding places. It is the same principle that starlings use when they follow cows about; they know that the lumbering brutes will be putting up invertebrates simply by moving about. Another good place to look is near bridges. Otters often like to leave their droppings (called spraints) in dry places under or near bridges.

The Ballinderry is the easternmost of a group of rivers in Northern Ireland which has a significant population of otters. The others are the Owenkillew and the Foyle system. These rivers communicate with other rivers in Donegal, which also have healthy populations. The Ballinderry is a small river. It is probably able to support a few female territories, but only a couple or three male territories. If this population becomes isolated, it is not large enough to sustain itself for more than a few years. The productivity of the river in terms of otter food and therefore of otters depends on its biodiversity. This in turn depends on how natural the channel is. If it has been modified to any degree not only is its biodiversity impaired, but there is a reduction in the bank-side habitat that encourages otters. This is not to say that otters are delicate creatures, liable to an attack of the vapours if confronted with a discarded beer bottle. In point of fact, their need to check things out for food means that they will hunt in places that human beings would consider unpleasantly polluted. What matters is not the pollution itself, but the way in which pollution reduces biodiversity.

The numbers of otters generally seemed to decline through the last two decades of the twentieth century, and the animal became extinct, or was extinct, through large parts of Europe. There seems to be signs of a recovery over the last number of years. In order for this to be maintained, there has to be strict monitoring of their numbers and of the productivity of the river. It is important to remember also that otters are not tied to rivers, and can wander quite a distance away from them. Each year a number of them, unfortunately, feature as road kills. When they are breeding, the females like a den where there is no danger of flooding. One such breeding den was discovered by one of the BREA directors some distance away from the river, in an old badgers' den.

Mink are a problem in some of the smaller tributaries, doing great damage to ducks and other waterfowl, although their main prey is fish. Superficially they resemble otters, to which they are related, but they vary in a number of ways. They are bolder, for a start, and will go about their business with a complete disregard for any humans in the vicinity. They are also smaller, which is a good thing, seeing the damage they do. They started to escape from mink farms back in the 1950s. The first recorded escape in Northern Ireland was in 1961, near Omagh, where thirty animals escaped. In England and other European countries thousands of mink have been released into the wild by self-styled animal rights campaigners. This was done as recently as 2003 in County Laois. These terrorists *manqué* think little of the rights of native animals. The decline of water voles – Ratty in *The Wind in the Willows* – is almost certainly linked to feral mink. The North American mink is an intelligent animal, active and playful, much like its cousin the otter. Domestic mink, bred for their coats, are not the same animal. After hundreds of generations born in captivity, they were found to have smaller brains than the original wild animal. Researchers speculate that the domestic version is not as able to survive in the wild as it should be and lives for a much shorter time. In Denmark it was estimated that they live less than two months.

This is unlikely to be the case in Ireland. Although at one time there were around forty mink farms on the island of Ireland, this is no longer the case. Mink farming has been banned in Northern Ireland since 2003 and the number of farms still operating in the Republic of Ireland is reduced to six. Mink are well established in the wild and it seems unlikely that they are dependent on new recruits in some ongoing great escape. One limiting factor is the fact that they are solitary animals and defend territories. Males will not allow male trespassers, but are less aggressive towards females. Within its territory the mink will have several dens. Favoured sites are among the roots of riverside trees, among boulders and in old rabbit burrows. The young are born between March and early May. The mother keeps the young with her during the summer, even after they are weaned, but the family disperses in the autumn, when the young make off to establish territories of their own.

Fishermen dislike mink because of what appears to be a wasteful method of fishing that they have. Time and again anglers will come across the body of a fish that has been killed by a single bite to the back of the head. They then come to the conclusion that the mink is a wanton killer, killing for fun. If we remember that this animal originates in the northern United States and in Canada, where winters are extremely cold, the behaviour begins to make sense. Like all hunters, the mink has to deal with times of glut and times of famine, when prey is hard to find. In order to cope with this it will attempt to stash food when times are good, in order to tide it through the lean times. In winter,

North America it is so cold that a fish, once out of water, will freeze immediately and can be recovered at any time before spring. The mink has not lived enough generations in the British Isles to have worked out that this system will not operate in our mild climate, so it keeps trying.

Otters do not like mink either. In the first decades that mink found their way into the Ballinderry, otters avoided them. Where a mink established a territory, the otters moved away. This might have been fatal for the otter population of the river valley but for one thing. Mink prefer very slow-moving or still water and so prefer the lower reaches of the river. Although some individuals may be seen near faster water, these are usually young specimens in search of a territory. The result has been that otters have been given a free hand in the Upper Ballinderry, while mink have tended to limit themselves to parts of the river nearer the lough. Interestingly, there is some evidence that otters are beginning to claim some parts of their lost territories.

Meanwhile, the mink get on with things in these lower waters and in some of the slower tributaries, like the Ballymully below Moneymore. Here they feed on fish, varied in spring by the eggs and young of ground-nesting birds, in particular moorhen and coots. In fact, the presence or absence of these birds from a section of river can be a good indication of whether mink are present. When mink first came to the Ballinderry, moorhens all but disappeared. The mink also feed on another of the Ballinderry specialities, the white-clawed crayfish.

This strange little monster is a relative of the lobster, which it resembles. It was once widespread across Western Europe, but declining water quality has affected it, as has degradation of its habitat. There are other ecological threats, such as competition from alien species of crayfish. The British Isles constitute the last stronghold of the white-clawed crayfish. Even here it is under threat in the Eastern Island (Great Britain), where it has to compete with the signal crayfish, a native of North America. So far, Ireland is the only part of the white-clawed range where it does not have to compete with its transatlantic cousin.

The greatest concentration of the species is in the limestone country of Fermanagh. When researchers started surveying the Northern Ireland population in the 1990s, it was here they concentrated. There were stories, however, that the Ballinderry had its own population, and some specimens had been taken at the inlet to a fish farm on the river. The valley of the upper river contains some of the richest and deepest sand deposits in the country. These had long been taken for building, and the washings had produced a watery environment that was very suitable for crayfish.

Since the Second World War, however, changes in agricultural practice have had a dreadful impact on the river. The intensity of the current agricultural regime has meant that farmers have had to use more fertiliser on their land. This has been exacerbated by the fact that modern animal husbandry has produced huge tanks of slurry that have to be emptied every now and again, and the only place to get rid of the smelly waste is on agricultural land. Excess nutrients wash into ditches and streams and find their way into the river. Here they encourage the growth of weeds to the extent that a stream might be choked. It is only when the weeds die in the winter that the real threat reveals itself. As the weeds decay they use up the oxygen, leaving nothing for the animals of the stream.

Other changes came about. The human population grew, and more people moved into towns to live. As living standards increased, families were no longer willing to live in decrepit houses, depending on well water and a chemical toilet. More and more houses were joined to the main sewage systems, so many that in places the ability to deal with sewage lagged behind the amount of sewage that was being produced. Sewage works were – quite literally at times – overwhelmed. The works at Cookstown were a particular problem, one that has only been dealt with in the last decade. Even now there can be problems. When a pump failed, water got into an old pipe and what was euphemistically called 'grey water' got into the river. Since BREA has an unofficial network of river watchers, this was soon noticed and reported and, to be fair, the authorities dealt with it straight away.

Crayfish

In more remote areas the septic tank was to be the great innovation. So it was, where the rules for looking after a septic tank were followed. Unfortunately, many young housewives treated the system as if it was attached to the main sewage network and, as a result, nobody knows how many of the countryside's septic tanks are still working. Another thing that people sometimes ignore is that there is still some effluent that drains from septic tanks; it is accepted that this is low grade and that the water system into which it is draining will be capable of dealing with it. There is still the danger however that building too many houses, all draining into the same waterway, will overwhelm the water-way's ability to purify itself of the pollution. Although modern houses in the countryside have much stricter building regulations to follow, the fact that no one knows what existing conditions are means that it is impossible to predict potential hazards before they occur. All of this has allowed the water quality in the Ballinderry to decline.

These were not the only problems that the crayfish had to survive. Along the lower river extensive flood protection work was carried out in the 1950s and 1960s. This involved both building flood banks and, more destructively, drain-ing the river. The use of dredges not only removed much of their habitat, but also must have killed many hundreds of crayfish. At the same time, increased demands for building materials encouraged less efficient management of sand washing, so the process which had helped crayfish in the past now became a threat. It was in the years following this that crayfish retreated to just a few stretches of the Ballinderry. This occurred at the same time as a decline in the numbers and range of dollaghan, salmon, the otter and the literal jewel in the Ballinderry crown, the freshwater pearl mussel, to which we shall return later.

The numbers of white-clawed crayfish became so low that a survey car-ried out in 1996/97 found none in the Ballinderry River. Alarmed at this result, BREA conducted its own survey in 2006 and found that there were populations in the lowest stretches of the river and, surprisingly, just below the Glenavon Weir in Cookstown. In conjunction with Queen's University Belfast, an approved system of monitoring was put in place. One of the problems with this species of crayfish is that it is very slow to recolonise even suitable habi-tats when the original population has been lost. After checking the literature, BREA decided that it would be possible to establish a breeding programme which would provide enough young to allow the reintroduction of the cray-fish into carefully selected areas. The chosen areas would be those which held white-clawed crayfish in the past. Once again individual volunteers and work-ers drew on the community for help. A local firm donated the use of a small lake near Pomeroy as a breeding pond. Queen's University encouraged students to carry out projects relating to the crayfish. Although the project has not yet reached the stage of liberating crayfish into the wild, the indications are that they are on track to do so. One limiting factor may be the Northern Ireland regulations that govern the movement of a species from one site to another.

Crayfish are not the only strange creatures that inhabit the river. Lampreys are strange, eel-like creatures that have existed so long on earth that they do not even have jaws. They are creatures of nightmare, if fish have nightmares. They get their food by attaching themselves to the bodies of fish, then, with their rasping teeth, they begin to consume the living flesh and drink their victims' blood. Lampreys come in three sizes. Luckily we are spared the largest of these, the sea lamprey. It can grow to almost 1m in length and its circular mouth contains concentric rows of sharp, pointed teeth, together with a rasping tongue that allows it to penetrate the scales and skin of its prey. The victim usually dies from loss of blood or from infection. Sea lamprey are born in fresh water and live in mud for up to seventeen years before metamorphosing into its parasitic form and going to sea. When they are sexually mature, they return to fresh water to breed and die. They do not come as far as the Ballinderry.

On the other hand, two species of lamprey do live in the waters of the Ballinderry: the river lamprey and the brook lamprey. The brook lamprey, as its name suggests, is the smaller of the two, growing to no more than 15cm. Its life history couldn't compare more extremely with its lumbering cousin, the sea lamprey. The brook lamprey spends all its life in the mud of its native river, filter feeding, eating any organic rubbish it comes across. It does not have a parasitic phase; the adult form simply breeds over the sediment where it has spent its life and dies.

The river lamprey is a very close relative of the brook lamprey, and it is very difficult to tell them apart except in terms of size; the river lamprey grows up to twice as big as the brook lamprey. It shows different aspects of behaviour as well. It does have a parasitic form, feeding on fish tissue and blood. It also spends part of its life cycle in the sea. There is a body of scientific opinion which has it that brook and river lamprey are two races of the same species but with different lifestyles. The comparison made is with brown trout and sea trout. River lampreys return to their spawning grounds in autumn and winter, and the most intense spawning activity is in the spring, after the water reaches 9°C. There is some evidence that river lamprey from the Ballinderry, and only from the Ballinderry, do not go all the way to the sea, but spend their parasitic stage in Lough Neagh. In this their habits resemble dollaghan trout rather than sea trout. For this reason the Ballinderry river lamprey deserves special protection.

In Britain, both brook and river lampreys are listed as species for which there is conservation concern. This is not the case in Northern Ireland, the reason – or excuse – given being that there is a lack of information about their distribution. The reason for the lack of information is that it is very difficult to tell the two species apart. Since both species are listed without priority being given to one or the other, it is difficult to see this as anything more than an excuse not to do anything to conserve a creature which is unlikely to gather much popular support.

The River Ballinderry suits these strange creatures. They like clean water which supports a high level of biodiversity. They need sediment to burrow into and they prefer it to be at least 8cm deep. The sediment can be anything from fine sand to coarse gravel. They like a slow flow, deep sediment, plenty of shade and less vegetation in the channel itself. Most of these factors apply more to the lower reaches of the river; this means that they are not protected by the current Area of Special Scientific Interest. Whether the area of conservation might be extended to include the waters of the lower river is probably as much a political as a scientific decision.

As we go further up the river we are following the path that the dollaghan trace each late summer and autumn as they make their way to their spawning beds. What they are looking for is a gravel ford that will allow them to lay their eggs in fast-flowing, oxygen-rich waters. Writing in 1950, Robert Lloyd Praeger claimed that dollaghan of 30lb had been common in the past, and that specimens up to 50lb had been caught. Most fishermen I have spoken to, even those who remember the glory days, felt that this was on the generous side, but they do remember catching enough double-figure fish to need a bicycle to bring them home. Sadly, those days are gone and dollaghan are diminished in both size and numbers. When BREA did a survey of the different tributaries of the Ballinderry, they found that the Ballymully River, which flows through Moneymore, was the only one which held significant numbers of the big trout. With the help of government experts they obtained fertilised eggs and (eventually) reared fingerlings that they could return to the wild. By repeating this process year after year (they have returned some 15,000,000 fish to the river) they have managed to restore a healthy population. In late October or early November it is possible to stand on the bridge at Coagh and watch large dollaghan, some of them weighing up to 14lbs, digging their redds and laying their eggs in the gravel below.

Moving up the river at the same time are the salmon. The word iconic is one that is almost used to death, but if it applies to anything it applies to the leap of a salmon over a weir, a picture that epitomises a healthy river. There has been concern going back to the 1980s about the welfare of the wild Atlantic salmon through its entire range. It is well known that salmon spend the first part of their lives in rivers, then go to sea, where they grow quickly on the excellent feeding. Traditionally, it was as they returned to their home rivers to breed that they became targets for fishermen. At about that time, however, the pressures that salmon were suffering as a result of drift netting and fixed nets in estuaries were compounded when trawlers discovered where they spent their lives at sea. Concurrently, intensive agriculture was degrading the salmon's spawning beds. The fact that deep-sea trawlers are catching salmon in great numbers is reflected in the drop-off in catches in coastal fisheries. An example can be seen in Lough Foyle. Back in the 1960s this was one of the most prolific salmon fisheries in Ireland. In the last few years catches have been so low that few fishermen even try for them anymore. Salmon nets remain in sheds and boats stay tied up to the quay.

The evidence of diminishing salmon stocks is not simply anecdotal. Detailed records have been kept on the River Bush and this has shown that the percentage of young salmon (smolts) that return as adults has been steadily declining. In 1997 it was over 30 per cent. This had dropped to 11 per cent in 2003 and as little as 6 per cent in 2005. Efforts to control catches and to eradicate poaching by tagging dead salmon seem no more than a drop in the river when compared to these realities, although the records that anglers are required to return do give some idea of the status of the species on a river-by-river basis. Many angling clubs also keep detailed records of fish caught.

At the beginning of its existence, BREA bought in 1,000 salmon fry and put them into the system. Their technique has changed since then, in the hope of giving the young fish a more substantial start to life. The fry are now kept in a specially adapted pond on the Lissan Water until they have developed into smolts. This is the stage at which they are ready to leave for the sea. In the pond they are allowed to decide for themselves when they are ready to leave. Those who leave are caught in a smolt trap at the outflow. This trap is checked every day and the young fish are marked by having their fins clipped and then released into one of the tributaries of the Ballinderry system. Salmon also breed naturally in the river, an increasing number each year. Although it seems as if the gravel they choose for their redds is little different from that chosen by dollaghan, groups of young fish tend to be either mainly salmon or mainly dollaghan. This probably comes from the salmon's preference for faster water and slightly coarser gravel.

One quick indicator of the suitability of a river for salmon is the presence of a modest green plant which waves elegantly in the flow, looking like the visible hair of some invisible naiad. When it blooms its white flowers show it to be one of the species of water crowfoot, a relative of buttercups. In the pampered waters of England's chalk streams it grows in such abundance that it has to be cut at regular intervals during the fishing season. Anglers on the Ballinderry are not confronted by this annual chore. They are glad to keep what they have, since beds of water crowfoot provide a habitat which is of great ecological importance. The species in the Ballinderry is the stream water crowfoot. The much rarer river water crowfoot lives in a small stretch of the Six Mile Water in County Antrim. Although the stream water crowfoot is commoner throughout the British Isles, the Ballinderry is the only river flowing into Lough Neagh, and one of only three rivers in Northern Ireland where it lives in substantial amounts.

The plant grows for some fifteen miles of the Ballinderry's length, where it often grows with water starwort. It can be found in many different states of the river – runs, glides and pools – but likes to grow on a gravel bottom. It seems to prefer shallow glides to shady pools, but is not limited to these areas. As a species, it is often found in the presence of other plants. For example it is associated with cuckoo flower, mud water starwort, curled pondweed, watercress, common spike-rush, marsh horsetail and a number of other lower plants. Another plant that is associated with it is hemlock water dropwort, an umbellifer that needs to be treated with caution, since it is reputed to be the most poisonous plant in the British Isles. This combination of plants indicate that the river is moderately enriched, but not overly so.

Since water crowfoot is a vital habitat for many of the invertebrate species that are vital to the welfare of trout, and gives shelter to young trout and salmon, BREA is very anxious to ensure that it continues to be a healthy part of the river ecosystem. They encourage farmers to put their fences slightly back from the river, so that banks are not trampled by cattle, since the resulting erosion can cause silt to build up on the water crowfoot. The same caution has to be taken when any engineering works, such as bridge repairs, are being undertaken. BREA also intends to look at the possibility of reintroducing water crowfoot to stretches of the river and its tributaries where it is currently absent.

There is a final species which lives in the Upper Ballinderry which is very precious to the natural heritage of Ireland, though at first appearance this seems a rather grand judgement on a rather nondescript organism. The animal with the accolade is the freshwater pearl mussel. These were once widespread on Irish rivers and were the basis of a substantial trade in pearls. Up till about a century ago there were pearl fisheries on many Irish rivers, including the Ballinderry. Its natural range spreads from Russia to the Atlantic and the north-eastern States of the USA and Canada. For some time now it has been declining along much of this range, and in some countries it has totally disappeared. Even where it has not, there is a great decline in breeding success. The pearl mussel is a long-living, slow-growing animal, and large adults can live on in a river for decades, giving a false impression that there is a healthy population. Almost half of those populations which are successful in their breeding, and which have young mussels as well as old, live in Scottish rivers. There are three active populations in Northern Ireland rivers: the Middle Ballinderry; the Clady River at Swanlinbar, and the Owenkillew. Another population has been found in the Tempo River. Although the mussels in the Tempo are actively trying to breed, young have not been able to develop because of the lack of suitable conditions. The largest single group (about 1,000 specimens) of pearl mussels lives in the Ballinderry.

Mussels in the riverbed.

Mussel adolescents.

The first study of the Ballinderry River mussels was carried out in 1995. The researcher was struck by the absence of juvenile mussels, that is, specimens less than about 2½in long. To understand his explanation, it is necessary to understand a little of the life cycle of the freshwater mussel. It is a very long-living creature, and can easily survive for more than one hundred years. They live partially buried under clean water in fast-flowing streams. They feed by sticking out an organ called their siphon into the water. This allows them to filter out the tiny organic particles on which they feed. In the past, large numbers of mussels were an important factor in keeping rivers clean enough for salmon and trout, fish upon which the mussels depend. Mussels are very slow growing, and do not mature until they are between twelve and fifteen years old, by which stage they are about 3in long.

In the early summer the males release sperm into the river. This sperm is taken in by the females and is used to fertilise their eggs, which they keep in a pouch within the shell. After several weeks, in the late summer these are released into the water as tiny larvae known as glochidia. These resemble minute mussels, but they float in the water with their shells wide open until they are, if they are lucky, taken into the mouth of a salmon or trout. As they pass over the fish's gills the shell snaps shut on a filament and the glochidia has a new address for the next six months or so. The vast majority of glochidia fail to find a host but since up to 4,000,000 can be ejected by a single female at a time, and all the females in a group release their offspring within a few days of one another, there are plenty to spare. Even for the lucky ones, the dangers are not yet over. Although they have an environment with a superabundance of oxygen in which to spend the winter, they do have to abandon it the following spring and have to trust that they will land in a clean, sandy or gravelly stream bed where they can settle, bury themselves and start to grow. Their period as a stowaway does not seem to harm the fish, and it means that there is a possibility that the young mussel will be dropped off further upstream. If fish were not involved, there would be a steady if slow migration downstream, till the mussel ran out of habitat.

In the Ballinderry River it was unlikely that it was the lack of salmon or trout that caused the problem with the pearl mussels, because BREA had already begun an intensive stocking programme in the river system. This idea was reinforced by the discovery of a large number of juvenile shells, indicating that young mussels were dying before they reached maturity. The finger of suspicion was pointed at pollution. This hypothesis was reinforced by the fact that mussels were being found in the less intensively farmed part of the river. The strategy for recovery, then, had to be two pronged; captive breeding would only succeed if it was accompanied by an improvement in habitat. It says a great deal about the team at BREA that the work they have done on captive breeding of the pearl mussel, together with the restorative work they have undertaken along the river, has placed them at the forefront of world knowledge of this species. A camera team actually arrived from a Japanese television channel to make a documentary about the project. It gives a childish delight to hear familiar scenes along the Ballinderry being described in an unfamiliar tongue.

The battle to save the river is not over yet. There are other threats to its integrity, but I like to think that its human guardians are being watched over by some natural ones. In the hills are ravens, probably descendants of ravens who watched as the first human family made its way gingerly along the banks of the river. Man always seems to have viewed the raven as a fellow toiler in the wilderness. Even today there is something uncanny about the way that, as you walk in any hills that the raven frequents, the resident pair will appear from nowhere to check out your intentions. If there is a dog in the party, the male will sometimes fly low over its head, hover even, with feet dangling. It is as if the bird is taunting the dog about its inability to fly.

Pairs of ravens occupy quite large territories. Somewhere in its acres will be a crag or a tall tree which the ravens consider a safe site for their nest. They are early birds as far as nesting is concerned, and will often be sitting on eggs by mid-March. They often have as neighbours that other bird of the wilderness, the peregrine. In those early days of the year there may be some animated discussion as to whose site this actually is. Each bird respects the other's weapons however, and in most years an armed truce prevails, with each species seeming to pretend that the other is not there.

The fact that ravens have been breeding successfully for a number of years now has created problems for the young birds. Although they may be tolerated for a year or so near the nest, helping out with big sister duties, the adults are not very comfortable with them about and the young ones eventually leave. The role of a solitary is a difficult one for the crow family. One pair of eyes is simply not enough to search for food and still look out for danger. Worse, if a solitary young bird does come across food, the territory pair is quite likely to come along and chase it off. The raven is a wise bird, however, even when young. Adolescent ravens stick together as a sort of gang. There are more birds to keep an eye out for danger or to search for food. Even better, if they do find a prize in the way of food – a dead sheep, for example – there are enough of them to intimidate even the local pair. I recently watched a group of seventeen young ravens soaring and landing on the southern slopes of Slieve Gallion. A few of them came close, to check that I wasn't a danger to them, before going back about their business. Business! It seemed pure enjoyment. As they soared and plunged, showed off by flying on their backs, or simply stood on the warm grass, I was reminded of a mixed group of teenagers at the beach on a summer's day. Long may they enjoy themselves.

Another bird soars over the river, though it prefers to be in lower country, and likes to have trees about. Thirty years ago the buzzard was nearly extinct in Ireland. A few pairs clung on at Murlough Bay, on the Antrim coast near Fair Head. Suddenly, in the mid-1980s, they began to expand their range and now thrive over most of Northern Ireland, although they seem to prefer river valleys with trees enough for roosts and nests. Their preferred food is rabbit, but they will take any rodent. Although they seem clumsy on the ground, where magpies delight in pulling at their tail feathers, they are strong and agile fliers. I have seen a sparrowhawk cower in a hedge, its yellow eyes for once full of fear, as a buzzard flew over. On another occasion a buzzard was flying too close to the nest of some hooded crows. The crows flew over the big bird, trying to strike it on the back with their beaks and claws. The buzzard simply flipped over on its back and showed the crows its talons, before going on its way.

But these are birds of the heights, and to finish I want to look at two birds which are intimately connected with the river. Everyone knows, or thinks he knows, the kingfisher. On television we see it in close up and slow motion, and we can pick out the colour of each feather. From the river bank, on the other hand, what we often see is a blur of electric blue, with a hint of warmer colours, as the bird flies away almost faster than we can focus. The truth is that the kingfisher is tiny and unless we move quietly and keep our eyes working on likely spots, we won't see it until we frighten it away. Quite a few breed by the Ballinderry and its tributaries and it can be quite easy to find a nest. One that I know is on a vertical bank where the Ballymully flows through a planting below Moneymore. The nest hole is easily spotted in summertime; its opening is stained with droppings and there is the faintest whiff of fish in the air. If you take a seat in the shade of a bush and remain reasonably still and quiet, the bird will ignore you as an irrelevance and will come and go quite confidently.

The other bird I have in mind is even more intimately involved with the river, and seems equally at home in it or on it. This is something of a surprise, because the dipper does not look in the least like a water bird. It is more like an overgrown wren that is wearing its best clothes to go out for the evening. Its main coat is a browny-black, but it has a white bib to set off the outfit. In spite of this pied effect, the dipper can be quite hard to see along the river, especially if it is standing near to an overhanging bank. Once again it is the flying bird that most people see; not a flight away from the observer this time, but simply past him or her. Dippers are quite bold birds, and will continue to feed near to passing people. They are difficult to see because their dull colouring blends in with the shadows. If you do see one, stand still and watch it operate. It simply walks into the water so that it is completely submerged, then turns over stones in search of the juicy invertebrates clinging to the underside. When its beak is full, it will pop out again and fly off to feed its

Children's Bridge.

Children at the Banks of Ballinderry Fair.

nestlings. Dippers seem to like building underneath bridges, so it is worth searching fast-flowing water near bridges if you want to find them. Avoid the temptation
of going under the bridge to find the nest itself, as there is the danger that you will
frighten a nestling enough for it to leave the nest. Young things need protection.

Luckily, there is a project that has begun which looks to protect the river and its
inhabitants in all their aspects. Working with WWF, and with additional funding
from the Heritage Lottery Fund, BREA has initiated the RIPPLE Project, which
is attempting to re-establish the link between the Ballinderry River and the people
living along it. People have been brought together to create a vision of the river as
they would wish it to be. A number of aspects have been chosen, from a clean-up
to improved access, and for each of these a group has volunteered to undertake
any action necessary. One of the great successes of the experiment so far is that
it has also established links between ordinary citizens and the agencies which the
Government has established to look after the environment. For people along the
river, bureaucracy is no longer a faceless abstraction. They have shared tea and buns
– and wet riverbanks – with scientists and engineers and politicians. Cookstown
Council has been generous with its help and a local MLA, Patsy McGlone, who is
Chairman of Stormont's Environmental Committee, has turned up to help in the
clean-up operation, as well as attending meetings when time allows.

It looks as if people have decided to give something back to the Ballinderry.

At last!

GAZETTEER

CREGGANDEVESKY COURT TOMB

Creggandevesky is set in a bright green field to the west of Lough Mallon, high on the watershed between the Ballinderry and the Owenkillew Rivers. It is easily missed, so the motorist approaching the site needs to navigate fairly carefully. If you are coming from the A505 between Omagh and Cookstown, there is a signpost pointing south just to the east of An Creagan Visitors' Centre. Alternatively, the route is also signposted from the B4, which runs between Pomeroy and Sixmilecross. The car park is little more than a slight widening of the road that is used by farm traffic, so it is important to park as tight to the side as possible.

The path to the tomb is about half a mile and is across a field, which may be wet or even muddy. The drier and shorter path seems to go to the right, but this is a dead end. The visitor must stay to the left, or south, of the lake. This approach has the advantage of keeping the remains hidden until the last minute, so that they are seen all at once, rather than revealed a little at a time. When the visitor does arrive at the site it is worth spending a few moments looking at the panorama revealed. The vista has a mixture of splendour and mystery in any weather (other than thick mist), and it is worth remembering that it is not all that different from the view that Neolithic man would have had: the trees would have been well cleared and the blanket bog, which has been cleared from most of the fields about, would have only begun to encroach on the farmland.

It was the bog that protected the site. When the owner of the land decided to improve it, back in the 1970s, all that there was to be seen above the soil was a collection of large stones protruding through the surface. The mark where moss had been growing in 1979 can still be seen on the lintel, and marks the old land

Creggandevesky Tomb.

surface before excavation began. After the archaeologists had cleared most of the peat away, they found a jumble of fallen stones which must originally formed a cairn which covered the tomb. This cairn may have been as high as 3m.

The court which gives this type of tomb its name faced to the east, towards the rising sun. Most archaeologists believe that this area was used for important ritual, possibly emphasising the tribe or clan's ownership of the land. This ownership was sanctified by the burial of ancestors in the burial chamber. The burnt remains of up to twenty-one human bodies have been found at Creggandevesky. It is impossible to tell whether others were simply buried, since the very acid soil would have destroyed all traces of this. Also found were flint arrowheads, scrapers, knives, the head of a javelin and the remains of a bead necklace, as well as pottery.

The burial chamber itself was made of corbelled stones, that is, each layer of stones projected slightly over the one below it, so that it eventually formed a domed roof. This roof had collapsed under the weight of the cairn. The tomb was probably abandoned as the climate deteriorated and the bog began to take over. There is evidence from pollen that hazel trees grew in the area after the farmers had left.

There are eleven other court cairns within a ten-mile radius of Creggandevesky.

BEAGHMORE STONE CIRCLES

Beaghmore lies north of the Ballinderry Valley. It is most easily found by following the signposts near Dunamore on the A505 between Cookstown and Omagh. Alternatively, the visitor can drive south from Draperstown along the Sixtowns Valley. Just after crossing the watershed he should look for Sheskinshule minor road to his left. After crossing a minor crossroads, he will see the complex of stone circles on his right. There is a very adequate car park.

This is a very complicated site at first glance, because there is a series of monuments here, some of them intertwined. The layout is further complicated by the fact that there are also the remains of Neolithic field boundaries, in the shape of low banks of small stones.

Originally a wooded site, it had been cleared for farming by 3500 BC. The stone monuments date from 2,000 or more years later, from about 1500 BC until 800 BC. Six of the seven circles are arranged in pairs. Each pair has a cairn either next to it or between the circles, although there are more cairns than this (twelve in total). All of the cairns were discovered to have cremated bones within them. The seventh circle is off by itself, and is very obviously different from the others, since it is completely filled with stones set close to one another. These stones are known locally as dragons' teeth.

There are so many stones here that it is almost like clutter, and it requires an effort of will, almost, to try to concentrate on one on the monuments. One experience that is worth trying is to be there before dawn on midsummer's day. As the light gradually fills the sky and the visitor becomes more aware of his surroundings, it becomes apparent that at least four of the stone rows point reasonably accurately towards the rising sun. The visitor should appreciate the moment when the sun breaks the circle of the horizon and before returning to his car, should look around him. The shadows will help him see just how many of Beaghmore's features stretch out under the bog. There is still a lot more to find.

THE HIGH CROSS AT ARDBOE

The high cross is the only remnant of a monastery that was established on the shore of Lough Neagh in the sixth century. The founding saint was Colman Mac Aed. The monastery buildings were of wood, and were destroyed in a fire in 1166. They were undoubtedly burnt before that, when Vikings made a camp only a mile or two away, at the mouth of the Ballinderry River. It had been rebuilt after that earlier catastrophe, but this second fire happened very soon after St Malachy, who was Archbishop of Armagh, had reformed the Christian Church in Ireland. There was no longer room for the old Gaelic form of monasticism; from now on only approved orders of monks would be allowed.

The nearby ruins did not form part of the original monastery. There was a parish church near the site all through the Middle Ages, but this ruin dates from after the Reformation, when the Established Church in Ireland followed the late Tudor version of Protestantism. A later, seventeenth-century building was erected for the small Church of Ireland congregation at Ardtrea, on the south bank of the Ballinderry River. Details like this did not put local families, mostly Catholic, off the desire to be buried within the ruined walls. The east wall of the church is not far from a low, clay cliff, which was the original shoreline of the lough before levels were lowered in the nineteenth and twentieth centuries. From here it is possible to see almost all the shores of Lough Neagh, and to pick out the woods of Ram's Island, almost opposite. To the north, a field or so away, is another ruined church known locally as the 'Abbey'.

Within the graveyard can be found remnants of a religion that was even older than Christianity. Priests attached to the local parish of Moortown have been distressed at a tradition which has persisted until the present day of hammering coins into living trees. In previous centuries it would have been pins that were hammered in. In the last half century at least three trees have died of metal poisoning. Local tradition has it that the original tree had been blessed by a monk, but the tradition surely goes back to a time when the mystery of metal was as awesome as the mystery of the Eucharist. Originally it might have been horseshoe nails that were driven in, each one asking a favour or a cure. Incidentally, to remove a coin is to draw the disease on yourself!

The cross stands near a bend of the road, in the shade of a row of tall trees. It is tall, at 18ft high, and gracefully slender. Unlike many other high crosses, the shaft and the head seemed to have been designed to be together, and the original collar which held the two pieces of stone together is still in place. Something of the magic is lost by the fact that the cross is enclosed within railings, but there was a tradition of emigrants taking a chip of stone with them, and you can still see the pock-mark damage that was done.

Crosses such as the one at Ardboe were originally designed as teaching aids. Scenes from the bible were carved in low relief and then, probably, painted in the same intense colours that characterise Irish illuminated manuscripts. There are twenty-two panels of sculpture. The side facing the graveyard, the east side, concentrates on scenes from the Old Testament: Adam and Eve; Daniel in the lion's den; the Hebrews in the fiery furnace. The same Old Testament theme is seen on the south side: Cain slays Abel; Samson and the lion; David killing Goliath. It also has a panel showing St Paul and St Anthony being fed in the desert by a raven.

The north and west sides concentrate on the life of Jesus. The north face shows scenes from His early, private life, culminating with his baptism. The west face has the public events: the Adoration of the Magi; the Miracle of Cana; the Miracle of the Loaves and Fishes; Christ's entering Jerusalem. On the head of the cross, the west side shows scenes from the passion and death of Christ, while the east side shows the second coming and the Last Judgement.

Ardboe High Cross.

TULLYHOGUE FORT

Although Tullyhogue Fort was the scene of the inauguration of the O'Neill chiefs from the twelfth to the sixteenth centuries, it was actually the clan seat of the O'Hagans. The clan name and the name of the fort are both derived from the Irish word for 'young' or 'youth'.

Although the enclosure is visible from a wide area, it is actually quite easy to drive past the small car park, which is situated in quite a twisty, wooded section of the road between Cookstown and Tullahogue Village. Having found the car park, the visitor makes his way up a concrete lane to the top of the hill. Even before entering the enclosure, it is worth looking at the views, and admiring the choice of site. The entrance is through a gap in the outer bank. It is clear that this was a ritual rather than a defensive site, since there is no outer ditch. There is a depression between the two banks, but it is much wider than usual. It is obvious that the layout relates to the fact that it is a royal power centre.

It is probable that it was a royal centre even before the Northern O'Neill expanded their territory to include the western shore of Lough Neagh, and the stone on which the O'Neill was 'crowned' may originally have been used as the inauguration site for the O'Hagans. Certainly the traditional burying place for the clan is in the circular, walled cemetery of Donaghrisk, less than a mile away. The last O'Neill inauguration was that of Hugh O'Neill in 1595. The Stone of the King was smashed into pieces by Lord Mountjoy when he captured the enclosure in 1602. Luckily, there exist two drawings, both probably made in 1601, which show the site before its destruction.

The first of these shows the site as an enclosure with two gates. There are two thatched buildings within the banks, while the Stone of the King is shown at some distance from the enclosure. There is also an enlarged drawing of the stone. It would seem to be a large boulder, with stone slabs added on each side and at the back to produce what looks like a throne. The second drawing, probably by the same artist, shows a group of men in Irish costume standing around 'Tullogh oge'. 'On this hill,' it goes on, 'the Irish created heir O'Neale.' The O'Neill is easily identified; he is the one sitting on the Stone of the King. One man, the O'Hagan, holds a shoe over the O'Neill, while another, the O'Cahan, holds the side of the throne. We can only speculate about the significance of these acts.

DERRYLORAN OLD CHURCH

The name indicates that there was a church here for a long time. Derryloran means 'the oak wood of Luran', whose feast day was celebrated on 29 October from as far back as 800. There is an entry in the annals that a church at Derryloran was plundered in 1195. These early churches were probably wooden structures, and it has proved impossible to find any trace of them. The twelfth-century restoration used well-dressed sandstone in the walls, and some of these can still be seen in the ruins. There exists a list of the parish priests from the late fourteenth century up to the mid-sixteenth century.

The current building was erected about one hundred years later, towards the start of the Plantation in the early seventeenth century. Alan Cooke leased the site from the Archbishop of Armagh in 1609 and used it to build the first purpose-built Protestant church to serve his new town of Cookstown. What remained of the old walls was demolished to ground level and the rubble used as the footings for the new building.

The ruins are of a long, narrow church. At the east end there remains the tracery of a window, looking down to the Ballinderry River. This was restored in the late twentieth century. An interesting feature is that on the north wall there are traces of a blocked door and a blocked window. It is possible that this had to be done because of some structural problem, but it is interesting to speculate whether the work was done to make the building more defensible during the 1641 Rising. There are signs of further alterations in the mid-eighteenth century, when the new Cookstown was being laid out.

Although the church was abandoned for a more convenient site within Cookstown in 1822, the graveyard continued to be used for some time after that. The tomb of the Stewarts of Killymoon is here, and that of Henry Lewis von Stieglitz of Gortalowry House, who was buried in 1824. Decay and a build-up of ivy threatened the building with collapse, but restoration was carried out by the DOE Historic Monuments staff in the 1980s, and it is now safe to visit, a quiet place which is evocative of 1,200 years of history.

SPRINGHILL HOUSE

Springhill was built in the years after the Plantation of Ulster. Until 1957, it was the family home of the Conynghams.

The Conynghams came to Ireland from Ayrshire and were granted land in Armagh. The family bought the Springhill Estate around 1630. The original farmhouse, probably built on the site of the present car park, was burnt by the rebel Irish during the Rising of 1641. When William Conyngham II got married to Ann Upton from Templepatrick around 1680, part of the agreement was that he was to build a 'convenient' lime-washed stone house which was to have all necessary facilities. His wife seems to have had to be patient, because analysis of the tree rings in the roof beams shows that the trees were not cut until sometime after 1690. Perhaps William, who was known widely as Good Will, was waiting until he was sure of a peaceful future before he made his substantial investment.

The estate prospered, and the Conynghams started to build the village of Coagh around 1755. To demonstrate their loyalty to the new German monarchs, they named the central square of the village Hanover Square. At around the same time, Col. William Conyngham added two wings to Springhill House, one as a ballroom, the other as a nursery for his children. In this last matter he was disappointed, for he married late and died without children. Since his brother also died without children, the estate passed to their nephew, George, son of their sister Ann. George obligingly added Conyngham to his father's name, and became George Lenox-Conyngham, a style maintained by the family until the present.

George was more fortunate in his inheritance than he was in politics, and had to resign his commission in disgrace in 1816. His nature was not robust enough to cope with this, and he committed suicide shortly afterwards. Strangely, it is not his ghost, but the ghost of his wife, Olivia, which haunts the house to the present day.

Lissan House.

A place to think.

George's son William inherited. He had been trained as a lawyer, and he married the daughter of a fellow lawyer, John Staples of Lissan House, the other Big House north of Cookstown. He built a large dining room at the back of Springhill House. An interesting feature of this was a seventeenth-century Italian chimneypiece that had been salvaged from Ballyscullion House, near Lough Beg. Later in the nineteenth century, changes in the law led to the sale of much of the estate, which was reduced to about 300 acres. Because of the loss of rental incomes, the family found itself less secure financially than it had been. Unwise investments did not help.

Lt-Col. William Lenox-Conyngham married Mina Lowry of Rockdale House in 1899. She outlived her husband, who died in 1938, and her son William, who signed a will bequeathing the house to the National Trust only three days before his death in 1957. Mina remained in the house till her death three years later. The only connection with the family now is that some of the woods on the west side of the Coagh Road are still owned by one of the Lenox-Conynghams, though they are managed by the Department of Agriculture and Rural Development.

The National Trust stripped back later accretions to return each room to the appearance it would have had when first built. The Gun Room still has its eighteenth-century wallpaper and contains a musket which was made about 1680. There are around 3,000 books in the library, many of them dating from the seventeenth and eighteenth centuries. The oldest volume in the collection is a small Latin psalter of 1541. There is a large collection of costumes housed in the laundry. A selection is displayed each season in the Costume Museum.

SPRINGHILL WALK

There is a circular walk starting and finishing at Springhill which gives a sense of the character of the local countryside. One of the highlights is the Yew Grove. Two of these trees were alive before the Plantation of Ulster, and may be the last remnants of the Great Wood of Glenconkeyne. The walk is signposted, and refreshments and toilets are available at its end.

KILLYMOON CASTLE

This imposing building is found just outside Cookstown. It is signposted from Church Street, which is one of the manifestations of Cookstown's long, straight main street. The approach is through Killymoon Street, which is found almost opposite the main road to Omagh.

The castle was originally built by James Stewart, who was of Scottish descent; his ancestors had come to Ulster at the time of the Plantation. In 1666 he bought the lease for Cookstown from Cooke, who had not been able to make a go of the settlement. The few houses he had built were at the opposite end of the main street from Killymoon. The house Stewart built in 1671 really did have defence in mind, since there were still bandits known as raparees roaming in the neighbouring districts. It was built overlooking the Ballinderry River.

The Stewarts were intimately associated with the growing wealth of Cookstown. When, in 1801, the original castle was destroyed by fire, the then owner, Col. William Stewart felt able to ask one of the greatest architects of his day, John Nash, to undertake his first Irish commission. The house that Nash designed was much grander than its predecessor. It is built on a terrace high above the river, and has wonderful views along the river valley. It took only a year to build and cost, it was said, £80,000.

The building is two storeys high, but seems higher. Its towers are interesting in that no two of them are the same. Around the castle are extensive stables and outbuildings, as well as the remains of labourers' cottages. Part of the castle itself is still used as living quarters, and the estate is still managed as a farm.

The grounds and the interior of the castle are popular venues for brides who want a grand setting for their wedding photographs. The gardens are maintained with this in mind, with a mixture of bright flowers and whimsical decorations. The castle is entered from the east side, up narrow steps opening unto a vestibule which opens in turn unto the main hall, which has a striking stone staircase to close the prospect. To the left is the oval dining room. Beyond this is the drawing room, the windows of which are in the form of six intersecting arches. It is laid out as an extended octagon, with mirrors in the short corner walls increasing the sense of light and space.

When building was completed, Col. Stewart had the entire estate (585 acres) enclosed by a 10ft-high wall. Access was by one of four gates, each of which had its own lodge. Nowadays the only motor access is through Killymoon Golf Club, but it is also possible to reach the grounds by foot along the river.

The Stewart family fell on hard times in the middle years of the nineteenth century, and the estate was sold in 1857 for £100,000, being sold again in 1865, 1875 and 1916, before being bought by the Coulter family in 1922 for £100!

During the Second World War Killymoon Castle was the headquarters of 82nd Airborne Division of the American Army while they were stationed in Northern Ireland.

THE CARRICKMORE HILLS

The Carrickmore Hills form an area of elevated plateau south of the Sperrins. Most of the ground is relatively undulating, with glacial moraines and rocky outcrops giving it a sense of repeating patterns. Above these ridges, however, rise rocky, granite summits, with distinctive silhouettes that can be seen for many miles around.

Most fields in the area are enclosed by hedges and wire fencing, although in some areas there are stone walls made up of boulders that have been cleared from the fields. Many of the hedgerows are made up of **gorse**, or whin as it is known locally. This gives them a rough, unkempt look for much of the year, but in late winter and spring the countryside luxuriates in the luminescence of the whin blossom and, on sunny days, the lanes are full of its coconut smell. In damp hollow areas where the farmer has given up trying to keep the drains flowing, scrubby woods of **birch** and **alder** grow back, giving a fresh pattern to the regular fields. In the low-lying areas, there are many **ash** trees along the hedges, particularly where houses are built at road junctions, or at the entrance to lanes leading to farms that are set back off the road. As the roads lead uphill, however, there are fewer hedgerow trees, and small blocks of conifers give an angular, alien look to the landscape.

Another alien presence in the landscape is the number of quarries that occur along the edges of the plateau. Although they give a sense of the depth of sand that occurs in places, they cannot avoid being bright scars on the landscape, only moderated in rain or mist, when the brightness of the exposed sand is dulled. In addition, there is the danger that a great deal of archaeological evidence is being lost.

Moss on stone.

This is marginal farmland where, as local farmers say, 'a living is hard wrought'. Field boundaries are not well maintained, so much of the land has been allowed to grow rank and waste. In some areas fly-tipping is a problem. The upland forms a landmark that is very sensitive to change. Even the current level of sand and gravel extraction is putting pressure on the infrastructure, as well as the landscape itself.

This is one of the least wooded parts of Northern Ireland, with a woodland coverage of less than 2 per cent. Drum Manor is part of an old demesne and some of the original planting predates 1830. Most of the trees have been planted; **Norway spruce**, **Japanese larch**, **beech** and **oak** are the most common, and there are some compartments of **Sitka spruce**.

Most of the woodland in the area is made up from old demesne woods, all of which were present in the 1830s. Wellbrook, Drumshanbo and Athenree all had patches of semi-natural woods as part of their make-up and it is probable that elements of this 'ancient woodland' can still be found in the herb level, particularly among the mosses and lichens. **Beech** is the dominant tree in most of these woods, but there are also **oak**, **Scots pine**, **sycamore** and **birch**. Where the ground is wet, **alder** and various species of **willow** are common.

Most of the Carrickmore hills are covered in grassland, and most of this is improved pasture. This has resulted in very poor biodiversity. While high levels of grazing and of cutting for silage, with the high input of slurry and fertiliser that goes with this, persist there is not likely to be any significant improvement. Perhaps any reduction in the intensity of farming that may result from the current slump may halt the process.

What biodiversity persists is usually concentrated in hedgerows. These tend to be confined to lower land and are associated with intense pasture. Even here they are poorly maintained, with gaps that are roughly blocked with wire. Most trees growing in the hedgerows are **ash**. Elsewhere they are allowed to be overwhelmed by **gorse**, with reinforcement provided by untidy strands of wire.

Acid grasslands are common in the high ground to the west of the hills, where there is widespread peat as well as peaty soils. The land cover here is quite intricate – cut-over bogs and untended pasture merge with rocky slopes and better-drained areas that have sand or gravel under them – and it is possible to find species that are associated with drier heath. Further east, on lower ground, the rough, acid grasslands tend to be found where the river valleys widen, in damp hollows surrounded by drumlins. They can be cut-over bog or simply places where the river is liable to flood. These areas have clumps of **rushes** with grazed grasses in between. Plants such as **meadowsweet** are good indicators of damp soil.

Land like this gives abundant cover for many birds which are Priority Species in Northern Ireland. These include **curlew, reed bunting, skylark, spotted flycatcher, song thrush, bullfinch, yellowhammer, linnet, lapwing** and **redshank**. It also supports **Irish hare**.

On the western uplands, among the steeper and rocky slopes, there is widespread upland heath, where **gorse, common heather** and **bell heather** can be found, and where there is still a breeding population of **red grouse**. The Murrins National Nature Reserve, above Creggan, gets its name from the small, round lakes, locally called murrins, which are common in the Carrickmore Hills. These small lakes have **mallard, teal** and feral **greylag geese**. Much of the blanket bog that protected these areas has been extracted and even where this has not been the case, there are few intact bogs left. It is hoped that restrictions on machine cutting of turf will allow some recovery to take place.

On the wetter bogs, some species of **sphagnum, Sphagnum cuspidatum, S. Papillosum**, and **S. acutifolia** (on drier hummocks) can be seen with **bog bean, common cotton sedge, sundew, bog asphodel, cross-leaved heath, hare's-tail cotton sedge, deer sedge** and **common heather**. These areas of blanket bog are of international importance. They provide habitats for breeding waders and for overwintering birds. The micro-habitats formed by the pools and hummocks support such insects as **water beetles** and **dragonflies**. The loughs in the hills are mostly peaty, but Lough Macrory and a few others have a middle level of nutrients in the water and contain some aquatic plants which are rare nationally.

The Upper Ballinderry River is one of the most important rivers in Northern Ireland in terms of biodiversity, containing as it does some rare aquatic life, including **water crowfoot**, and, more importantly, the **freshwater pearl mussel**. The Ballinderry is one of the few rivers in Northern Ireland which has a big enough population of these to remain viable. To help in their protection and in monitoring the river environment, the **Ballinderry Hatchery** is managing a breeding programme for these valuable and slow-growing little animals, which can live for over one hundred years. Another important species in the upper river is the **brook lamprey**. This small, eel-like creature is the descendant of a line which goes back many millions of years. Like sharks, its skeleton is made of cartilage rather than bone and its round mouth has only two teeth which are designed to fasten onto fish while the lamprey's rasping tongue obtains nutrition from the fish's tissues. The river has a good population of **brown trout** to keep them fed.

Perhaps the most spectacular animals to live along the river are the **otter** and the **kingfisher**, which can be found along the entire length of the Ballinderry.

COOKSTOWN FARMLANDS

This is drumlin country, with the drumlins shallow in the Cookstown area, but becoming more pronounced as you travel west into the higher, steeper country round Beaghmore or north-west towards Slieve Gallion. As you travel towards Lough Neagh, east of Cookstown, floodplain becomes more pronounced, particularly where the Killymoon and Ballymully Rivers join the Ballinderry. Farms and villages are scattered within a landscape of fields, hedges and small copses. Most of the fields even today are relatively small, but there are larger arable fields where the land is shallow enough. The drumlins do not dominate the landscape as they do in Down or Monaghan, and the gentler scale somehow makes it easier to appreciate hedgerow trees or how a house may snuggle into shelter within trees or against a hillside.

The areas along the floodplain have a character of their own. Around and between the fields are large areas of wet woodland. The roads that cross these areas are raised on embankments to protect the traveller from the flood. There are also several estates in the area which have wooded parkland attached. The best of these are at **Loughry**, **Killymoon** and **Drum Manor**. They are surrounded by high stone boundary walls. The Killymoon River has a particularly attractive river corridor, which has a sequence of woodlands and small-scale riverside pastures.

Cookstown is the principal town and is the major centre for general services. Villages on the floodplain are along roads, with clusters of buildings at principal road junctions. Farms tend to be small, with the farm buildings at the end of long tracks, well away from the roads. There is a sense that views are closed in

Lissan Water.

by drumlins, hedges and trees. Some hedges have been lost where farmers have wished to operate more intensively, and the landscape would lose its regular structure if any more hedgerows and the trees they contain were lost.

There is poor woodland cover in the district, less than half the Northern Ireland average. Most of it is broadleaved, with only two major areas of conifers, in the state forests at **Drum Manor** and **Lissan**. The Drum Manor woods we have dealt with already. In Lissan, the coniferous wood has been planted on ground that was woodland in 1830, so it too has relics of long-established, if not ancient, woodland. The Ordnance Survey Memoir for the area, written in the 1830s, said that Lissan had a great deal of old timber. The **Lissan River**, as it passes through the demesne, is lined with beech, oak and lime, as well as specimen trees like **redwood, London plane, Chilean pine** and **yew**. In the state forest, **Sitka spruce** and **Japanese larch** are the predominant trees, together with some **Scots pine, beech** and **oak**.

There are the remains, or the actuality, of several estates in the area, and it is here that most patches of woodland are found. Some of the most interesting are along the Killymoon River: Killymoon Castle; Loughry College; Desertcreat, and Tullylagan Manor. Rockdale and Bloomhill are further to the south, while Orritor and Lissan Rectory are in the foothills of Slieve Gallion. Although most of the planting in these estates was done around 1830, in some of them seventeenth-century planting incorporated older, semi-natural woodland. This happened particularly in damper areas with alder and willow and steeper areas with ash and scrub. These are the most likely areas to contain ancient woodland, and it is certainly worth searching these places for the flowers, mosses and lichens that are restricted to such woods.

Most of the estate woodlands have beeches as the most plentiful species, together with **oak, ash** and **sycamore**. There are usually some specimen trees scattered around the parkland. In parts of most woods, **laurel** and **rhododendron** have formed an impenetrable understorey.

Tirnaskea Wood near the Rock is associated with an old estate, but most of the wood is semi-natural, with a rich ground flora and native trees dominating most of the area. 'Planted' trees include **beech** and **western red cedar** with a shrub layer of **rhododendron, cherry laurel** and **Portuguese laurel**. The main native trees are **ash, oak, willow, hazel** and some **wych elm**. Within the wood are **holly, blackthorn** and **hawthorn**. The ground flora includes **wood anemone, wood sorrel, pignut, goldilocks buttercup, early purple orchid, common dog-violet** and **primrose**. A long-established wood nearby is **Tullyreavy Wood**, known locally as the Oak Wood.

Most other woodland in the district is to be found on cut-over bogs, which are well scattered. In the south and west they tend to be found between drumlins, while in the east they are to be found in broader areas along the tributaries of the Ballinderry. Most of them are semi-natural in the sense that they have regenerated themselves. The drier parts are mostly **birch**, while **willow** and **alder** grow on the damper margins.

Over 80 per cent of the land is grassland and over 80 per cent of this is improved grassland. This means that over two thirds of the land in the area is of little use to wildlife, since they have a very low biodiversity resulting from their intensive management. In places like this any wildlife there is is concentrated in the hedgerows. These are very important refuges for woodland plants and animals. Because of the small size of fields in the area, hedgerows make a really important contribution here, although it diminishes towards the east where wetter land means that many fields are bounded by ditches.

Arable seems to be a disappearing land use in the district, other than where a farmer chooses to reseed grass. There is some rough grassland, often associated with the outskirts of towns and villages or with large sand pits and quarries. Some of the land between drumlins is poorly drained and in the wettest of these patches may develop into marshy grassland, where **rushes**, **sedges** and **meadow sweet** are common.

In spite of the intensity of agriculture in the district, several priority species of bird still breed in the area. Among them are: **linnet**; **song thrush**; **reed bunting**; **skylark**; **bullfinch**; **curlew**, and **spotted flycatcher**.

LOUGH NEAGH SHORES

This is a relatively flat landscape on the fringes of Lough Neagh. There are some drumlins which seem almost like islands – in the past many of them were – surrounded by flat, open pasture. Tucked on them are farmsteads and some mature trees, many of them in hedgerows. The fields can be large, surrounded by straight ditches which are essential for drainage. There are many roads which lead straight from the main road down to farms at the lough shore. Along these there is considerable ribbon development of mostly modern houses.

Many of the rivers are enclosed by embankments, and there are often extensive woodlands of **willow**, **alder** and **birch** making access to the river difficult. Even the low-lying land is, for the most part, intensively managed, although there are still areas of poor drainage and scrub. There are many ruined or derelict buildings which are hidden from view by their distance from the road and by tall hedges.

There are two sections of state forest in the area. In the smaller one, known locally as the **Birch Wood**, there are: **sycamore**; **oak**; **beech**; **alder**; **spruce**; **Douglas fir**, and **Japanese larch**. The other section is coniferous, with **Sitka spruce** and **Lodgepole pine**, but it has a fringe of **birch** and **alder** on the south side. Much of the woodland is on cut-over bog. The large bog of the **Gort Moss** has been colonised by trees. **Killycolpy Wood** is also on cut-over bog and consists mostly of **alder** and **birch**. Within it are quantities of **regal fern.** Along the lough shore itself, wet woodland and scrub is colonising the wet grasslands.

More that 80 per cent of the grassland has been 'improved' and is of low value as far as biodiversity is concerned. What native flora and fauna there is is concentrated in the hedgerows. Most of these are **hawthorn** and still dense, with mature **oaks** growing in some of them. Unfortunately, the hedges are mostly situated on the drumlins. In the flat-ground fields boundaries tend to be marked by ditches. Where there are damp pastures and fields with rushes, there is improved habitat for birds and you can find **bullfinch, song thrush, curlew, linnet, reed bunting, tree sparrow, yellowhammer, spotted flycatcher** and **skylark.** As you approach Lough Neagh itself you find more wet meadows, as well as fen, reedbed, and woods and meadows that are regularly flooded in winter. Here waders breed, and there are good numbers of **lapwing, snipe** and **redshank.** This area also supports a good population of **Irish hares.**

KEVIN JOHNSTON

Kevin Johnston was born towards the end of the Second World War in the City of Derry. He went on to train as an English teacher in Belfast, where his tutor for three years was Seamus Heaney. After qualifying he returned to Derry, where he married Maura, and with her had two children. Confronted by the troubles in Derry, he chose to go to Swaziland, in southern Africa, where he taught for three years. He now lives in Moneymore with his wife, two children and two dogs. His hobbies are hill-walking and birdwatching. He has written a history of Belfast's shipyards, *In the Shadows of Giants*. *O'Neill's Own Country* is his second book.